SAGE was founded in 1965 by Sara Miller McCune to support the dissemination of usable knowledge by publishing innovative and high-quality research and teaching content. Today, we publish over 900 journals, including those of more than 400 learned societies, more than 800 new books per year, and a growing range of library products including archives, data, case studies, reports, and video. SAGE remains majority-owned by our founder, and after Sara's lifetime will become owned by a charitable trust that secures our continued independence.

Los Angeles | London | New Delhi | Singapore | Washington DC | Melbourne

Curriculum Development

A Guide for Educators

Bill Boyle and Marie Charles

Los Angeles | London | New Delhi
Singapore | Washington DC | Melbourne

Los Angeles | London | New Delhi
Singapore | Washington DC | Melbourne

SAGE Publications Ltd
1 Oliver's Yard
55 City Road
London EC1Y 1SP

SAGE Publications Inc.
2455 Teller Road
Thousand Oaks, California 91320

SAGE Publications India Pvt Ltd
B 1/I 1 Mohan Cooperative Industrial Area
Mathura Road
New Delhi 110 044

SAGE Publications Asia-Pacific Pte Ltd
3 Church Street
#10-04 Samsung Hub
Singapore 049483

Editor: Marianne Lagrange
Assistant editor: Robert Patterson
Marketing manager: Dilhara Attygalle
Cover design: Wendy Scott
Typeset by: C&M Digitals (P) Ltd, Chennai, India
Printed and bound by CPI Group (UK) Ltd,
Croydon, CR0 4YY

Library of Congress Control Number: 2015940529

British Library Cataloguing in Publication data

A catalogue record for this book is available from
the British Library

ISBN 978-1-44627-329-6
ISBN 978-1-44627-330-2 (pbk)

At SAGE we take sustainability seriously. Most of our products are printed in the UK using FSC papers and boards.
When we print overseas we ensure sustainable papers are used as measured by the PREPS grading system.
We undertake an annual audit to monitor our sustainability.

Contents

About the Authors

Professor Bill Boyle was Professor of Education, the Chair of Educational Assessment and Director of the Centre for Formative Assessment Studies (CFAS) in the School of Education, University of Manchester (UK) from 1989 until January 2014.

During his time at the University of Manchester, Professor Boyle was director of many assessment reform projects nationally and internationally including the ten year longitudinal assessment project for the UK government's Qualifications and Curriculum Authority (QCA, 1997–2008), which collected, analysed and reported on a nationally representative sample of primary and secondary schools' curriculum and assessment data. He also contributed to the UK government's parliamentary Select Committee Report on the National Curriculum and its Assessment (2008–9).

Professor Boyle publishes extensively on teaching, learning and assessment and works with schools, pre- and in-service organisations, ministries of education throughout the world on curriculum, teaching and assessment research and development, and policy and practice consultancies. These include leading World Bank projects in Russia, Armenia, Vietnam and Jamaica on teacher development and the development of national education assessment systems in Russia and Pakistan from conceptual design through to item development and analysis and reporting phases. He has worked with the Gulf Arab States Education Research Council in developing a curriculum manual for benchmarking standards and presents workshops on Quality Assessment in Higher Education in the Kingdom of Saudi Arabia. Since 2001, he has supported developments in teaching, learning and assessment in the United Arab Emirates, Saudi Arabia, Oman and Bahrain. He is currently a member of the Expert Council of the World Bank on an innovative Russian Educational Aid and Development project which supplies teaching, learning and assessment educational technical support to a number of countries in Eastern Europe, Africa and Asia.

Most recent publications with Marie Charles include: *Formative Assessment for Teaching and Learning* (London: Sage, 2013) and *Using Multiliteracies and Multimodalities to Support Young Children's Learning* (London: Sage, 2014).

Marie Charles is a formative assessment researcher, consultant and author whose work demonstrates that she believes passionately in the learner (rather than measurement or grading) being at the centre of the education process – a belief that she carries into her classroom practice.

Marie Charles and her co-author, Professor Bill Boyle, publish their research work in academic and practitioner journals, present at international conferences and workshops, and design and support developments in formative teaching, learning and assessment. Currently, they are working with colleagues in Pakistan, Russia, Armenia, Oman, Saudi Arabia and the USA on understanding and using formative strategies for more effective teaching and learning.

Acknowledgements

The most terrifying question of all: What sort of human being will you be from the womb to the tomb? We begin with courage to cut against the grain, to be committed to something bigger than ourselves. To stir up Socratic energies – which unnerve, unsettle and unhouse. (Cornel West, 2012)

Thanks also to Paulo Freire, Alexander Jones, Bob Dylan, Lana Guinier, James Joyce, Tom Christie, Philippe Perrenoud and Mark Rothko for steering me through a 35 year research journey.

Bill Boyle
Marie Charles

Introduction

The teacher is no longer merely 'the-one-who-teaches', but one who is him/herself in dialogue with the students, who in turn while being taught also teaches. They then become jointly responsible for a process in which all grow. (Paulo Freire, 1970)

This book addresses designing, developing, reviewing and using a national school curriculum, a complex subject critical to the success of the teaching, learning and assessment process within any country's educational system. Our starting point on this 'curriculum research journey' can be summarised by the following statement – which also neatly encapsulates our end point and emphasises the reiterative nature of a learner's journey: the intention of a curriculum is that it provides a breadth of structured learning opportunities and experiences which will support the progressive and measurable development of pupils within that range of differential pace of assimilation, understanding and challenge found in the complexity of a school situation (Crawford, 2000; QCA, 2002; White, 2004; Boyle and Bragg, 2006).

Once the 1988 Education Reform Act (ERA) passed as legislation and introduced a first ever National Curriculum in England, education became highlighted as a political domain in the same way as 'health', 'economy' and 'defence' had traditionally occupied that role. Under Tony Blair's governance (1997–2007), 'education, education, education' became, at first the unwilling, but then the inevitably passive and submissive victim and object of political soundbites and more and more political control. The curriculum and its assessment ceased to be a method for supporting the learner but became a means for constructing a measurement framework, a minimum competency one at that, by which schools could be ranked and graded. In 2004, Ofsted, long utilised as a disturbingly powerful arm of that political control, in one of those instances of historical irony, itself highlighted the curriculum issue that should be being addressed and which we attempt to address in this book: 'We face a challenge to make sure that every subject is taught well in schools, and that every child gets the benefit of a rich, well-designed and broad curriculum. This needs to include a wide range of in-school activities like dance, sport and drama and the chance to study music and a foreign language' (DfES, 2004: 34).

Study of the research literature, commentaries and evaluations of the educational policy and structural reforms (Apple, 1996; Popham, 2001; White, 2004) which have taken place in the majority of the countries around the world in the last 20–25 years locates 'the curriculum' at the centre of these changes. A curriculum and its related curriculum standards (which are globally used for performance assessment or testing purposes) would seem to be the signposts for policy makers around the world to determine the effectiveness and the need for change of their schooling systems. This demand for curriculum reform, redesign and development has spawned a number of key research and development questions, not always worded the same in every country case but voicing the same issues. These questions include the following: Who determines the aims of a curriculum? What are these aims? How can the aims be addressed and achieved through curricular arrangements? What is the role of a 'subject'? How can a curriculum structure manage both 'breadth' and balance across subjects? How can progression be ensured within the need for breadth and balance of curriculum experiences? What is the link between the curriculum and effective teaching, learning and assessment?

These questions will provide the focal points for this book and our attempts at addressing them will hopefully throw light on the roles of learner, teacher, school leadership, policy maker and the range of stakeholders who have interests in effective education systems.

What are the roles of teaching and learning and how does the curriculum influence pedagogy? The literature suggests one definition as that pedagogy is the translation of the curriculum into the operations of teaching and learning (Dunphy, 2008). The traditional distinction was curriculum as 'content' and pedagogy as 'delivery of that content'. This is not a helpful distinction – even in methodological terms, pedagogy is relational or transactional. The pedagogical experience conveys norms and values (albeit, on occasions 'poor' or 'rich' norms and values) based on the teacher's role, style, inputs and beliefs. If the assumption is that the teacher's role is to develop the learner and that the learner is an active subject in the process of becoming autonomous and self-determining (a self-regulated learner: Zimmerman, 2000), then the margins between teacher and learner, curriculum and pedagogy become less fixed, flexible and, to a formative thinker, more positive (Perrenoud, 1991; 1998; Allal and Ducrey, 2000).

Apple describes the international movement of the 1980s to 1990s which served to introduce a plethora of new or reformed national curricula with the following cautionary note: 'While the proponents of a national curriculum may see it as a means to provide social cohesion and to give all of us the capacity to improve our schools by measuring them against "objective" criteria, the effects will be the opposite. Rather than leading to cultural and social cohesion, differences between "we" and the "others" will be produced even more strongly and the attendant social antagonism and cultural and economic destruction will worsen' (Apple, 1996: 63). This has sadly proved to be the case in England where an over-emphasis on the 'tested subjects' (Boyle and Bragg, 2006) and using these to rank and inspect schools led to 'what gets measured gets taught' (Rothman, 2001). Twelve years after the introduction by legislation of the first National Curriculum for England and Wales, Popham stated: 'in an evidence-oriented enterprise, those who control the evidence-gathering mechanisms control the entire enterprise' (2001). Popham reviewed the history of testing practices in education and addressed the ways in which using high-stakes tests (end of key stage assessments for example) to measure school accountability changes the essential questions on which educators focus: since Popham wrote that review, of course, education has become even more of a political tool ('Education, education, education' – Blair, 1997) and no reviewer today would assume that the educator's focus would or could out-vote the political imperative! However, Popham's key question still remains valid as follows: 'How do we teach Tracy the things she needs to know?' This has become: 'How do we improve Tracy's scores on the high-stakes test she will be taking?' (2001). The warning for the 'death' of the curriculum is implicit here. Standardised tests assess low-level knowledge (minimum competency coverage testing) in a specific subject area and ignore everything else (for mark allocation purpose). Once the standardised test *becomes* both curriculum and learning goal, its omnipresence subverts learning. 'In the USA, the "bottom" 30% in the achievement scale come from the poorest 30% of the population and are those most likely to "drop out", be unemployed and go to jail' (Christenson, 2011).

A national scenario: in the mid-1980s, as a major part of the policy development in the UK towards the first ever National Curriculum for England and Wales, the UK government's Department for Education and Science produced an influential report called *Better Schools*. The report defined the school curriculum as follows:

> A school's curriculum consists of all those activities designed or encouraged within its organisational framework to promote the intellectual, personal, social and physical development of its pupils. It includes not only the formal programme of lessons but also the informal programme of extra-curricular activities as well as those features which produce a school's ethos such as the quality of relationships, the concern for quality of opportunity, the values exemplified by the way the school sets about its tasks and the way in which it is organised and managed. Teaching and learning styles strongly influence the curriculum and in practice they cannot be divorced from it. (DES, 1985)

However, there are tensions within that definition and recent history has revealed these. In the majority of countries, national curriculum developments and designs tend to focus on a linear subject structure (i.e. a body of work taught as a single subject, for example mathematics Grade 1 through to mathematics Grade 12) with what has become the elevation of a number of priority or elite subjects into a 'core curriculum' – this core is usually identified by the inclusion of subjects which are tested externally and whose tested results are used as data for student and school performance measurement, often with a ranking or judgmental aspect. This focus on accountability through measurement as conceptual framework for curriculum design soon descends into skewing the balance heavily towards the 'tested subjects' and reduces the opportunities for pupils to experience the non-tested or non-testable subjects.

This seemingly inevitable consequence of the linear structure of subjects and progression by the pupil through sets of competencies or curriculum standards is that a narrow concept of curriculum (and by association, a narrow definition of assessment as 'testing' rather than 'scaffolding' learning) reinforces poor teaching and learning becomes 'the recitation script' (Alexander, 2005). Catalogues of subjects and lists of skills or competencies as highly packaged content, do not make a curriculum, nor should assessment be defined as narrowly focused written tests.

The book addresses questions which are as relevant now as they should have been when the Educational Reform cycle began [in the UK] in 1989. Namely:

- Who should determine the aims of the curriculum?
- What should these aims be?
- How can the aims be realised in curricular arrangements?

1

Curriculum Evolution

Chapter summary

The historical underpinning and antecedents of the Education Reform Act (1988) and the thinking behind the first National Curriculum in the United Kingdom.

The idea of a broad and balanced curriculum is not new, according to the Education Reform Act:

> the curriculum for a maintained school should be a balanced and broadly based curriculum. (DES, 1988)

From 1996 until 2007, the author (Bill Boyle) was contracted by the UK government's Qualifications and Curriculum Authority (QCA) to carry out the longitudinal monitoring of the nationally representative sample of primary schools (initially key stage 1 and key stage 2, but subsequently a representative sample of Early Years settings was included). The type of data collected included school type, percentage of free school meals, length and timings of teaching week, curriculum priorities by subject (were 'breadth' and 'balance' as stated by the 1988 Education Reform Act being achieved?), programmes of study (how was the appropriate programme being covered and what were the issues of difficulty in covering the programme, if any?), percentage teaching time allocation (by year group, by subjects specified as statutory core and foundation), combined/separate subject teaching (the extent that subjects are taught discretely or combined with another subject or element of another subject), planning for 'inclusion' (meeting individual learning needs) and finally but not least, success at meeting government expectations (will the majority of pupils meet the expected levels at the end of the relevant key stage?).

With the pressure 'to raise standards' in English and mathematics exerted by the Department for Education increasing steadily over that 11-year period, the introduction of national numeracy and literacy strategies and percentage 'success level targets' set centrally for pupils' national test outcomes, a reduction in the teaching time for the (untested or 'unSAT-ed') foundation subjects was probable. It was the extent of the reduction in the teaching time afforded to those 'other' subjects and the consequent disproportionate 'unbalancing' of the curriculum evidenced by the monitoring survey data that was alarming.

The 1988 Education Reform Act which instituted the National Curriculum and its assessment stated that the curriculum should be 'a balanced and broadly based curriculum which promotes the spiritual, moral, mental and physical development of pupils at the school and of society and prepares such pupils for the opportunities, responsibilities and experiences of adult and working life' (DES, 1988).

This short preamble to the Act had its origins in and extended the statement in the 1944 Education Act that children should be educated 'according to their age, ability and aptitude'. However, the 1988 ERA drew more from the proposals of the 1985 White Paper, *Better Schools* which set out a list of the purposes of education in schools. These were to help pupils to:

> develop lively enquiring minds, the ability to question and argue rationally, and to apply themselves to tasks and physical skills; acquire understanding, knowledge and skills relevant to adult life and employment in a fast changing world; use language and numbers effectively; develop personal and moral values, respect for religious values and tolerance of other races, religions and ways of life; understand the world in which they live and the interdependence of individuals, groups and nations; appreciate human achievements and aspirations. (DES, 1985: 14)

The major revision of the National Curriculum by Dearing (SCAA, 1993) reduced and clarified the understanding, knowledge and skills to be taught. Dearing's report provided a more extensive description of aims for the school curriculum:

> Education is not concerned only with equipping students with the knowledge and skills they need to earn a living. It must help our young people to use leisure time creatively; have respect for other people, other cultures and other beliefs; become good citizens; think things out for themselves; pursue a healthy lifestyle; and not least, value themselves and their achievements. It should develop an appreciation of our cultural heritage and of the spiritual and moral dimensions to life. It must moreover be concerned to serve all our children well, whatever their background, sex, creed, ethnicity or talent. (SCAA, 1993: 18)

Aims and purposes of the 1988 ERA sadly were 'after the event' outlined in non-statutory guidance for schools produced by the two bodies, sometimes competitively, responsible for keeping the curriculum under review. These were the National Curriculum Council (NCC) and the Schools Examinations and Assessment Council (SEAC). In 1997 sense prevailed and the two bodies were subsumed into the newly created, multi-purpose Qualifications and Curriculum Authority (QCA). These organisations disseminated advice and guidance for teachers aimed at helping them understand the curriculum and its aims and issues such as the relationships of subjects within cross-curriculum skills, themes and dimensions. However, commentators (Johnson, 1991; Boyle and Bragg, 2008) refer to the 'astonishing silence' on issues such as multicultural education, social studies, personal and social education, political education, etc. which within the framework of this 'new' (although post-Dearing already in its second iteration) National Curriculum. In fact, during the period prior to the consultation for the millennium revisions (Boyle, 2001) the only statement of curriculum aims, purposes and values appeared in *Curriculum Guidance 3: The Whole Curriculum* (NCC, 1990).

Historically there are precedents and a number of reports from the Consultative Committee of the Board of Education (established 1902) and from the Ministry of Education's Central Advisory Council (established 1944, replacing the Consultative Committee) articulated educational aims and purposes. These committees and advisory council reports officially had the status of advice to the Secretary of State. The Hadow Reports from the Board of Education Consultative Committee – *The Primary School* (1931) and *Nursery and Infant Schools* (1933) – set out in detail the aims, content and methods for the primary stage. The most significant of these reports was the Central Advisory Council's Plowden Report (DES, 1967).

In the Plowden Report the aims of primary education were reviewed. The society of the 'future' was discussed and aspirational conclusions reached that children would need to be 'adaptable and capable of adjusting', 'be able to live with their fellows appreciating and respecting differences', 'need the power of discrimination and be able to withstand mass pressures', 'be well balanced with neither emotions nor intellect giving ground to each other', and to 'understand that in a democratic society each individual has an obligation to the community as well as rights within it' (DES, 1967: 185–8).

The Consultative Committee consulted a range of stakeholders from headteachers to philosophers of education in the course of their review of evidence for the Plowden Report. Headteachers were reported as emphasising the all-round development of the child and the acquisition of the basic skills necessary for contemporary society. However, Plowden was critical that the aim of securing the co-operation of school and home and 'with it that of making good the deficiencies of their backgrounds' was barely mentioned by these school leaders. The Report concluded that most schools' general statements of aims 'tended to be little more than expressions of benevolent aspiration which may have a rather tenuous relationship to the educational practices which actually go on there' (DES, 1967: 186).

Plowden stated that 'a recognisable philosophy of education' emerged from its deliberations and included the following statements about aims and values:

> a school is not merely a teaching shop, it must transmit values and attitudes. It is a community in which children learn to live first as children and not as future adults ... the school sets out deliberately to devise the right environment for children, to allow them to be themselves, and to develop in the way and at the pace appropriate to them. It tries to equalise opportunities and to compensate for handicaps. It lays special stress on individual discovery, on first hand experience and on opportunities for creative work. It insists that knowledge does not fall neatly into compartments and that play and work are not opposite but complementary. A child brought up in such an atmosphere at all stages of his education has some hope of becoming a balanced and mature adult and of being able to live in, to contribute to and to look critically at the society of which he forms a part. (DES, 1967: 187–8).

Although it was without any associated legislation (unlike the 1988 ERA), the Plowden Report was highly influential in the development of the primary school curriculum and its pedagogy – and its invocation against the 'teaching shop' philosophy is highly significant in 2015 England with more and more discontent about the model of school as 'exam factory' (Boyle and Charles, 2015). Much of the post-Plowden 20 years of debate about the need for a National Curriculum in England and Wales centred round the influence of the 'Plowden philosophy' and the extent to which its philosophy and ideas had been put into practice. Indeed, even later, in 1999 when the author (Bill Boyle) was contracted as the researcher to manage the national consultation and analyse the data for the QCA's report to the Secretary of State for the millennium National Curriculum revisions, many of the issues from Plowden re-emerged. Did schools have aims for their curriculum and did they prioritise those aims in their response to the consultation? Did schools recognise the difference between their aims and their priorities? Did schools define their aims and priorities specifically enough for those comments to be meaningful and or measurable as achieved or not? Would the schools' responses contribute to the debate on whether a revised National Curriculum should depend on a subject structure or a whole curriculum underpinned by a values agenda? Was there an alternative to a state-imposed curriculum? Was this alternative supported and derived from a school-based version of the National Curriculum?

Through their role of setting out future government policy, White Papers are therefore important in articulating rationale for legislation. However, unfortunately, that rationale might not in many cases be included in the ensuing statutes. In furthering the cause of prioritising aims of the curriculum *Better Schools* (DES, 1985) was an influential White Paper as it included the statement that schools should develop, based on their Local Education Authority's (now Local Authority) Curriculum Policy, their own detailed aims and priorities (DES, 1985: 13). These would be reviewed over time by all those involved in the partnership of the local education service. *Better Schools* endorsed the principles of breadth, balance, relevance and differentiation (DES, 1985: 88) and stressed that the preparation of a pupil for working life was one of a school's principal functions: 'academic achievement should be complemented by the capacity to apply knowledge ... and the ability to work as part of a team' (DES, 1985: 15). It also emphasised the (Conservative) government's view that 'every element of the primary and secondary curriculum and every learning area is concerned with the development of personal qualities and attitudes' (DES, 1985: 17).

Better Schools provides a stronger articulation of the rationale for the subject-based structure of the (proposed) National Curriculum than other succeeding documents. However, it also stated that the curriculum is described in subject terms for the sake of convenience and that it is not in dispute that the purposes of education in school go beyond learning the traditional subjects (DES, 1985: 53). Two years later, the DES paper, *The National Curriculum 5–16*, did not ignore whole curriculum issues and there is a clearly discernible direct line from *Better Schools*:

> there are a number of subjects or themes which can be taught through other subjects ... it is proposed that such subjects or themes should be taught through the foundation subjects. (DES, 1987: 8)

However the same document is clear that:

> the description of the National Curriculum in terms of the foundation subjects is not a description of how the school day should be organised and the curriculum delivered. (DES, 1987: 9)

It stressed that there is a need for the attainment targets and programmes of study to 'reflect cross-curricular themes' (DES, 1987: Annex A, para. 3).

Curriculum philosophy

> Virtually all the enlightened views on curriculum planning are now agreed that subjects should be regarded as important only if they help to reach other objectives. (Lawton, 1987)

It is a fact that in the course of the implementation of the first version of the National Curriculum (Education Reform Act, 1988) during the period 1988–92, no explicit linkage was formulated between the overall aims of that curriculum and the orders which established the ten subjects. The real issue, the question of why a school curriculum was built around the subject structure, and to what ends, was never adequately addressed at national level and was (O'Hear and White, 1993; White, 1993) and still is (Boyle and Bragg, 2006; 2008a; Boyle et al., 2009) a matter of frequent criticism. It has been regularly suggested that a more sensible and cogent method of proceeding would to have been to establish a coherent set of aims and then agree on the best method of implementing those aims:

> [Outline the] aims in various areas of the curriculum, the sequence of development which can be expected in children and the methods through which work can be soundly based and progress accelerated. (DES, 1967: 198)

Such a starting point would have provided a firm basis for critical reflection about values. However, there remains strong opinion that the political objective for the DES at the time was to:

> get teachers to accept, understand and implement a National Curriculum free from the distraction and competition provided by the 'whole curriculum' debate. The political decision was that publishing guidance on the 'whole curriculum' during 1989 was unhelpful. (Crawford, 2000: 629)

Similarly, with the political interventionist resonance that teachers have come to know and fear in the intervening years, 'the desire [by politicians] to exert direct influence over the curriculum was more important than the precise nature of its form and content' (Chitty, 1988: 329).

Research literature on the National Curriculum includes significant detail on issues related to educational purposes: much of it emphasising the fundamental importance of a clear vision for the purposes of the curriculum and the lack of appropriate debate on that issue. Concern about this lack of debate and its implications for the Curriculum 2000 revisions were raised by Alexander: 'there is little point in proposing a grand statement of educational purposes for the next century of the curriculum as prescribed and transacted does not reflect them' (SCAA, 1997: 42).

The Le Métais and Tabberer study (1997) provided a background against which to consider the vigorous debate about educational purposes which had become more intense since the introduction of the National Curriculum through the 1998 Education Reform Act. In those years, White was one of its strongest critics: 'the structural weakness of the 1988 curriculum is plain. Its basis is the ten foundation subjects.

What these are all supposed to be *for* has never been made clear, beyond the virtually uninformative prescription in the ERA that they are to promote the spiritual, moral, social and cultural development of pupils and prepare them for adult life' (White 1993: 3). Following the introduction of the National Curriculum in 1988, O'Hear and White (1991) presented their alternative National Curriculum in which they took their argument further by emphasising not only the importance of articulating the curriculum's aims and purposes but of 'outlining its basis in the fundamental values of liberal democracy' (O'Hear and White, 1991: 3).

This principle of democratic values as the precursor to establishing curricular aims was taken up by Carr (1997) who emphasised the importance of articulating a vision for the educational future, 'firmly grounded in democratic values and which can provide strategies for the future development of the National curriculum with a strong sense of purpose and direction'. He also requested that 'we re-engage with fundamental questions about the relationship between education and democracy as such a vision would transform the style and substance of educational debates' (Carr, 1997: 3).

There is considerable consensus in the literature about the need for the inclusion of democratic values in underpinning curriculum aims. Woodhead (1993) took issue with this point of view and questioned the extent to which it is necessary or indeed helpful to 'return to first principles' arguing that 'the relevant paragraph [Section 1 ERA 1988] is certainly terse but it points clearly enough to the essential and complementary aims of any educational system' (Woodhead, 1993: 26). This is a minority view in the literature and the claim that 'terse' statements are sufficient may require further elaboration when set alongside the Le Métais and Tabberer study (1997). The latter study pointed to the possibility that a more comprehensive exposition could prove beneficial not only in relation to practice but also to educational outcomes.

The argument was pursued by curriculum analysts with considerable research experience and sound acquaintance with the practicalities of curriculum provision. Invited to consider further curriculum developments, Anning (1997) described the current curricular aims for key stage 1 as not radical enough for the twenty-first century. Richards (1997) called for a creative millennium project which considered the nature of childhood and of the education required for the future. He floated the premise that there was no more apt national agenda for the first decade of the new millennium, urging that the debate should be widespread and involve the wider community and especially the young themselves. The point was pursued by Wragg (1997) who expressed concern about earlier debates taking place behind closed doors (a common thread throughout the iterations of the National Curriculum which have taken place since 1988).

Alexander rebutted the idea that this was a discussion no longer relevant to the present. He acknowledged the 'understandable nervousness' not least on the part of an 'exhausted teaching profession' but argued for a fundamental rethink within the context of the 'millennium factor'. He looked for a shift 'from a view of state education still enslaved by the elementary/grammar legacy of the nineteenth century to one which was attentive to the needs and circumstances of the twenty first' (Alexander, 1997: 37).

The general call for a more explicit articulation of underpinning values was reflected in the QCA's own work in this area, firstly in relation to its 'values forum' (SCAA, 1996) and secondly in its attempt to survey a representative sample of schools' views of their curriculum aims (Boyle and Christie, 1996). A keen critic of these initiatives and of attempts to establish a consensual value position was Marenbon (1996) who took issue with the process in its entirety, arguing that the entry of the QCA into the debate was philosophically misplaced, ill-timed and unworkable. Tooley (1997) pursued a similar argument objecting to any official definition of values in a multicultural society. The Marenbon/Tooley position is not substantially reflected in the overall literature which favours the attempt to identify common ground.

A central point in this argument is that the debate about values is a necessary prerequisite to any description of aims since value positions predispose us towards particular aims. The expression of values helps us to see why we should have a National Curriculum at all and what its nature, scope and aims should be. Alexander is clear that the debate now is about values first, structures and content second (1997: 35–44).

Nevertheless Le Métais and Tabberer's analysis (1997) of values and their comparison of the 'ideal' and the 'real' emphasised that 'there is no point at which education can start with a clean slate', that we do not live in an ideal world where national values are clearly understood and shared and in which there is no dissonance between legislated aims and those pursued by teachers, parents and others with a legitimate interest. Elliott (1994) and Roe (1994) both reflected this view in describing the 'paradoxical' nature of values. Elliott, in arguing for 'greater clarification', warned that this cannot be an 'abstract or armchair' activity but is a dynamic process. He made his argument in the context of schools and individuals but it is one that has obvious relevance to the wider debate about the curriculum.

The distinction between the process of expressing democratic values and the reflection of those values in educational aims may be an important one for several reasons. For example, Elliott addressed the issue of 'values in use' – those ideologies and values that are perceived as underpinning curriculum reform, notably economic, market-led values, but without the benefit of a wider debate. The lack of this debate is viewed by several policy analysts as having had negative effects on the structure and content of the curriculum subjects and themes and resulting in considerable disenchantment by members of the teaching profession.

A second reason why the debate about values is currently important is its emphasis on the central concept of citizenship in a democratic society and what that might involve beyond the consumerist principles of a market economy, Bottery's 'Citizens Charters' (1986). Bottery (1986), Fogelman (1991), McLaughlin (1992), Buck and Inman (1993) and White (1997) all argued that this is the essential issue which needs to be addressed as the foundation of the curriculum for the twenty-first century.

Alexander summarised what he perceived to be a short-sighted approach to curriculum aims and associated curriculum structures. 'The sentiments in the ERA's first chapter are meaningless. It is clear that of the various purposes which a state education could properly pursue, utilitarian, and more specific economic, imperatives have been paramount. In relation to all the other imperatives arising from a complex pluralist society such as ours, and from the needs of the individuals trying to make their way in that society, the National Curriculum may be fairly broad but it is not balanced and balance not breadth is the real issue here' (Alexander, 1997: 5). He called for a more generously conceived balance of curricular aims and purposes – economic, occupational, personal, cultural, moral, social and civic – that would lead logically to a different curriculum structure from that currently in place.

The idea that the curriculum is designed to preserve certain interests provides the basis for a realistic assessment of the barriers to curriculum change and the extent to which changes are resisted for ideological as well as educational reasons.

In England in 1988 Kenneth Baker (Secretary of State for Education and Science), in outlining his government's intention to regain control of the curriculum through a national core curriculum gave weight to the country's needs in an age of acute international economic competition. 'Raising the quality of education in our schools is the most important task for this Parliament' (*Hansard*, 1987). This device of control has never been far beneath the surface of the English National Curriculum and its assessment's legislation, a legislation designed to increase England's status in the global arena of international 'standards' competitiveness.

International perspectives

Le Métais and Tabberer's research (1997) on the values and aims evidenced through the curricular frameworks of sixteen countries provided a useful starting point for considering how educational purposes were defined in different cultural contexts. Le Métais and Tabberer's study identified 'immense' educational diversity among (and within) the 16 countries investigated and indicated several aspects which have proved to be influential in shaping those differences. Relevant to this analysis was the diversity in educational aims and values and the ways in which these are expressed. Le Métais and Taberrer drew attention to three issues: the extent to which national governments' statements of values and aims reflected popular aspirations and expectations, whether stated aims and values were evident in practice and how stable over time values and aims proved to be.

Despite these open-ended issues, Le Métais and Tabberer's study identified some commonly articulated aims across the 16 countries in relation to developing the capacity of the individual, promoting equal opportunity, preparing young people for work, establishing a foundation for further and higher education, providing knowledge, skills and understanding and promoting citizenship and cultural heritage.

It is interesting that while there were common features across the expressions of educational aims and values, countries varied considerably in the level of detail with which these were expressed or prescribed in legislation. Curriculum frameworks in many other countries include a fuller specification of aims than in the current National Curriculum in England. The approach in England prior to the year 2000 revision fell into the 'minimal' reference to values category while in Japan, Korea, Singapore and Sweden, aims and educational and social values were enunciated very specifically. In Sweden, the basic values underpinning the education system were clearly prescribed and included 'the inviolability of human life, individual freedom and integrity, equal value, solidarity with the weak and vulnerable, understanding and compassion, open discussion, the internationalisation of Swedish society, and empathy with the values and conditions of others' (Le Métais and Tabberer, 1997: 11).

In Norway the *Curriculum Guidelines for Compulsory Education* (Norwegian Ministry of Education and Research, 1990) consisted of 300 pages covering every aspect of schooling including the 'core task' of schools and 'the role of school in society'. Underpinning values were stated through a lengthy description of the aims of the education system. 'The daily activities of the school must reflect democratic values ... Through examples and guidance the school shall help pupils to be broad-minded and tolerant. However, if the assumption of intellectual freedom and tolerance is to have any meaning the school must represent specific values and concepts. Pupils must learn that a personal stand point is no obstacle to showing respect for others ... The school shall promote a democratic view of society and stimulate the pupils to become actively involved in society' (Norwegian Ministry of Education and Research, 1990).

Seven countries describe the curriculum in terms of key or essential areas of learning: Australia, Hungary, The Netherlands, New Zealand, Singapore, Spain and the USA. Seven countries group their subjects together: Canada, France, Germany, Japan, Korea, The Netherlands and Sweden. Three countries teach their curriculum in multidisciplinary or interdisciplinary ways: Italy, The Netherlands, Singapore. All the other countries studied define their curriculum in terms of areas of learning or subject groupings. England is the only country in the group of 16 studied which defines its curriculum in terms of ten discrete subjects.

The study also suggested further similarities but Le Métais and Tabberer suggested that there is 'superficial evidence of convergence between different systems' and warned against simplistic comparison, when closer analysis often revealed subtle differences. For example, 'the structure of moral education content in early education in Japan is similar to that recently debated in England although there are significant differences in the degree to which the two countries emphasise this content within the primary curriculum as a whole' (Le Métais and Tabberer, 1997).

Other differences emerged in content analysis: Le Métais and Tabberer found that 'labels could be misleading, in one case the science curriculum proves to be relatively heavy in geography' (1997). The differences can be even deeper: 'In different countries, subjects, educational concepts and teaching techniques or organisational approaches can mean quite different things. These hidden differences are in such realms as teacher discourse, teacher–pupil interaction, attitudes towards learning and the ways in which subjects and knowledge are constructed, conveyed and validated. These differences can be more profound even than the hidden differences in what subjects mean' (Le Métais and Tabberer, 1997: 11).

Relevant analyses of the impact of these differences can be found in collaborative work undertaken by Broadfoot et al. (1996) and Osborn et al. (1997) in England and France. Their work addressed the impact of curriculum change on children's educational experiences, attitude to school and learning outcomes.

Vulliamy and Nikki's (1997) comparative study of school experiences of curriculum change in Finland and England was an in-depth study of 12 schools using case study methods. This study chronicled the differences between English and Finnish primary schools as they moved in apparently opposite directions in relation to the balance between national prescription and local determination. Following the determination of a highly prescriptive and centralised curriculum in the 1970s (soon revealed as unworkable, expensive and fragmentary) Finland moved towards the development of local curricula within national guidelines. 'Schools are encouraged to clarify their values and aims, devising new curricula, monitoring their implementation by devising school self-evaluation strategies and feeding the results back into school-based and wider regional in-service training [teacher professional development] programmes or courses' (Vulliamy and Nikki, 1997: 4).

A similar approach was advocated by Campbell who suggested that to encourage schools to think more creatively about the curriculum it would be useful to follow Margiotta's maxim of 'encouraging experimental approaches to the whole curriculum amongst a selected group of schools who have shown high performance in the statutory curriculum as evidenced through inspections' (Campbell, 1997: 5). In 1997 no curriculum researcher could have realised how that theory was going to turn around and bite as Ofsted's power grew as the arm of government policy on 'failing schools, failing teachers'.

Granheim (1997) also made an important point when comparing Norwegian principles and procedures with practice in England and Wales. Because of scepticism among the teachers, the Norwegian Ministry of Education laid down the following principles: 'The aim should be to evaluate the degree of achievement in the whole range of objectives defined in the curriculum. The results of various evaluations should not be used to rank schools or municipalities. A system of evaluation should not involve the collection of more data than will be for certain made use of' (Granheim, 1997: 6).

During this post-Dearing review period, Alexander's voice was prominent in raising issues which should be included in the millennium revisions for England and Wales:

> We find the critical point of variation with countries with demographic and economic circumstances not unlike our own is the extent to which children in their primary schools engage with the question of what it means to be a social being or, as a user, inheritor or custodian of finite resources, or as part of an independent community of nations. It seems to me to be not insignificant that these are precisely the areas which feature most prominently in the SCAA/National Forum for Values in Education Framework (1997). On the basis of international comparison and national consensus then, we have a pointer for curriculum review that we cannot afford to ignore. (Alexander, 1997: 3)

These specific differences represent only part of the picture. Le Métais and Tabberer forecast an increasing dialogue between countries about curriculum and assessment options and suggested that this dialogue will produce practical effects. As one country moves towards a more regulated curriculum with greater emphasis, for example, on basic skills, 'it will encounter others with those same qualities, interested in deregulating and trying to achieve a better balance with an extended curriculum or higher order skills' (Le Métais and Tabberer, 1997: 17).

Maden drew upon several international studies of over 25 countries in her analysis which identified not common curricula but common global concerns. She argued that 'the curricula challenges confronting schools in England and Wales in the post-industrial world are basically the same as elsewhere' (Maden, 1997: 2). Maden was less concerned with specific curriculum models than with what she described as the 'common range of pressures and developments which result in a broadly shared needs analysis and agenda for action' (1997: 2). Le Métais and Tabberer argued that the agenda for action will be shaped by cultural differences which will almost certainly result in different approaches to provision.

Maden's view of global curricular commonality in part mirrored the findings of Meyer's international examination of primary curricula (1992). Meyer identified a common cross-national spine of language and mathematics. Campbell pursued this issue within the framework of the, at that time, public and political perception of the importance that teachers have consistently attached to 'the basics'. Meyer stated that empirically the phenomenon of 50% of time on these two subjects (English and mathematics) – what we might call the basic instinct – is firmly established. Indeed, Meyer argued that this phenomenon has been a global constant – irrespective of region or political economy or state of development (Meyer 1992: 4). Fast forward a dozen years and Boyle and Bragg's research showed the dramatic increase in the time spent 'teaching' (coaching) mathematics and English for end of key stage 2 SAT tests, and made this 50% figure of Meyer's look like a balanced curriculum! (Boyle and Bragg, 2006).

Curriculum analysts of the structure in England consistently made the point that the greatest weakness of the pre-2000 National Curriculum was its lack of an underpinning set of values and aims. It is a recurring argument that prefaces much of the reflective discourse on curriculum structure, for example, Elliott (1996), Alexander (1997), Campbell (1997), Carr (1997) and Daugherty (1997) are representative of a much wider field of researcher critics.

The need to think more creatively about the curriculum for the twenty-first century was reiterated by Anning (1995; 1997) who was critical of Dearing's redefinition of the 'distinctive purposes of the key stage 1 curriculum' (SCAA, 1993: 31). Anning (1995) acknowledged the need to 'develop basic skills' to introduce young children to 'an interesting range of content' and to 'promote positive attitudes to learning' but argued that while these might be laudable they were not radical enough for the twenty-first-century agenda. Holt, in setting out the rationale for the arts in the curriculum, re-examined the concept of entitlement (as set out in the 1988 Education Reform Act) and called for a better overall balance, arguing that it is only through a more far-sighted view of curricular aims that the position of the arts will be ensured in the face of the 'worst excesses of the current basics drive' (Holt, 1997).

The Revised Ofsted Framework for the Inspection of Schools (1996) described areas considered of value in the curriculum. The Framework's focus on areas to be evaluated and reported on made it clear that judgements about curriculum provision and teaching quality should take account of breadth and balance in the curriculum in conjunction with aspects such as equality of access and opportunity for pupils to learn. The Revised Framework set out in a document (which was in the public domain) what is valued in relation to pupils' attitudes, behaviour and personal, social and moral behaviour.

The Department for Education and Employment report, *All Our Futures: Creativity, Culture and Education* (DfEE, 1999a) strongly supported the QCA view that the millennium curriculum revisions should be based around a clear rationale. The DfEE report took issue with the Education Reform Act (1988) requirement for all schools to provide a curriculum 'which prepares young people for adult life' as the ERA text did not explain what preparation for adult life was likely to mean at the end of the twentieth century or at the commencement of the twenty-first. Of more concern was that the objective of preparing for adult life gave no indication how that objective was to be met in the context of the ten subject structure that ERA had introduced. The *All Our Futures* report (DfEE, 1999a) expressed concern that 'while accepting the need for a sustained strategy in numeracy and literacy, it is vital that this emphasis in key stages 1 and 2 should not marginalise other areas of intellectual and personal development which are equally important in the early years and during primary school' (DfEE, 1999a: 77) (see also, Boyle and Bragg 2005; 2006, House of Commons, 2009).

2

Developing a National Curriculum: Consultation

> ## Chapter summary
>
> A description and critique of the research project which supplied the national consultation data for the Curriculum 2000 revisions.

In 1997 the author (Bill Boyle) was contracted (subsequent to open competitive tendering, already an experienced Director/Principal Researcher on six national projects for the Qualifications and Curriculum Authority (QCA) and five projects for the Northern Ireland Curriculum Council) by the QCA to develop and maintain a nationally representative sample of primary (1,000 approximately) and secondary (500) schools for the purpose of an annual monitoring survey of each of these schools' curriculum provision. This ranged across aspects such as subject timetabling, planning, subject department issues, etc. The reports from the analyses of these data were to supply core data for the QCA's curriculum monitoring reports to a range of stakeholders ranging from Select Committees of the House of Commons to the Department for Education to the national population of schools. In 2001 QCA expanded the survey to include a nationally representative sample of foundation stage settings, i.e. within and without of school locations. The methodology for the survey was determined by the QCA as a centre-periphery postal questionnaire to collect large scale quantitative data; from these data, emerging issues, interesting profiles or models of curriculum planning and provision were further investigated by the QCA and myself and my research team through focus groups, telephone interviews or case studies. A range of reports on issues from the data, e.g. trends over time

(Boyle and Bragg, 2002; Boyle and Bragg, 2003), foundation stage education (Boyle and Bragg, 2004), the impact of assessment on the curriculum (Boyle et al., 2007) were authored for the DfES and QCA; the latter further distilled and disseminated some of the information through its annual curriculum reports to schools.

We were aware that there were methodological issues with the survey instrument for a longitudinal study, for example changes in the wording of question stems and significant changes in the style and format of questions over the period of the survey. An extreme example in the later years was the jettisoning of questions which had already collected data over a number of years in favour of almost 'vox pop' type items which probed for approval of government policy changes. However the principal questions collected data to enable the development of a longitudinal profile of subject teaching time allocations and separate and combined subject teaching implementation and these were retained throughout the ten years of the survey with only minor format or wording amendments. As an example of these issues in the years 1997 to 2001 inclusive, the sub-categories of the 'combination of subjects' question were; 'nearly always separate', 'separate half the time' and 'never/hardly ever taught separately'. While for the years 2002 and 2003, the sub-categories were: 'hardly ever/never combined', 'combined half the time' and 'nearly always combined'. For 2004 and 2005, the question addressed only the subjects of English, mathematics and information communication technology (ICT) and looked at a whole key stage rather than by each year group.

Another issue which was debated with the funding agency was the reliability and limitations of 'self-report' data. The accuracy of self-reported personal or other data has been extensively researched. In the area of educational research there are contrasting views. For example, Jeff and Julie (1991) reported finding that students' self-reported coursework was accurate enough to be used for research purposes. However, the same study recorded that self-reported grades were not accurate enough to be used in decision making concerning the educational development of individual students. Smith and McCann (1998) found that less than 40% of higher education students correctly reported their family income. Maxey and Ormsby (1971) reported that students tended to inflate their grades when asked to report them and that different groups of students over-reported by different degrees. Similarly Taylor et al. (1998) found little evidence to support the use of self-reported student data.

Little research was found about the accuracy of teacher self-reported data and most of the existing information is contradictory. Traub and Weiss (1982) suggested that teachers provided accurate self-reported information in a school-based research context but Resnicow et al. (1998) found that the teacher self-report questionnaire they used was not a valid measure of implementation of the school health curriculum. Fletcher and Barufaldi (2002) and Lambert (2003) suggest that the use of teacher self-reported data cannot be a substitute for other more rigorously tested measures and indicators. Porter (2001) argues that 'education indicators must be accurate. There are two aspects of accuracy. One is an issue of measurement. For example, if an indicator is based on self-report questionnaire data, can self-reports be trusted to be valid. Sometimes the answer is yes and sometimes no ...'. However, much education research is still based on self-reported data for the principal reason that it is significantly easier and cheaper to collect this data this way. This is why the centre-periphery data collection design was the design of preference for this large scale survey; any other option for a longitudinal large scale sample was unfeasible in terms of both budget and time (Boyle et al., 2005).

Despite the random selection of a representative sample and a healthy response rate (e.g. 45% in 2005), completion of the survey by the schools, although government funded, was not government mandatory. Therefore a significant percentage of schools chose not to respond and this would lead one to anticipate some bias in the outcome. For example, do the more 'successful' schools choose to participate and therefore 'skew' the responses accordingly? Therefore the findings of the survey are reliable to the extent that the self-reported information is accurate. In the context of the survey, with anonymity and confidentiality guaranteed to the schools, the expectation would be that respondents had no reason to supply inaccurate responses.

Over the ten years of the survey the longitudinal data have supplied a uniquely evidenced profile of change in curriculum patterns, planning and provision in a representative sample of schools. The data have been used for reports to government education sub-committees, for QCA's statutory monitoring reports on and to schools for evidencing trends and changes over time for DfES and QCA (see above) and have enabled evidenced commentary on a range of issues such as changes in the curriculum linked to government interventions in that period. For example, two of my selected publications address how the introduction of national strategies for primary schools in literacy and numeracy brought about changes in teaching provision not just for English and mathematics, but so influenced the teaching time allocated to science and the foundation subjects that the balance of the curriculum offered to children was disproportionately affected (Boyle and Bragg, 2005; 2006).

The disparity between the emphasis on literacy and numeracy and the concept of a broad and balanced curriculum was commented upon by David Bell (Her Majesty's Chief Inspector) (HMCI) when authoring Ofsted's annual report (2002a): 'the strong focus on raising standards in English and mathematics and on meeting targets exerts considerable pressure on the time devoted to the teaching of other subjects' (Ofsted, 2002a: 3). He emphasised the point: 'the gulf between what pupils achieve in the core subjects and in the rest of the curriculum remains a concern' (Ofsted, 2002a: 5). Five years later in 2007, Christine Gilbert (the current HMCI) reiterated the continued existence of this 'two tier curriculum' in her annual report (Ofsted, 2007). The introduction of the revised curriculum in September 2000 did not initially redress the balance – despite the accompanying *Handbook for Primary Teachers* (DfEE, 1999b) suggesting and identifying specific opportunities for planning connections between subjects. The high level of external auditing and accountability for following the strategies and hitting national test targets resulted in a pronounced reduction in cross-subject planning, linkage and teaching alongside an increased concentration of teaching time on English and mathematics which reduced the time allocated to the foundation subjects (Boyle and Bragg, 2006). The survey data for 2001 evidence that the emphasis on single subject teaching was as strong as it had been prior to the revised curriculum. Gradually, supported by *Designing and Timetabling the Primary Curriculum* (QCA, 2002), by *A Strategy for Primary Schools* (DfES, 2003) and a more supportive attitude from Ofsted (Ofsted, 2002), schools began to demonstrate increased flexibility in their planning for subject teaching (Boyle and Bragg, 2008a). There have to be reservations about the extent of this flexibility as our recent research in primary classrooms is evidencing rigid, inflexible lessons planned in direct modelling from the national strategies and ignoring the intentions of a more flexible planning model envisaged by the Revised Framework (2006) (see Boyle, 2008, Boyle and Charles, 2010).

During the period October 1997 to April 1998, the QCA funded the author (Bill Boyle, in his role as Director of the Centre for Formative Assessment Studies (CFAS) of the University of Manchester) to conduct a national survey of the aims and priorities of the school curriculum. The principal outcome of this research exercise was to be an evidenced report to the Secretary of State for Education on the responding schools' expressed aims and priorities. The report was to be based on quantitative and qualitative analysis of a national questionnaire survey sent to all schools in England including maintained, foundation, voluntary controlled, voluntary aided and independent schools (no Academies or Free Schools existed at that time) covering the primary and secondary phases.

Context

The Dearing Review (1993) mandate that there should be a 'period lasting five years in which no major changes are made to the curriculum'

(SCAA, 1993: 39) had been more honoured in the breach (or more specifically by the many breaches) than in the observance. The most recent changes had been those made by David Blunkett as Secretary of State in 1997. His revised primary curriculum included reduced demands for the teaching of the foundation subjects and a plethora of changes to the end of key stage assessment rubrics. However, it was widely anticipated that a major and hopefully enduring revision would take place in time for the implementation of the latest model in the millennium year itself.

The government decided to give all schools the opportunity to have a voice in the process of revision and to do this through a national consultation exercise. That decision was mainly as a reaction to previous versions of the (still young) National Curriculum being regarded by the teaching profession as the product of wrangling between subject working parties and government pressure groups.

The research instrument was an open-ended questionnaire designed by the QCA (the design being subject to internal debate with much reservation about this structure expressed by the researchers). 'Questionnaires are capable of producing large quantities of highly structured standardised data. The quality of the information they provide is largely dependent upon the design of the questionnaire' (Clarke, 1999: 69). For its instrument, the QCA chose to ask the schools just one direct open-ended question: What are the aims and priorities of your school curriculum? The question was repeated for each key stage within the pre-populated school distribution to try and encourage potential responses by key stage. The questionnaire was titled 'Aims for the school curriculum: What does your school think?' and was addressed to the headteacher in each case. The headteacher was requested to 'please consult your colleagues before completing this questionnaire for your school [by appropriate key stage]'.

To the researchers, and probably to the recipient schools, a sub-set of research questions was located within this overarching aims and priorities framework question: these sub-questions included: Did schools have aims for their curriculum and did they prioritise those aims? Did schools recognise the difference between their aims and priorities? Was there a link between a school's aims for its curriculum and its priorities?

The invitation to participate and the distribution to schools was also the responsibility of the QCA and the organisation couched the language of the accompanying letter very much in terms of contributing to the review of the curriculum leading to a completely revised National Curriculum for the year 2000.

> Our monitoring suggests that a sensible first step in any review should be to establish a broadly agreed set of aims for the school curriculum and priorities at each key stage. This is your opportunity to tell us your views on this matter. (QCA, 1997: 2)

The sole contextual information supplied within the questionnaire was derived from the 1988 ERA and at that time was the only statement in legislation setting out the aims for the school curriculum. 'The 1988 Education Reform Act stated that the curriculum for a maintained school should be a balanced and broadly based curriculum which: promotes the spiritual, moral, cultural, mental and physical development of the pupils at the school and of society, and prepares such pupils for the opportunities, responsibilities and experiences of adult life'.

The author and the whole research team had misgivings about the open-ended structure based on our prior experience of working with open-ended questionnaires. However, the questionnaire was designed by the QCA as open-ended and determinedly retained as such despite the author's team piloting two alternative more structured models with a small sample of schools. The feedback on our piloted structured versions indicated at least 'ease of access and completion' and the provision of an 'any other comments' box, supplied an opportunity for (analysable) unstructured comments if the headteacher and colleagues so desired.

> Open-ended questions allow respondents to answer in their own words rather than being restricted to choosing from a list of pre-coded categories. They have the advantage of giving respondents leeway to elaborate on their answers. However, they also have their disadvantages particularly when used in self-completion questionnaires. They can generate a wide range of responses some of which can prove difficult to categorise. (Clarke, 1999: 70)

However, QCA's rationale for adhering to the open-ended strategy can be interpreted as based on: 'minimising the imposition of pre-determined responses when gathering data ... it is critical that questions be asked in a truly opened-ended fashion ... to permit respondents to respond in their own terms' (Patton, 1990: 295).

The QCA wanted to avoid the limitations of the 'closed' questionnaire in which the response possibilities are clearly stated and made explicit in the way in which the question is asked (Patton, 1990). However, it appeared that the organisation was equating lack of structure with a desire to offer schools the opportunity to communicate as fully as possible their aims and priorities. However, Patton further cautions that: 'many think that the way to make a question open-ended is simply to leave out the structured response categories. Such an approach does not however make a question truly open-ended, it merely makes the pre-determined response categories implicit and disguised' (Patton, 1990: 296).

The questionnaire is an instrument for 'measuring the ideas that go into its design. For this reason the questions not only reflect the survey's aims but also must be understood by respondents in a clear and unambiguous way' (May, 1993: 75).

The responses from the schools evidenced that the author's misgivings had been well grounded. From scrutiny of the initial influx of responses it was apparent that because of the lack of a coherent (and therefore non-standardisable) structure to the questionnaire, the headteachers' responses evidenced that they lacked guidance on structuring their responses and therefore did not recognise the link that the QCA had anticipated (but not accounted for in their design) between a school's stated aims and its priorities. Unfortunately while there is an opportunity for the researcher to clarify any ambiguities in situations where a questionnaire is administered by means of a face to face or telephone interview, there is no such opportunity in the case of self-administered questionnaires (Clarke, 1999: 69). That unfortunate 'window of ambiguity' resulted in many responses which were composed of isolated words or random (disconnected) phrases – virtually unanalysable with any degree of confidence. This was further compounded by the fact that many schools clearly found identifying their priorities as an ambiguous process. Their responses indicated that they were finding it difficult to determine whether 'the priorities' that were being sought were those that related to their own priorities or a general set of agreed national priorities, and furthermore, whether these priorities related to the present situation or to a future envisioned scenario (QCA/CFAS, 1998).

By suggesting alternative versions of the questionnaire offering classifications, frameworks and structures to offer schools guidance for their responses, the author and the research team had anticipated this potential (likely) scenario of invalidity of data. The QCA however was determined on the 'open-ended' format and it was their version which they distributed to all schools in England in October 1997.

Methodology

Data collection and coding procedures were used to produce categories, themes and conceptual understandings inductively from the data (Blasé, 1990). Data were coded by the research team according to qualitative research guidelines for grounded theory research. This approach to qualitative enquiry begins with open-ended questions rather than hypothesis. Data are generated and scrutinised concurrently through an inductive process designed to produce description of theoretical ideas. In essence, grounded theory research focuses on the discovery of substantive categories and hypotheses relevant to the subject under investigation. This research methodology permits categories, themes and theory to be conducted directly from the data (Glaser and Straus, 1976; Glaser, 1978; Bogdan and Biklen, 1982; Le Compte and Goetze, 1982). Data analysis was completed by use of an adaptation of the Miles and Huberman (1984) coding system. This consisted of categorical coding of data and selection of descriptive quotations.

The relatively large number of returned questionnaires made the use of a software package for analysis of the responses a necessity. However, currently available standard qualitative packages, such as NUD*IST, were not found to be practical enough for the task. Although the first goal of the analysis was to draw the main concepts from the responses and then classify them into broader categories (a standard task for a qualitative analysis package), the second goal was to use those categories to quantify the qualitative data, i.e. to prepare statistical tables to describe efficiently and accessibly what main categories of aims and priorities were most frequently mentioned by the schools. A home-built software was used which, like other standard qualitative analysis software, enabled the assignment of concepts to school responses and the formulation of broader categories but also enabled the monitoring of the frequency of each concept and category in the responses. It was therefore possible to build and expand or collapse categories of concepts in a near-optimal way. The software also enabled the transfer of the data to other popular software such as MS Access or SPSS for further analysis.

The key themes across the whole sample emerged from analysis and generalisation of the volume of replies for both aims and priorities. The findings at each key stage were organised for reporting purposes within these key themes. The numerical reporting at key stage level was based on the number of statements made by schools within these themes. Odds ratios were then calculated to identify how schools' responses cross-related by theme, i.e. if a school reported 'academic development' as a priority, which other themes were they likely to report? This method of calculating confidence intervals for relative risks (odds ratios) seemed to offer more information on relationships than the Pearson correlations which were also run (Morris and Gardner, 1988).

The sample

Questionnaire returns were received from 3,022 schools – a very disappointing return for a national consultation. From a national population distribution (21,822 schools) this was an approximate one in seven (14%) return. Although a disappointing rate of return, in all data collection exercises involving schools there were the usual range of acceptable excuses: e.g. wrong time of year/term, exam time, etc.; OFSTED inspection due/being reacted to; staff shortages; better things to do, etc. Schools drafted their responses as individual statements from headteachers or as an agreed statement from whole-staff meetings, department or key stage meetings, year group meetings or any combination of these. There was virtually nil indication of which of the above categories applied to each school response as the QCA had not indicated any requirement for responders to indicate status within school.

After 'cleaning' out 'blank' and indecipherable returns, there remained 2,706 responses for analysis. Those 2,706 were not consistent with 2,706 schools which supplied 'aims' and 'priorities' responses – after 'cleaning', the useable sample consisted of 2,484 schools who supplied details of what they considered to be the main aims of their school and 2,433 schools who detailed their curriculum priorities.

Findings at key stage 1 and key stage 2

At key stage 1, although the development of the values agenda was well supported in the schools' aims responses, it was apparent that the subject agenda had pre-eminence when priorities were being reported. There were six main aims themes reported by level of response: development of self-awareness (personal development); physical, social, moral, spiritual and cultural (PSMSC) values and development; broad and balanced curriculum; curriculum related to real world and real life; academic development and development of skills; emphasis on English and mathematics. Of these six, four are 'value' themes and only one represents the core subject agenda. However, when schools reported their priorities there were two themes which predominated: the core subjects theme with emphasis on English and mathematics, and then the PSMSC values theme.

The big 'losers' at key stage 1 between the aims and the priorities responses were the 'softer' themes of academic development/development of skills and development of self-awareness, which seemed from the evidence of their response rates to be regarded as fine by schools as aims but not the stuff of which priorities were made. Could it be because they were seen as less measurable (or reportable) than tests in English and mathematics? These 'values' themes reported on a par with the core subject agenda as aims but emphasis on English and mathematics accumulated far more support when the priority responses were counted.

It was interesting to note that key stage 1 schools which reported physical, social, moral, spiritual and cultural values as an aim were more likely to also report development of self-awareness and academic development as aims – however, they were also more likely to report emphasis on English and mathematics as another aim. More specifically, the schools which reported PSMSC values as an aim were 3.1 times more likely to report development of self-awareness and 2.2 times more likely to report academic development as aims. On the other hand, those schools were approximately twice more likely to report emphasis on English and mathematics as another aim.

When the aims statistics were run against the schools' priorities at key stage 1, the strongest relationship was between those schools prioritising physical, social, moral, spiritual and cultural values and the development of self-awareness (odds ratio 2.3). However, schools prioritising PSMSC values were almost twice more likely to prioritise emphasis on English and mathematics (odds ratio 1.8).

Odds ratios were then explored across schools' aims and priorities responses to establish relationships between themes. There was a strong likelihood that a school which reported physical, social, moral, spiritual and cultural values as an aim would have reported development of self-awareness as a priority. There was an even higher chance that if a school reported PSMSC values as an aim it would also have reported the same theme as a priority. Although school–community–parent partnerships were reported as a low priority (surprising because although this was 1998 – before Every Child Matters and safeguarding legislation – there were many 'Community primary schools' established), it was highly likely from the odds ratio analysis that it would be schools that had reported PSMSC values and development as an aim which had then reported the school–community–parent partnerships as a priority. There was less likelihood that schools which reported emphasis on English and mathematics as an aim reported school–community–parent partnerships as a priority. While there was every chance that schools which reported the emphasis on English and mathematics theme as an aim would have selected the same as a priority.

At key stage 2 the pattern was similar. The development of the PSMSC values theme was clearly the highest aim reported, followed by the fellow value themes of development of self-awareness and broad and balanced curriculum. The core subject agenda (emphasis on English and Mathematics) was reported as an aim by just over 50% of schools.

Table 2.1 Themes reported as aims by key stage

Key stage/question	KS1	KS2
Physical, social, moral, spiritual and cultural values and development	80%	76%
Development of self-awareness (personal development)	58%	63%
Academic development and development of skills	59%	59%
Emphasis on English and mathematics	57%	53%
Broad and balance curriculum – all-round education	53%	56%
Curriculum related to real world and real life	42%	43%

Key stage/question	KS1	KS2
Positive learning environment	38%	33%
Principles of curriculum planning	32%	39%
Excellence – high expectations – future targets	28%	31%
School-Community-Parent partnerships	27%	24%
Quality of teaching – good teaching strategies	21%	29%
Empower teachers	13%	13%
Stress individual subjects	11%	12%
Provision of feedback through alternative forms of assessment – self-assessment – record keeping	6%	7%
Stress the importance of exams	1%	1%
Information technology – New technologies	10%	13%

However, as schools reported their priorities, the core subject agenda rose in volume of responses leaving the values and academic development/ development of skills categories with reduced support. Apart for those four themes, there was very little support for any other theme as a priority. In comparison with key stage 1, both broad and balanced curriculum and principles of curriculum provision were better supported as priorities for schools at key stage 2.

The low priority at both key stage 1 and key stage 2 given to school–community–parent partnerships was unfortunate evidence of closed-door policies in schools, far from the inclusive partnership rhetoric expressed in the majority of school brochures and Ofsted reports (Ofsted, 1999). Similarly the concept of a positive learning environment was honoured far more as an aim than as a priority. When odds ratios were estimated across the 16 reported themes, as at key stage 1 the relationship between English and mathematics and PSMSC values was the largest (odds ratio 2.1). However, schools who prioritised PSMSC values were also approximately twice more likely to promote academic development, self-awareness and ICT. A very strong relationship was also found between emphasis on English and mathematics and ICT. More specifically, schools that prioritised English and mathematics were 5.3 times more likely to prioritise ICT as well. When schools' aims and priorities selections were analysed it was clear that if a school reported emphasis on English and mathematics as an aim, it was highly likely that the school would report the same theme as a priority. There was a similarly strong relationship at key stage 2 between the reporting of PSMSC values and development of self-awareness as both aim and priority. PSMSC values and development of self-awareness as aims were strongly linked with the reporting of curriculum related to the real world as a priority. As might have been expected, schools which reported the PSMSC values as an aim were then likely to have reported development of self-awareness (personal development) as a priority. Conversely schools which reported emphasis on English and mathematics as an aim were less likely to have reported either a positive learning environment or quality of teaching as priorities.

Conclusion

There are so many issues surrounding both the size of the sample and the methodology employed on the survey that one hesitates to support the findings from this research too strongly. From a national population distribution, 14% was a very low and disappointing return, supplying no more than 2,706 school returns capable of being used for any valid analysis – admittedly when being further disaggregated by question and key stage, these totalled 9,433 responses which provided a respectable amount of data for analysis.

In methodological terms there are (were) issues about the interpretation of the data produced through the use of an open-ended questionnaire which did not offer any guidance to schools on how to structure or to prioritise their responses. However, it is interesting to note that the QCA in their own published report of the consultation exercise defended the structure of the questionnaire robustly:

> These questions were posed within a deliberately unstructured open-ended format devised by QCA in order to give respondents maximum opportunity to express what they wanted to say. Accordingly, no definitions about aims or priorities were provided, and no guidance on expectations was given. (QCA, 1998: 18)

To return to the question with which the research began. Do schools have aims for their curriculum? The data show that they certainly stated aims and that those aims were not very different across key stages. Physical, social, moral, spiritual and cultural values was heavily supported as the main aim throughout. Do schools prioritise their aims? In the main, the response again is affirmative; there was some reordering but in general the same themes in almost the same order emerged as both aims and priorities. The dominant themes throughout the priorities responses were the same two, i.e. an emphasis on English and mathematics and the development of PSMSC values. The failure of the 'softer' themes reported as aims to be confirmed as priorities is noticeable and may be attributed to the atmosphere of heightened accountability that has existed since 1988 ERA but has been markedly 'hyped up' by the standards agenda and percentage success at levels introduced by New Labour in 1997. The responses then could be, cynically, viewed as an expression of 'real politic' practised by survivors.

Victims of this pragmatic reporting included school–community–parent partnerships, a positive learning environment and the development of self-awareness – all crucial issues in learner development but not measured in SATs (Standard Assessment Tasks) – all significantly supported as aims but not as priorities.

Did schools define their aims and priorities specifically enough for them to be meaningful and/or measurable as achieved or not? The answer is, in the main, 'no' although the structure (or lack of one) of the questionnaire did not encourage specificity in responses and on occasions left too much to the deductive skills of the researcher. The responses ranged from single words or context-free phrases to pasted-in segments of the school brochure, leaving the author in some doubt on many occasions as to whether he was analysing a 'wish list' or a litany of platitudes.

In the context of the consultation informing on any baseline philosophical decisions for the review of the structure of a revised national curriculum, there was strong support in the responses for a development of values agenda both as an aim and as a priority. This was argued in the dominant and inclusive PSMSC values theme but also through the support for the development of self-awareness as an aim across all key stages. This level of support for a values-based system was acknowledged by the QCA in their report to the Secretary of State 'on the broad nature and scope of the review of the National Curriculum' (QCA, 1998) subsequent to the author's submission of the research report to the QCA.

> We recommend that building on QCA's recent consultation, a draft document is published setting out (i) the core values and aims which should underpin the school curriculum and (ii) the aims and priorities for each key stage and (iii) the distinctive contribution of individual subjects in meeting these aims and (iv) the place of the national curriculum within the school curriculum. (QCA, 1998: 21)

However, the (moderate level of) support for numeracy and literacy as the main priorities of the first two key stages was clearly taken more notice of by the policy makers. The QCA advice stated that: 'We recommend that in order to provide stability and to minimise disruption to the work of schools, particularly at key stages 1 and 2, changes to the Statutory Orders in English and mathematics should be kept to a minimum' (QCA, 1998: 21).

3

Curriculum Development: Case Specific

> ## Chapter summary
>
> Research principles for the development of a national curriculum within a local and international context.

Research indicates that, for a curriculum to be productive and efficiently deployed, it should be presented in a structure which would enable coherence, a learning continuum that allows for the differentiated pace of individual learning needs, and measurement of progression against clearly stated learning outcomes (Perrenoud, 1998; Alexander, 2005; Boyle and Bragg, 2006; Wyse et al., 2007; Alexander, 2008; Boyle and Bragg, 2009; Halloun, 2011b). National curricula that have high expectations of their students and that are explicitly designed to empower their citizens to successfully compete in the global economy, should in particular satisfy those conditions among many others discussed in this chapter. As also discussed, ambitious but realistic curricula should also take advantage of major lessons learned from comparative international studies such as TIMSS (Trends in International Mathematics and Science Study) and PISA (Programme for International Student Assessment).

This chapter lays the theoretical foundations for a curriculum review using as its model a review carried out by the authors of the Qatar pre-school (K) to Grade 12 science and mathematics curricula presented in the *Early Years Foundation Curriculum* (EYFC) documents, and in the various science and mathematics *Curriculum Standards* and *Scheme of Work* documents pertaining to Grades K through to 12 (SEC, 2010). The chapter consists of six sections. Section 1 discusses some general premises of national curricula like those in the State of Qatar. Pedagogical premises are further discussed in section 2, from a general perspective, and in section 3, from the perspective of international assessment programmes that the Qatari curricula try to account for. Three critical aspects of any curriculum are discussed in the following three sections. These are, in order, assessment (section 4), cross-disciplinarity (section 5) and systemic sustainability (section 6).

Towards a national curriculum

A curriculum should be structured in a way to extend beyond the teacher-controlled classroom and include learning beyond the school context and beyond school years through the concept of the 'lifelong learner' who constantly works to become self-determining. This model fits the needs of employers and politicians. They are constantly urging schools to help students develop flexibility of mind, initiative, adaptability, creativity, communication skills, competence in problem-solving, multi-skills, ability to collaborate and work in a team situation, etc. If schools are to respond effectively to these calls, they need to work in collaboration with families and the local community in seeking to achieve two broad aims through the curriculum. These aims provide an essential context within which a curriculum needs to be developed.

> Aim 1: A curriculum should aim to provide opportunities for all students to learn and to achieve.
>
> Aim 2: A curriculum should reflect and influence the values of society, as it aims to promote students' spiritual, moral, emotional, social and cultural development and prepare all students for the opportunities, responsibilities and experiences of life.

These two aims mutually reinforce each other. The personal development of students spiritually, morally, emotionally, socially and culturally plays a significant part in their ability to learn and to achieve. Development in meeting both aims is essential to raising standards of attainment for all students, and to preserve and enhance one's own heritage.

When a curriculum is defined and implemented at a national scale, it should further aim to fulfil the four following purposes:

1   To establish an entitlement

To secure for all students, irrespective of social background, culture, race, gender, differences of ability and disabilities, an entitlement to a number of areas of learning and to develop knowledge, skills and dispositions necessary for their self-fulfilment and development as active and responsible citizens.

2   To establish standards

To make expectations for learning and attainment explicit to students, parents, teachers, employers and the public, and to establish national standards for the performance of all students. These standards can be used to set targets for improvement, measure progress toward those targets and monitor and compare performance between individuals, groups and schools.

3   To promote continuity and coherence

To contribute to a coherent national framework that promotes curriculum continuity and is sufficiently flexible to ensure progression in students' learning. It facilitates the transition of students between schools and phases of education and provides a foundation for lifelong learning. Good curriculum design plus reliable information about each student's strengths and weaknesses can help to offset any regressions in progress at times of transition across schools or phases.

4   To promote public understanding

To increase public understanding of and confidence in the work of schools, and in the learning and achievements resulting from compulsory education. It provides a common basis for discussion of educational issues among lay and professional groups, including students, parents, teachers and employers.

From a practical perspective, there are at least three major principles that need to be accounted for. First, teachers need to know about their students' learning progress and difficulties and misconceptions in learning so that teaching plans can be adapted to meet these learning needs. Teachers ascertain these learning needs through assessment and evaluation. This process can be described as the integration of teaching, learning and assessment of the curriculum defined in its simplest form. As a matter of principle, all three processes are interdependent and mutually strengthen the teacher's ability to support the progress of the student. Once this first principle has been accepted, it requires action in the context of the school's planning for the delivery of the practical aspects of the curriculum, i.e. the programme of work, programme of study, syllabus, unit of work, lesson plan.

The second principle involves the value placed upon the organisation of a curriculum. Is it based on the philosophy of the superiority of subject based knowledge? Does the curriculum organisation place a higher value on subject knowledge than on knowledge of the relationships between subjects? All research-supported best practices seem to lead us away from isolated, discipline-based curricula towards cross-disciplinary curricula that promote a coherent big picture not only within a given field but across various fields that may appear for some as independent from each other, such as science and arts or humanities.

The third principle defines curriculum as both an orienting and a mediating device. Through the right kind of curriculum, students can be oriented towards the worlds of knowledge, culture, social experience and relationships. But the curriculum cannot be conceived as some kind of final and fixed entity, a list of finite 'learning areas'. Rather it emerges or is constructed as an intersection between:

- the perceived or hypothesised learning needs of the individual students
- the structure and evolution of knowledge conceived as disciplines and tools for learning
- changing realities, beliefs, values and ideologies of society. (OECD, 1990)

It is in this definition and designing of the curriculum, the planning of its implementation and its practical expression in the teacher–learner relationship that we find the visible expression of the core values and organised learning of society in the setting of the school. The curriculum is increasingly being recognised as a selection from the culture, a mode of addressing the culture, as a mediation of cultural experiences and processes in a living situation where teachers, students, parents and community interact on a common project. All this, for public account-ability purposes, must be accessible through documents and web pages but also physical, with parents feeling that they are welcomed in and have access to the learning environment of the school.

Curriculum and pedagogy

Pedagogy allows the translation of curriculum into the operations of teaching and learning. The traditional distinction was curriculum as 'content' and pedagogy as 'delivery of content'. This is not a good distinction: even as method, pedagogy is relational or transactional, not transmission. The pedagogical experience conveys norms and values, based on the belief that the teacher's role is to develop the learner and that the learner is an active subject in the process of becoming. In this analysis, the margins between curriculum and pedagogy become less fixed. 'Education can either socialize students into critical thought or into dependence on authority', that is, according to Shor (1992: 153), 'into autonomous habits of mind or into passive habits of following authority, waiting to be told what to do and what things mean. Unfortunately in traditional schooling, the latter most often occurs'. According to this definition, the teacher's pedagogical positioning is at the centre of the 'how' and the 'what' of teaching and learning. In short pedagogy is dichotomous: it can encourage and support growth for children, locate and empower children at the centre of learning or it can stultify and reduce the process to following externally prescribed schema (Edwards, 2001; Dunphy, 2008).

Within this accountability-compliant model there was no place for 'teachers shifting from control of knowledge to creation of processes whereby students take ownership of their learning and take risks to understand and apply their knowledge' (Graziano, 2008: 157). And there was certainly no way that the factory-product technicians would understand that 'teachers and children are partners in teaching and learning transactions. We need to find ways of interacting with children to co-construct shared meanings in ways we cannot do if the children themselves are not active participants in exploring the situation' (Makin and Whiteman, 2006: 35). And there was even less understanding that 'child-centered teaching includes behaviours that actively involve children in guiding the learning process, such as offering choices, encouraging activity and suggesting solutions' (Hayes, 2008: 433).

Researchers have chronicled the sterility of the pedagogy designed, like in England, to improve test scores within a minimum competency model and restricted definition of the term 'standards' (Edwards, 2001; Patrick et al., 2003; Alexander, 2005; Wyse et al., 2007; Alexander, 2008; Dunphy, 2008; Boyle and Charles, 2010b). 'Pedagogy is so palpably the missing ingredient ... and it is so obviously vital to [students'] progress and to learning outcomes that we have no alternative but to find ways of remedying the deficiency' (Alexander, 2008: 22). So teachers and their trainers have to rethink the basis of pedagogy: synonymous with this process is an understanding that a student as an autonomous learner should be involved in sharing the construction of his/her own learning, i.e. self-regulated learning. For Schunk and Zimmerman (1997: 14), 'self-regulation refers to self-generated thoughts, feelings and actions that are planned and cyclically adapted to the attainment of personal [learning] goals'. For Perry et al. (2007: 29) students 'develop the process of self-regulation through instrumental support from teachers and peers through the forms of modelling and scaffolding attitudes and actions'; note the focus across both those definitions on enabling the students to systematically monitor their own learning. The importance of Perrenoud's philosophy is evident as he states that 'the roles of teacher and student have to be deregulated from the traditional transmission and passive reception model' (1998) and therefore as a minimum requirement for teaching, teacher training should stress avoidance of the 'recitation script' style of pedagogy so criticised by Alexander (2005). The current summative metric model and didactic pedagogical style are producing students who cannot self-regulate (because they are not offered the experience of working that way) and teachers who are still located in the traditional model of whole class teaching and didactism. Ruttle (2004: 75) warns the didacts to reflect whether their 'preconceived learning objectives, however well-intentioned and meta-cognitively "pure" get in the way of actually working with how some children think about their own writing'. Ruttle is cautioning teachers (and the teacher-trainers) against both the rigidity of the pre-planned package version of teaching and the dangers of ignoring individual learning needs to keep the majority moving at pace through the weekly objectives.

Students will not arrive at this self-regulated position overnight nor by accident nor will the trainee teacher understand self-regulated learning without tutoring and support, both theoretical and empirical. Meyer and Turner (2002: 23) recognise the student's achievement of self-regulation as a learner by describing the process as 'assuming responsibility, this becomes contingent not only on the classroom climate and growing competence but also on the opportunities afforded to demonstrate that competence'.

It is important to draw the distinction between an inclusive model of formative teaching which has the child at the centre of a learning agenda and the complex pedagogy required for that process to be supported and to compare it with the present situation in which the child is reduced to a provider of statistical data within a metric driven model of teaching (Perrenoud, 1996). For example, the current teacher training model in England is based on the formal 'surface' accretion of 33 standards (TDA, 2008). These standards are based on process competencies rather than on the development of teacher professionalism through a focus on understanding and using differentiated formative teaching practices, developing an active pedagogy and engaging in innovative approaches to involve both teacher and student in self-regulated learning (Perrenoud, 1996). In contrast to this prevailing model, Rowsell et al. (2008: 115) suggest that 'pedagogy refers to an educational position or approach that includes both theory and practice'. This definition focuses on the strength or weakness of the connection between theory and practice in the teacher's pedagogical development. There should be no end point in the teacher's development as a practitioner and for that development to produce a truly reflective formative practitioner there has to be a synthesis between theory and practice (Shepard, 2005).

Curriculum alignment with international programmes

No national curricula today may ignore the international comparisons created by many international cross-country testing programmes.

This can be illustrated by examining the international monitoring studies, which demonstrate the advanced examples of developments in assessing student achievement. Here one can refer to PIRLS (Progress in International Reading Literacy Study), TIMSS (Trends in International Mathematics and Science Study), PISA (Programme for International Student Assessment), the results of which cause great interest for educational policy makers internationally and nationally (Mullis et al. 2003; OECD, 2003; Mullis et al., 2006; IEA, 2008; Osborne and Dillon, 2008; OECD, 2009; Mourshed et al., 2010).

The test materials of these studies are developed on the basis of one or another cognitive classification (Nezhnov and Kardanova, 2011), which determines adequate activities for different aspects or levels of learning content attainment. In other words, the starting point in test development is the hypothetical cognitive structural picture of evaluated features (degree of training, attainment). For example, in the TIMSS test package for monitoring mathematics mastery, a differentiation of four types of activity is introduced which makes a source of taxonomy: Knowing Facts and Procedures; Using Concepts; Solving Routine Problems; Reasoning. This qualitative typology serves as a basis for developing a set of test items.

However, later on the package is evaluated by statistical processing of received data to create a scale which no longer indicates the initial classification of the four types of activity. Instead of this, four levels of mastering mathematics appear (advanced, high, middle, low) thus meeting particular statistical (quantitative) criteria.

Statistical analysis is also performed to determine test items completed by every group of students. Therefore every level, with a certain probability, is referred to a set of items and then to a relevant list of skills, i.e. levels of competence and probability parameters. Thereby, test results, being scaled, give the basis not only for ranking the examinees but also for grouping them into four categories, with regard to mastering a certain set of skills. However, the qualitative difference between the four groups of skills turns out to be rather vague and requires additional conceptualisation which seems to be problematic in this case.

Such an approach to developing toolkits for the assessment of school students' achievements for international comparisons prevails nowadays. The main reason for this is a complicated situation about the use of taxonomies of educational goals – hierarchical classifications, which model an education process and are necessary prerequisites for quality assurance of education results.

The first peculiarity of the situation is the substantial number of different taxonomies. Following the classical version of Bloom (Bloom et al., 1956) a variety of level-related schemes have been developed, which differ from their original, one way or another. In particular, the versions of Lerner, Simonov and other authors appeared in Russian education (Lerner, 1980; Simonov et al., 1999). In the international education environment, the cognitive classifications developed in TIMSS, PIRLS and PISA became widely known. The second peculiarity is a lack of a common theoretical background, which would provide the possibility of rational comparison and mutual criticism of various versions with the further generalisation. The implicit compliance of pedagogy with mechanistic approaches (association psychology, behaviourism) not adequate for the interpretation of education processes makes the majority of existing taxonomies of equal worth from the philosophical point of view. As a result, the subject of discussion moves to the area of pedagogical expertise, thus partly explaining why this multiplicity is so stable.

One can hope to overcome this difficult situation by developing integral, theoretical approaches which bring into the system concepts from the main constituents of education process (such as learning, development, educational results, understanding, competence, etc.), and by giving footholds to pedagogical taxonomies suitable for making an assessment instrument. Some prerequisites for providing a solution to this problem have been created by the Russian psychological school of Vygotsky (1978).

Curriculum and assessment

Assessment plays a crucial role in the development of the learner and has to be integrated within the dynamics between teaching, learning and curriculum. There has to be a balance between summative and formative strategies for uses of assessment. Assessment in many countries now has three paradigms and one result. Paradigm one is dominated by the accountancy model, beloved of policy makers and at the core of the school effectiveness debate (Gorard, 2010). It is best defined as 'teach to be measured', in which the sole purpose of teaching is to deliver or cover material that will later be tested; there is no involvement of the student in that learning process. Paradigm two is dominated by the banking model (Freire, 1970) in which the teacher teaches and the students are taught, those are the fixed and immutable roles; there is no deregulation of that role (Perrenoud, 1998; Allal and Ducrey, 2000; Zimmerman, 2000). This was traditionally described as the 'topping up' model in which the child was an 'empty vessel' and was topped up or filled up with knowledge, which they 'recited back to the teacher to prove that learning had taken place (Tharp and Gallimore, 1991; Smith et al., 2004; Alexander, 2005; 2008). How sad that it is still in evidence in 2011. Paradigm three is governed by the 'testocracy' in which the metric is prescribed and the teaching and learning process conforms to that testing metric. Its limitations and the humanistic and social implications (as follows) are not even considered as flaws in the system: 'test scores correlate with parental income (and even grandparents' socio-economic status) rather than actual student performance' (Guinier and Torres, 2003: 68). The fact that the testocracy reduces merit and a meritocracy to a meaningless pre-destined ordination is ignored. 'Test-centered techniques are used to ration access to elite higher education as appropriate measures of merit' and '... at no point was any attempt made to reconcile this with an elitist rationing process' (Guinier and Torres, 2003: 69). Guinier and Torres assert that alongside the testocracy even the vagaries and lack of standardisation of teacher assessment stand out like a beacon of fairness and equity: 'reliance on teacher ratings excludes fewer people from lower socio-economic backgrounds than does reliance on test scores' (Guinier and Torres, 2003: 71). The testocracy knows no boundaries but income, it even, as Guinier and Torres found in their research in the USA, redefines merit: 'it moved from an assumption that tests are meritocratic for everyone except people of colour to a larger critique of the way in which the conventional testocracy denies opportunity to many deserving white applicants as well. It changed the definition of merit' (Guinier and Torres, 2003: 72).

The three paradigms of assessment, as outlined above, have contrived to produce one result: a reduced pedagogy so that the complexity of the individual learner is ignored through the insistence of the system that the learner conforms to the (narrow) norms of the metric (Guinier and Torres, 2003) as defined by political intervention. This soon became and is now firmly established as centralised control of a minimum competency 'standards-based' accountancy and accountability system.

In practice national developments of curriculum tend to focus on a subject-centred curriculum with the inevitable elevation of a number of subjects into a 'core' curriculum. This then equally inevitably leads to the establishment of national testing of this 'core'. The inherent danger of this is that narrow concepts of curriculum reinforce poor teaching and learning practice. Catalogues of subject content are not curriculum, neither are packaged information and high stakes narrowly focused written examinations.

Curriculum and cross-disciplinarity

Concepts of knowledge are sanctioned in the curriculum programme of many countries through a process of social stratification that reflects the power of some groups to assert their view of knowledge as beyond dispute. This can lead to dangerous assumptions such as:

- the superiority of subject-based knowledge
- the undervaluing of practical knowledge
- the priority given to written as opposed to oral forms of presenting knowledge
- the superiority of knowledge acquired by individuals over that developed by groups of students working together.

These are analytical hypotheses about the school curriculum. They do not imply statements of value. Their value is that, as teachers, curriculum policy makers or researchers, they enable us to question the origins of particular ideas about knowledge that are expressed in the curriculum and the educational goals and vision of society that they imply. The idea that the curriculum is consciously or unconsciously designed to preserve certain interests provides the basis for a realistic assessment of the barriers to curriculum change and the extent to which changes are resisted for ideological as well as educational reasons.

The general educational progress of children and their competence in the basic skills appear to have benefitted where they are involved in a programme of study that includes art and design, history and geography, music and physical education and science as well as languages, mathematics and religious education. The coherence of the curriculum, whether at primary or secondary levels, can be strengthened by linking or even combining aspects of one subject with those of another. Through lesson planning, teachers can link or combine related or complementary aspects from two or three subjects, and plan similar units, or even a common unit of work. Learning objectives for each individual subject continue to be planned for and taught over the course of this unit of work.

Alternatively, a curriculum can be designed on cross-disciplinary grounds that highlight and promote common patterns in knowledge structure and thought in various fields. Research on differences between novice and expert knowledge structure and reasoning skills, and on aspects of expertise and excellence in a given profession, have long shown that what distinguishes experts and high achievers in various professions from other people at the level of content knowledge is the way professionals organise their knowledge rather than the amount of knowledge they possess. Furthermore, research shows that there are common patterns in the way distinguished members of different professions organise their knowledge. The same goes at the level of knowledge acquisition and deployment, and reasoning skills and meta-cognitive factors that govern such activities (Gentner and Stevens, 1983; Johnson-Laird, 1983; Lakoff, 1987; Casti, 1989; Bower and Morrow, 1990; Giere, 1992; Novak, 1993; Ericsson and Charness, 1994; Giere, 1994; Viau, 1994; Halloun and Hestenes, 1998; Glas, 2002; Halloun, 2004; 2006).

Therefore, if a curriculum is to prepare students for distinguished achievement in the workplace and life, it should concentrate on and promote such patterns shared by professionals from various fields, and bring coherence and consistency among various curricula. This can best be achieved in cross-disciplinary based curricula as called for by many international organisations. For example, the National Assessment Governing Board (NAGB, 2011a; 2011b) that oversees NAEP (National Assessment of Educational Progress) in the US calls for 'scientifically literate' people who can connect ideas across disciplines: for example, the conservation of energy in physical, life, Earth, and space systems. The American Association for the Advancement of Science (AAAS, 1993; 1994) and the National Research Council (NRC, 1996; 2011) put an emphasis on unifying cross-cutting themes in science (e.g. constancy and change; patterns, systems and models) that allows students to realise a coherent big picture of science.

A cross-disciplinary approach is now formally encouraged even in countries such as England, where the curriculum is structured in terms of individual subject areas (QCA, 2003). For example, in Japan curriculum content has been reduced to make space on the timetable for experiential learning. The aim is to encourage and promote cross-disciplinarity, individual expression and positive engagement. The curriculum in many countries complements the compulsory subject areas with cross-disciplinarity. Known as 'common themes' in the USA, 'cross-curricular areas' in Australia, 'common essential learnings' in Canada, 'key issues' in Ireland, 'key skills' and 'thinking skills' in England, 'cross-curricular objectives' in Hungary and Holland, 'essential skills' in New Zealand, 'core skills and values' in Singapore, 'cross curricular themes' in Spain, they usually comprise a set of interrelated categories of conceptions (content knowledge) and habits of mind (skills and dispositions) across subjects (INCA/QCA, 2003).

Curriculum and systemic sustainability

No curriculum, especially a national curriculum, can be sustained without instituting proper monitoring and support mechanisms for various actors, especially teachers. These sustainability mechanisms should be instituted in the national educational system, and in participation with various stakeholders and the community at large.

According to the McKinsey report, the most improved school systems around the world sustain improvement by balancing school autonomy with consistent teaching practice, and by ensuring 'leadership continuity'. They keep getting better because of 'six interventions [that] occur with equal frequency across all the improvement journeys'. These are 'revising curriculum and standards, ensuring an appropriate reward and remuneration structure for teachers and principals, building the technical skills of teachers and principals, assessing students, establishing data systems, and facilitating the improvement journey through the publication of policy documents and implementation of education laws' (Mourshed et al., 2010: 26).

The most critical requirement for curriculum efficacy and sustained impact is a well-trained teaching workforce. This teaching force will understand the importance of constantly interrogating the curriculum and reviewing its applicability to the range of learning needs of the relevant populations of students. Student assessment, again, plays a crucial role in this respect:

> Assessment ... can provide a framework in which educational objectives may be set and students' progress charted and expressed. It can provide a basis for planning the next educational steps in response to children's needs. By facilitating dialogue between teachers, it can enhance professional skills and help the school as a whole to strengthen learning across the curriculum. (TGAT, 1988a)

In a curriculum system driven by an 'assessment for learning' (AfL) philosophy, the focus on students' learning needs will cause teachers to think more about their teaching and contribute to their professional development.

- Teachers will gradually think less about 'What am I going to teach and what are the students going to *do*?'. Then they will move towards '*How* am I going to teach this and what are the students going to *learn*?'
- The teacher should look for ways to encourage and involve the students in taking responsibility for their learning. This will inevitably lead to more interactive learning activities in the classroom. The use of formative teaching, learning and assessment strategies will lead to fundamental changes in teaching and learning.
- All the teachers in a subject department in a school could come together to scrutinise each other's marking of a sample of students' work and bring each other's judgements into line. Teachers will see professional development through good practice in such 'moderation' or 'standardisation' meetings – good practice through the selection of work (the exemplary function: Sadler, 1989) and also the use of selected work samples to demonstrate to their students how to achieve to expected levels (the formative function).

In developing and writing curriculum assessment tests for the attainment of seven-year-old students in the UK, Boyle and Christie (1990) modified the procedure and introduced Standard Assessment Tasks which were samples of typical classroom activities, centrally designed and written by 'teacher-experts'. Teachers administered and marked these tasks over a period of two or three weeks and held within-school agreement trials to authenticate standards. The process of discussion of standards and 'how' the teachers had taught to achieve those standards proved to be a powerful teacher development activity with peers sharing best practice in teaching and learning (Clarke and Christie, 1995).

The great advantage of group moderation goes beyond assessment to all aspects of classroom practice (Linn, 1992; Radnor and Shaw, 1994). It has been found that where teachers come together to discuss performance standards or criteria, that moderation process becomes a process of teacher development with a beneficial feedback to their teaching. Professional learning communities, action research and focus groups are some of the many platforms that bring teachers together to share their experiences with the aim of continuous professional development. A curriculum should be structured so as to facilitate teacher interaction for continuous professional development.

4

Curriculum Reviewing Criteria: Case Specific

Chapter summary

Perspectives, questions and review criteria for curriculum auditing.

A curriculum review is optimised when carried out in two broad and complementary perspectives: theoretical and practical. From a theoretical perspective, the review should answer specific questions about the curriculum architecture, and the content and mechanisms associated with various curricular dimensions. From a practical perspective, the review should look into curriculum deployment at a representative sample of schools, and ascertain the strengths and weaknesses, as well as threats and opportunities, that are reflected in the classroom implementation of the curriculum, and that are associated with students, teachers and various other stakeholders. The review would even be better consolidated when involving these stakeholders in the actual review process and the preparation of the review report.

This chapter consists of four sections. Section 1 draws on the previous chapter to set the major premises underpinning the construction of a national curriculum. Section 2 formulates the review criteria in the form of a series of questions pertaining to various facets of a curriculum. Section 3 presents the review template that guided the review process carried out in the manner outlined in Section 4.

Premises of a national curriculum

The discussion in the previous chapter indicates that a national curriculum, for general pre-K–12 education, should satisfy at least the following conditions:

1. A national Early Years (Kindergarten)–12 curriculum should be grounded into a well-structured educational framework with a clear and viable philosophy that is aligned with local constitutional and cultural aspects.
2. A national Early Years (K)–12 curriculum should empower graduates with a profile for success in life, especially in higher education and the workplace.
3. A national Early Years (K)–12 curriculum should adopt a sound, research-based pedagogy that provides well-defined and viable tenets, principles and rules (or educational standards) for curriculum design and implementation within the context of the local educational system. The pedagogy should bring into consonance the gradual development of student intellect and the historical development of any field of study from an epistemological perspective.
4. A national Early Years (K)–12 curriculum should include clear mechanisms, i.e. means and methods with explicit rules, guidelines and protocols, for translating the target student profile into measurable outputs (e.g. benchmarks, expectations, learning outcomes) that can be readily deployed in specifying the programme of study for any field or discipline (or set of fields).
5. A national Early Years (K)–12 curriculum should stipulate classroom implementation of the programmes of study in the most efficient ways possible, with coherent mechanisms of learning and instruction that promote mediated, student-centred, experiential learning and that are guided by authentic assessment for meaningful learning of programmes of study.
6. A national Early Years (K)–12 curriculum should include clear mechanisms for continuous evaluation and refinement of the curriculum.
7. A national Early Years (K)–12 curriculum should be well-situated in the existing educational system, and should provide for the institution in such system of support and sustainability mechanisms, to be maintained by various stakeholders, especially teachers, and by the community at large.

Basic questions

Curriculum review should be carried out according to well-defined criteria pertaining to various facets of a curriculum. The facets are normally defined by the original curriculum writers in accordance with the adopted curriculum architecture. The Qatari curriculum documents made available to the reviewers do not include a detailed description of the architecture in question, and do not specify the required facets. The reviewers had to begin their work by identifying a generic set of facets that may apply to any curriculum, and subsequently set their review criteria in the form of questions pertaining to each facet.

Different architectures of well-defined dimensions and facets may be adopted in the development of a curriculum. However, various facets may well fall in two broad structural and practical dimensions, complemented by a viability dimension. The structural dimension pertains to curriculum design, and comprises theoretical or foundational facets that include the framework of the curriculum and its scope, in relation to other curricula, along with its philosophical and pedagogical foundations. The practical dimension pertains to curriculum deployment, and comprises facets that set the form in which the curriculum should be reified, along with the physical and methodological requirements for its deployment and continuous evaluation. The viability dimension sets the terms and conditions that the curriculum should satisfy, or that should be satisfied for it, internally, in relation to its design and deployment, and externally, in relation to the educational system in which it is situated, the community it is supposed to serve, and various stakeholders, especially teachers.

Various facets addressed by the reviewers in each of the three dimensions are listed in the following, along with samples of questions that the reviewers tried to answer, among others, about each facet, and that give the reader an idea about what each facet is about. More ample details about each facet are given in the following text.

Curriculum design

- *Architecture*: How is the curriculum configured? What elements does it consist of, and how are they related to each other? What format is used in various documents, and how consistently is it being followed?
- *Philosophy*: What philosophy governs curriculum design and deployment? Where does it come from? What measures are taken to uphold it in all practical respects?
- *Framework*: What type of educational framework is the curriculum laid in? What are its foundations, and what does it call for? How systematically is it being followed in putting together various aspects of the curriculum?
- *Scope*: What field or set of fields does the curriculum cover? What content and practical aspects of this field or set of fields does it emphasise, and to what extent? On what basis are various elements chosen? How are they spelled out and organised?

- *Outputs*: What outputs are expected of the curriculum regarding target students? Are they classified according to a specific taxonomy? How are they specified? How well are they spelled out in terms of expected student achievement?
- *Hierarchy and progression*: Is there a specific hierarchy in the scope structure? How does it match the structure of the field(s) it covers? Is there a learning progression for output reification? How does it match cognitive development at various ages? How consistent is the content hierarchy with the cognitive progression?
- *Integration*: How does each covered field relate to other fields within and outside the defined scope? What interfaces govern the interaction among various fields? Are there mechanisms (tools, rules, protocols) for integrating new topics or new fields?

Curriculum deployment

- *Programme of study*: How is the programme of study configured? What elements does it consist of? How are they chosen? How are they related to each other? How are they sequenced? What time allocations are proposed?
- *Learning and instruction*: What mechanisms of learning and instruction does the curriculum prescribe, and why? How are they organised? How do they account for differences among students?
- *Assessment*: What types and forms of assessment does the curriculum promote? How do they guide learning and instruction? What sort of feedback does assessment allow, and how is it provided?
- *Resources*: What resources are needed (paper and electronic media included)? How should these resources be managed?
- *Environment*: What school and classroom settings are necessary for curriculum deployment? How should these settings be managed?
- *Evaluation*: What internal and external criteria are specified for continuous curriculum evaluation? How related are these criteria to the expected outputs? What mechanisms are prescribed to this end? How is feedback provided to various stakeholders at various stages of curriculum deployment? How does assessment serve continuous curriculum evaluation?

Curriculum viability

Structural viability

- *Coherence*: Are various elements within a given dimension coherently related to each other? Are various dimensions consistent with each other? Are there explicit linkage or bridging mechanisms between design and deployment components? Is the curriculum coherently related to other curricula?

- *Continuity*: How does the curriculum help learners evolve from one level to the next within a given grade and across various grades? How smooth and affordable is the evolution for both students and teachers?
- *Practicality*: Is the curriculum well-founded from theoretical and practical perspectives? Is it transparent enough to teachers and other actors? Is it affordable to students, teachers and other stakeholders? Are various mechanisms systematic enough and consistent with the framework? Can teachers readily follow these mechanisms?
- *Flexibility*: Does the curriculum explicitly account for different student aspirations and achievement levels? Can teachers readily adapt or extend the curriculum beyond its scope? Can the curriculum accommodate changes implied by deployment data or critical findings in educational and cognitive research?
- *Suitability*: Is the curriculum suitable from cultural and other national and/or local perspectives? Is it well-situated in the educational system?
- *Universality*: Is the curriculum aligned with internationally acclaimed and corroborated pedagogy? Does it empower students for smooth transition within the same educational system and to other local and international systems? Does it empower them for success in modern life?

Systemic viability

- *Sustainability*: What support systems are needed at various levels (from school to national educational authorities) to ensure successful curriculum deployment and to sustain its impact? Does the educational system provide necessary requirements? Are there proper monitoring mechanisms and accountability conventions? Are there proper contingency mechanisms to counter the rise of unforeseen negative matters?
- *Ownership*: Can teachers readily own the curriculum? What background is required of them for successful curriculum deployment, and do they possess it? What modalities of in-service professional development are required to sustain the curriculum? What about other stakeholders?
- *Community support*: What is the role of the community in curriculum design and deployment? What mechanisms are desired to allow constructive community involvement?

Review template

Based on the above, a template was formulated to guide the review process, and to report findings in the most efficient way possible. As shown in Table 4.1, the template is meant to ascertain, in three respects (constituents, mechanisms and structural viability), the extent to which each facet in curriculum design, deployment or viability is covered in

Table 4.1   Curriculum Review Template

Dimension	Facet	Constituents	Mechanisms	Structural viability	Notes
Curriculum design	Architecture				
	Philosophy				
	Framework				
	Scope				
	Outputs				
	Hierarchy & progression				
	Integration				
Curriculum deployment	Programme of study				
	Learning & instruction				
	Assessment				
	Resources				
	Environment				
	Evaluation				
Structural viability*	Coherence				
	Continuity				
	Practicality				
	Flexibility				
	Suitability				
	Universality				
Systemic viability	Sustainability				
	Ownership				
	Community support				

*The extent to which each of the structural viability facets is explicitly treated in the various curriculum documents is hereby being ascertained like all other facets. In contrast, and as indicated in the corresponding column, the structural viability of each facet, in all three dimensions, is ascertained following the four criteria as discussed above.

the Qatari curriculum documents (Early Years Foundation Curriculum or EYFC booklets, K–12 science or mathematics standards and schemes of work).

The 'constituents' column pertains to the coverage of various elements that make up a given facet, and their functions. The 'mechanisms' column pertains to tools and other means, as well as rules, protocols and other methodological aspects that are necessary to bring about and put together various constituents, and to ensure that the facet is duly respected in curriculum design and/or deployment. The 'structural viability' of each facet is ascertained in the third column in accordance with the corresponding six facets outlined above and as discussed in Chapter 3.

The 'notes' column in Table 4.1 is reserved for reviewers to put their detailed findings and own thoughts regarding any of the three preceding columns. These findings and thoughts are reported, as necessary, during the course of discussion in the following three chapters. They do not appear in the various tables included in those chapters, and in which various Qatari curricular facets are rated as discussed next.

The coverage of a given facet, in each of the three curricula (EYFC, K–12 science, K–12 mathematics) is ascertained, in each respect, on a three-point scale: S (satisfactory), P (partial), N (not or poorly addressed).

The coverage of a given facet, in each of the three curricula (EYFC, K–12 science, K–12 mathematics) is ascertained, in each respect, on a three-point scale: S, P, N. The coverage is said to be 'satisfactory' in any given respect (indicated by S in the template) when all aspects are fulfilled, in one form or another, in one or more of the documents pertaining to the curriculum in question. It is judged to be somewhat or 'partially' satisfactory (P) when only some but not all aspects are fulfilled, and/or when some superfluous or undermining aspects figure in the documents in question. A facet is judged not to be covered to an acceptable level (N), when it is superficially covered or not covered at all in any of the Qatari curriculum documents that were available to the reviewers.

Review process

The template above was used in the review of each of the Qatari curriculum documents (EYFC, science and mathematics). Reviewers took necessary notes about each facet as covered in the various documents, and used these notes to report their findings and set their ratings of each facet in Table 4.1. Except for certain facets in the EYFC, findings about a given facet are reported not for each document separately, but in all documents pertaining to a given curriculum (EYFC, science or mathematics). Notes taken by the reviewers are not reported verbatim in the following four chapters. They have been edited, and necessary excerpts presented during the discussion to clarify or support a given point pertaining to curriculum design, deployment or viability.

It should be noted here that facets addressed in the review often did not figure explicitly in any of the Qatari documents at hand. They had to be inferred from an analysis of one or more texts that may or may not pertain directly to the facet in question. For example, there was no mention of 'taxonomy' anywhere in all documents. However, a classification of outputs or goals figures under 'assessment' in the standards document that reveals that a certain form of taxonomy was actually at the foundations of the 'standards'.

Findings of the review process are reported in the following three chapters, beginning with science and ending with EYFC. Recommendations for the revision of all three curricula are given together in the last chapter. Many recommendations are given directly or indirectly in the next three chapters. Some of these recommendations are recapitulated in the last chapter along with new recommendations. Findings are first reported for science and mathematics in K–12 because of the broader coverage of these curricula. Discussion in the next chapter about the science findings includes details that are common to all three curricula, especially from theoretical and foundational perspectives. Such details, which also clarify a number of issues about various facets, are not repeated in the subsequent two chapters where findings are reported about the mathematics curriculum and the EYFC.

5

Science Curriculum: Case Specific

Chapter summary

A case study focus on an international 'standards-based' science curriculum model.

The science curriculum documents consist of the *Curriculum Standards* (Education Institute, 2004) and the *Scheme of Work for Grades K–12* (Education Institute, 2005), with Grades 10–12 presented at two levels, foundation and advanced (the two-level detailed Grade 10 scheme of work being not made available). Table 5.1 shows the overall rating of various curricular dimensions, using the template discussed in the previous chapter. Detailed findings in the documents in question are discussed in the following about the design, deployment and viability of the science curriculum. More emphasis is put on curriculum deployment than on the other dimensions, since the corresponding facets are the ones mostly covered and elaborated in the documents at hand.

Curriculum design

The Qatari science curriculum for Grades K–12 is a 'standards-based' curriculum that sets out what students should 'know, understand and be able to do, leaving it up to schools and teachers to decide on the appropriate resources and various means and methods of learning, instruction and assessment (Education Institute, 2004: 9, 11; Education Institute, 2005: 5). The science standards, like all other standards, are meant to prepare Qatari students to 'compete successfully in the worldwide economy' while developing 'a feeling of identity with their country, and a deep understanding of Qatar's traditions, achievements and culture' (Education Institute, 2004: 9).

Standards-based education originated in the USA with the publication of the *Curriculum and Evaluation Standards for School Mathematics* (NCTM, 1989) and related publications (NCTM, 1991; 1995; 2000), and then the *National Science Education Standards* (NRC, 1996). Standards were then meant as 'guidance and vision' (NCTM, 1989, 2000), or at best 'criteria that people at the local, state and national levels can use to judge whether particular actions will serve the vision of a scientifically literate society (NRC, 1996). In 2011, the National Research Council (NRC, 2011) recommended that 'standards should set rigorous learning goals that represent a common [performance] expectation for all students'.

In the Qatari K–12 science curriculum, 'standards are goals for students' learning' and 'focus on the content' along with specific reasoning and problem solving skills, and aim to provide enough detail to give teachers a clear understanding of conceptions and reasoning skills students should develop by the end of each grade (Education Institute, 2004: 10). As presented in the various documents, the Qatari K–12 standards look like the 'performance expectations' called for recently by NRC (2011) or 'benchmarks' defined by some US states, or more like the UK 'qualifications'. In fact, in numerous places, the Qatari documents speak of 'performance standards', or simply 'performance by the end of' a given grade, and often mix between performance and 'knowledge' of a given fact or concept.

The philosophy behind that choice is not spelled out explicitly in the Qatari documents at hand, and neither are paradigmatic or pedagogical premises that lie at the foundations of the various standards. Moreover, the difference between such K–12 'goals' and the EYFC counterparts or 'learning outcomes' is not clarified or justified, and neither is the shift away from the integrated approach followed in the EYFC document. The philosophy of a curriculum normally consists of a set of tenets, or principles of axiomatic nature, that set the foundations of a curriculum from national and cultural perspectives, and especially from cognitive and pedagogical perspectives. There is brief mention at the beginning of the *Curriculum Standards* of, say, the necessity to adhere to local heritage and culture, and for content to be relevant to modern life. However, it is nowhere evident in this and other documents how such premises need to be upheld in curriculum design and deployment. Pedagogic premises figure implicitly in various curriculum documents, and are not explicitly stated as philosophical tenets (e.g. experiential learning, instructional flexibility, breadth–depth balance and helicoïdal or spiral sequencing of materials).

Table 5.1   Curriculum Review Template completed

Dimension	Facet	Constituents	Mechanisms	Structural viability	Notes
Curriculum design	Architecture	P	N	P	Design not explicit
	Philosophy	P	N	P	Little, vague statements
	Framework	P	P	P	Minor details provided
	Scope	P	P	N	Mostly traditional, field specific
	Outputs	P	P	P	No taxonomy, no dispositions
	Hierarchy & progression	P	N	N	Traditional sequence
	Integration	P	N	P	Gets thinner towards upper grades
Curriculum deployment	Programme of study	S	P	P	Episodic, unbalanced content
	Learning & instruction	P	P	P	No learning cycle
	Assessment	P	N	N	Not authentic
	Resources	P	P	P	Mostly equipment
	Environment	P	N	N	Not evident
	Evaluation	P	N	N	Not evident
Structural viability	Coherence	S	P	S	Limited to scope
	Continuity	P	N	P	Somewhat consistent with framework
	Practicality	P	P	P	Depends on the state of schools
	Plasticity	P	N	P	In theory but not practice
	Suitability	S	P	S	
	Universality	P	N	P	Not evident
Systemic viability	Sustainability	P	N	N	Not evident
	Ownership	N	N	N	
	Community support	N	N	N	

The scope of the science curriculum is defined in five 'strands' for K–9: scientific enquiry, physical processes, life science, materials, Earth and space. It is defined, in two different 'pathways' for Grades 10–12, foundation and advanced, in four strands each: scientific enquiry, biology, chemistry and physics. The advanced pathway covers the topics of the foundation pathway, with more in-depth reasoning and problem solving. The scope includes not only 'scientific' knowledge, but also 'ethical and moral issues raised by scientific advances' as well as other issues about science, technology and society (Education Institute, 2004: 26).

This constitutes a major step forward in the Qatari science curriculum, and is aligned with the latest science education trends around the world, especially in Europe (Osborn and Dillon, 2008) and America (NRC, 2011).

The Qatari science curriculum moves gradually from a declared integrated scope in EYFC (pre-K–2), to a single-field scope in grades 10–12. The scientific enquiry strand is a cross-cutting strand at all grade levels. The 'skills and procedures' promoted in this strand help maintain a cross-disciplinary cognitive and, to a lesser extent, behavioural thread among the other strands. Cross-disciplinarity is further maintained, to a certain level, from an epistemic perspective as well as from a cognitive perspective, specifically with mathematics and language. A similar epistemic thread though does not explicitly tie up conceptions (concepts, principles, etc.) together in various scientific strands, especially not in Grades 10–12. As we shall see below, cross-disciplinarity could have been better realised among scientific strands, as well as with other strands, especially from an epistemic perspective, if the Qatari curricula were more aligned with scientific paradigms, like standards-based science curricula elsewhere in the world, and promoted model-based episteme and cognition.

A systematic specification of the outputs of a curriculum, like learning outcomes or performance goals or expectations, requires cognitively and pedagogically grounded taxonomy and learning progression. The taxonomy of outputs provides a classification scheme along three (or four) dimensions: epistemic, cognitive (and metacognitive), and behavioural. The epistemic dimension guides the specification of content knowledge or conceptions (concepts, laws, principles, etc.) that students are expected to 'know' and 'understand'. The cognitive dimension helps specify habits of mind, or reasoning skills and dispositions (metacognitive outputs), that students should be 'able' to develop. The behavioural dimension sets dexterities or performance skills that students should be 'capable' of showing in performing specific actions. The learning progression provides an evolution map that students are expected to follow, across the (age) years, in the development of various outputs (conceptions, reasoning skills, dispositions and dexterities), a map that should be aligned with the paradigmatic hierarchy (of content and processes) recognised in the field(s) that the curriculum is about.

Taxonomy is implicitly spelled out in the sections on the 'aims' and 'assessment of the science standards' (Education Institute, 2004: 11, 15–17). The implicit Qatari taxonomy is aligned in certain respects with Bloom's taxonomy (knowledge and understanding, application, analysis and evaluation, leaving out Bloom's synthesis), and with US standards and UK qualifications in others (scientific enquiry skills and procedures). It is also aligned in some of these respects with international testing programmes such as TIMSS and PISA, especially with the reasoning skills and dispositions outlined in the 'aims' section. The discussion on assessment in the *Curriculum Standards* (Education Institute, 2004: 16–17) sheds some light on what is expected of students in each of the three categories (knowledge and understanding; application, analysis and evaluation; scientific enquiry skills and procedures). The *Scheme of Work* gives even more detail on scientific enquiry. However, everything said anywhere seems to be underlined by the assumption that readers, especially teachers, know why and how these three categories came about, and what is meant exactly by each promoted conceptual or procedural output. This may not be necessarily true, especially that there is no clear consensus as to what the used terms (outputs) mean in the related literature.

The 'standards are based on the premise that all Qatari students are capable of learning successfully and of achieving high levels of performance' aligned to international expectations in high-demanding curricula. 'Key performance standards' that should be achieved by all students are spelled out in this direction, along with 'non-key standards' that target either low achievers or high achievers. This constitutes a good feature of the standards that 'do not imply that each student in a grade is necessarily at the same level of achievement. Teachers should exercise flexibility and imagination when they are planning lessons' (Education Institute, 2004: 11).

The learning progression that may take students to 'high levels' of achievement is not explicitly identified in the standards documents, neither from a cognitive perspective nor from a paradigmatic perspective. From a cognitive perspective, a generic evolution path needs to be identified for various types of outputs. Such a path would sketch out a learning progression across a finite number of developmental stages, from an 'initiation' stage where an output is barely known to, or developed by, a learner, to an 'innovation' stage where the output is mastered by the learner to the extent that they can deploy it in novel situations. From a paradigmatic or pure scientific perspective, various scientific models and related conceptions and habits of mind are classified, and ordered, into increasing levels of complexity, from structural, functional and procedural perspectives. The model hierarchy is then matched with the cognitive hierarchy in order to specify the appropriate sequencing of materials across consecutive grades (Halloun, 2011b).

Curriculum deployment

> The standards are intended to help schools to meet students' learning needs but are not in themselves a 'syllabus' … Decisions about how individual teachers might best teach the standards are left to schools. There are no prescribed teaching methods … Equally, there are no prescribed textbooks or other teaching and learning resources … no prescribed methods of assessing and recording students' progress. (Education Institute, 2004: 11)

> Each school can develop its own policies for lesson planning, teaching and learning, and assessment ... There is no requirement for Independent Schools to use the scheme of work. (Education Institute, 2005: 5)

The Qatari standards may in this respect be trying to give greater authority to schools in curriculum deployment, perhaps in alignment with OECD's recommendation based on PISA's findings that 'in countries where schools have greater autonomy over what is taught and how students are assessed, students tend to perform better' (OECD, 2011), and with the McKinsey report that shows that the 'most improved school systems' around the world achieve and sustain improvement by increasing the responsibilities and flexibilities of schools and teachers to shape instructional practice (Mourshed et al., 2010). Countries such as Finland where individual schools have full authority across a broad range of issues perform best on PISA, which may indicate that this perhaps positively affects student performance on such tests. However, along with this authority goes the need for appropriate regulations and pre-service and in-service teacher and administrator preparation. In the absence of adequate professional background and continuous professional development, teachers and schools are not necessarily able to make appropriate choices regarding any aspect of curriculum deployment.

No matter how good their background might be, teachers and other school actors need explicit guidance in the deployment of any curriculum. This guidance should cover all practical facets of the curriculum, from the programme of study (outlined in the *Curriculum Standards* document) and necessary mechanisms for monitoring its implementation, to all aspects of learning, instruction, assessment, evaluation and necessary resources and environment. The *Scheme of Work* provides in part necessary guidance in some of these respects.

Programme of study

The science programme of study is laid out in the form of 'standards', often 'performance' standards or goals, in the *Curriculum Standards* document. As mentioned above, the science scope is laid out in a limited number of 'strands' at various grade levels. Each strand, other than scientific enquiry, consists of a number of 'themes' that cover classical and modern-day science. The Qatari curriculum has duly gone the extra mile by including valuable, but delicate, themes that are considered controversial by some, and even abhorred by others, such as the big bang theory and the theory of evolution. Standards have been carefully defined for such themes to avoid culturally sensitive or highly debatable and controversial issues.

All in all, the scope of coverage is reasonable for various grades, and so is the sequence from one grade to another. There are, however, two major issues with the programme of study. One issue relates to the relative weights of the four types of outputs (conceptions, reasoning skills, dispositions and dexterities), the other to the way outputs are organised.

The relative importance or distribution of the four types of outputs in a given strand, in a given grade, should be about the same in all practical facets, from programme of study to learning and instruction, and assessment. The table about the 'weighting of assessment objectives' (Education Institute, 2004: 15) gradually increases the allocation to conceptions ('knowledge and understanding') from 20–30% in Grades K–2, and to 45–55% in Grades 10–12. The allocation to reasoning skills and certain dexterities associated with communication, ICT and scientific enquiry decreases in that direction. No explicit allocation is made to ascertaining dispositions, especially those pertaining to students' 'feeling of identity with their country, and deep understanding of Qatar's traditions, achievements and culture'. Aside from the dispositions drawback, the proportions allocated in that table to conceptions, reasoning skills and dexterities seem reasonable. However, these proportions are not quite reflected in the programme of study of various strands.

For example, the table in question allocates, in Grade 3, 35–45% of assessments to conceptions, 20–30% to certain reasoning skills ('application, analysis and evaluation'), and 30–40% to other skills and dexterities ('scientific enquiry skills and procedures'). Such weights are not quite reflected in any strand. For illustration purposes, consider the 13 'physical processes' key and non-key standards and their illustrations in that same grade (Education Institute, 2004: 87–95). The statements of all 13 standards pertain to 'knowledge' of certain 'conceptions' or so-called facts about forces and light propagation. The illustrations given with the standards allude to certain aspects of scientific enquiry and ICT, which, if handled properly, may help students develop certain reasoning skills (e.g. classification and analysis) and dexterities (e.g. graphical representations and equipment handling). However, the ratio of conceptions to skills and dexterities is here almost the inverse of the one allocated in the assessment table, and conceptions are given far more importance than the other outputs, while it should be the opposite. Another point is worth noting here. Teachers have to figure out promoted skills and dexterities on their own, since these outputs are not stated explicitly in the standards.

In Grade 10, and according to the same assessment table, 45–55% of assessment concentrates on 'knowledge and understanding'; 25–35%, on 'application, analysis and evaluation'; and 20–25%, on 'scientific inquiry skills and procedures'. Looking, say, at the chemistry strand in that grade, one may notice that with topic 15 on atoms and molecules are associated 15 key and non-key standards (Education Institute, 2004: 193–5). The statements of virtually all standards fall in the first category (knowledge and understanding). When a standard requires students to 'describe', 'explain' or even 'deduce' certain issues about atoms or molecules, it does not require them to reason on their own, but actually to be informed of what chemistry says about these issues. Even when asked to 'make a display' or a 'model' of a given structure, students are not actually required to build such representations on their own, but often simply to retrieve them from the internet or from other resources.

Cognitive and educational research often shows that, thanks to their paradigms, scientists concentrate on specific patterns in the world, coherently organise their episteme (conceptions) around specific models or systems, follow systematic reasoning and behavioural processes, and consistently adhere to their dispositions. In contrast, ordinary people's knowledge (students included) of and about science often consists of a loose bundles of conceptions (often misconceptions) and operational routines that they apply following rules of thumb for solving familiar problems (Helm and Novak, 1983; Halloun, 1986; Novak, 1987; Cobern, 1993; Hake, 1995; Halloun and Hestenes, 1998). Research also shows that unless students are explicitly guided to develop and organise various outputs in a science curriculum in accordance with scientific paradigms, students will not learn science meaningfully, and will retain little, if any, of what they learn in science courses (Donovan et al., 1999).

Scientific enquiry is a cross-cutting strand that covers four areas: methods of scientific investigation, how scientists work (starting in Grade 7), processing and communicating information, and handling equipment and making measurements (Education Institute, 2004: 17, 18, and 31ff). The strand is meant to help students develop scientific reasoning skills and dexterities, especially in relation to the experimental approach, and a better understanding of what science is about and how it benefits from technology, especially ICT. These aims are highly valued in the Qatari science curricula. The strand could still be improved, especially in the methods area, by explicitly focusing on model construction, evaluation and deployment as discussed above. The area on how scientists work could also be enhanced by relating student conceptions and processes about the world, and their views about science, to similar ideas in the history of science in an approach where 'ontogeny recapitulates phylogeny'.

A rich variety of scientific enquiry standards is promoted at various grade levels. However, certain generic standards appear sporadically rather than constantly in various grades and strands. The long list of sporadic appearance includes, among others: 'identifying patterns', 'making models', 'asking questions', 'hypothesis making and testing', 'description', 'explanation', and 'prediction' of structures and phenomena.

Various science outputs in the field-specific strands are listed in a traditional way for various grades. They figure in episodic lists of conceptions, reasoning skills or dexterities. They could have been more coherently organised, and better aligned with scientific paradigms, should they have focused explicitly on specific patterns, and been presented in the context of a limited number of scientific models in each grade, and across various grades (Halloun, 2004/2006; 2007; NRC, 2011). According to Giere (1994), laws and principles in a scientific theory 'function more like recipes for constructing models than like general statements'. All major reform movements in science and mathematics education have lately emphasised the importance of models for coherent knowledge organisation and of modelling for the development of scientific methodology (NCTM, 1989; NCTM, 1991; NRC, 1996; NRC, 2011).

Let us illustrate this point with the concept of force in physics, and especially in classical mechanics. Research shows that this concept, especially in Grades 8 and above, cannot be meaningfully understood outside the context of all Newton's laws of dynamics discussed together in the context of a limited set of 'particle' models (Halloun and Hestenes, 1985a; 1985b; Halloun, 2007; NRC, 2011). There is no account anywhere in the physics strand for this fact. The concept of force is discussed in a very traditional approach across various grades (force effects, types, pressure, moment, equilibrium, with no mention of Newton's first law, etc.). In a modelling approach, discussion of mechanics starts with the free particle model and not with individual kinematical or dynamical concepts, including the concept of force (Halloun, 2004/2006; 2007; 2011). A free particle model allows description, explanation and prediction of the translation of any physical object under no net force. Following the discussion of this model, the concept of force is introduced as a necessary 'cause' to 'change' the motion of a free particle, more specifically to change the magnitude or direction of its velocity. Models of increasing complexity can then be built, beginning with the model of a particle under a net constant force, followed by models of a particle in translation under binding or other variable forces. In each model, new conceptions of mechanics can be introduced only on a need basis. Various scientific reasoning skills can also be developed in the context of these models in accordance with a well-defined taxonomy.

'The standards reflect a spiral approach' (Education Institute, 2004: 19). Some themes figure in many grades, and are progressively built up in breadth and depth. The progression across grades seems reasonable for individual outputs. However, it is not explicitly justified from cognitive and paradigmatic perspectives. Coherence, efficiency and meaningfulness could have been better maintained should the sequence be not about individual outputs, especially conceptions, but about specific models being gradually elaborated across grades. In depth, a model could first be constructed to fulfil simple functions such as description of a pattern, and then gradually developed to engender explanation, then prediction, then control, then change of the pattern. In breadth, the model could gradually engender in its domain more and more complicated systems that manifest the pattern in question. A maximum of a handful of models can be selected in each 'theme', in a given strand, to do the job.

Learning and instruction

Major premises for implementing the programme of study through learning and instruction are outlined in the *Curriculum Standards*, and specific 'optional' mechanisms prescribed in the *Scheme of Work*. The former document calls explicitly for student-centred, experiential learning through individual and group work:

> Teaching the standards requires teaching methods that are varied and experiential. Effective lessons will incorporate an experience in which the students actively participate, followed by a period of consolidation during which the main issues are distilled from the experience. Learning should be facilitated by practical hands-on activities for students. The standards include the scientific enquiry strand, the effective teaching of which will require teaching spaces to be used flexibly to allow a range of different activities, from class-based activities, through group work, to individual work. (Education Institute, 2004: 25)

The document in question duly acknowledges that teachers 'may use direct instruction and explicit teaching, or may guide students to learn through experimentation and discovery. Traditional methods might have a place but students will need a much wider range of active experiences' for meaningful learning (Education Institute, 2004: 11). Some guidelines are given in the *Scheme of Work* to fulfil those objectives.

'The optional scheme of work for science is a long-term teaching plan... [about] how the standards can be taught' (Education Institute, 2005: 3). The proposed plan consists of a closed 'planning-teaching-assessing' cycle for which the *Scheme of Work* 'develops sufficient detail in each unit about what to teach and how to teach [about a specific group of standards in a given disciplinary strand] for teachers to be able to create a series of lesson plans' (Education Institute, 2005: 7). All units in the document in question have exactly the same structure: (a) a title page for each unit, followed, in order, by (b) a reminder of key- and non-key standards covered in the unit, (c) teaching and learning activities, and finally (d) assessment activities.

The title page includes a common introduction for all units followed by four sections entitled 'Previous learning', 'Expectations', 'Resources' and 'Key vocabulary and technical terms'. The introduction also stresses the right of teachers to use extra or alternative activities for teaching any of the standards from their schools' textbooks and other resources. However, criteria are given nowhere in any of the documents at hand according to which teachers should select appropriate activities. This may leave many teachers at a disadvantage, especially when they do not have the necessary background to understand the pedagogy behind the standards, and to make critical choices like those of the appropriate learning activities.

The 'Previous learning' section gives, where appropriate, a list of prerequisites required for the students to develop the standards in a given unit. The list consists entirely of conceptions or scientific 'facts', and includes no reasoning skills or dexterities. It is not accompanied by specific propositions on how to ascertain whether students actually possess the prerequisites, and how to compensate for any gaps in this respect. The document acknowledges in many instances that students often come to their science courses with misconceptions about the natural world and the realm of science. Such misconceptions impede far more students' learning than the lack of any knowledge about what they are about to learn. The Scheme of Work would have been more helpful to teachers in this respect if it had taken advantage of the pertinent science education literature.

The 'Expectations' section sets what the students are expected to know and be able to do at the end of the unit for regular students and those 'who progress further'. The latter students are expected to develop key standards and not non-key extension standards. This leads to confusion since all students are expected to develop key standards. Furthermore, this section could benefit from a discussion of the cognitive demands imposed by various standards, and of the hurdles that teachers should expect along the road due to various factors, especially those pertaining to expected student difficulties.

The 'Resources' section lists the main equipment needed for carrying out the proposed activities. As such, it helps teachers acquire what they need and afford ahead of time. The section though may be improved by listing other resources such as references, software, and internet sites that are specifically helpful for the discussed unit (instead of having a generic list of such sites in the introduction of the *Scheme of Work*).

The 'Key vocabulary' section helps teachers identify key terms which they need to concentrate on or pay special attention to. This section may become more beneficial for teachers if it were to include a glossary of such terms, and call teachers' attention to common misinterpretation of, and confusion among, various terms, as revealed in the science education literature, mostly due to the lack of appropriate semantics and correspondence rules in commonly used science textbooks. In its introduction to various units (Chapter 3), the *Scheme of Work* stipulates for some 'language objectives' and for 'teaching science in the medium of English'. There, it stresses the importance of proper discourse among peers and of scientific verbal and written communication. It also stresses that 'science lessons should promote students' reading strategies' and 'should include opportunities for informal writing' in various forms. However, the document in question does not suggest explicit mechanisms for achieving these objectives in various units. Such mechanisms are especially crucial when English is the medium of instruction, and when 'a teacher who is not completely fluent in English may have difficulty explaining a science concept' and lead students to confusion (Education Institute, 2005: 39, in Grades 10–12).

Under 'Activities', the *Scheme of Work* presents the key standards for each unit as the unit's 'objectives', and proposes for every standard, or set of standards, 'possible teaching and learning activities', along with the needed time, specific 'notes' and necessary 'resources'. The recommended teaching time for different standards and units, and subsequently for various science strands, looks reasonable in various grades. However, there are minor differences in the recommended teaching time among the three different timetables pertaining to periods of 60, 50 and 45 minutes (Education Institute, 2004: 13, 14). Some issues may also arise from the liberty of having periods differing that much in length.

Activities include a mix of lecture, peer discussion, and hands-on activities (often prescriptive experiments) associated with specific enquiry standards. The enquiry standards are listed by their numbers in the 'notes' column. It would have been more convenient if those standards were explicitly stated just like their content counterparts. Overall, proposed activities are suitable for the corresponding key standards. However, they could benefit from a better structuring as discussed next. But before we do that, let us turn one more time to non-key standards.

The common introduction in the title page refers teachers to prior or subsequent units for consolidation or extension activities pertaining to non-key supporting and extension standards listed in the following page. This may not be adequate for both types of non-key standards. First, students who had trouble developing specific outputs in previous grades, in meaningful, long-lasting ways, often do so because they were not originally afforded the appropriate learning activities. Remedial would then necessitate following an approach different from the one followed before, in a previous grade, and recommended for the 'supporting standards'. Second, non-key, 'extension standards' correspond in fact to outputs that are different from, though complementary to, outputs targeted in key standards. Instead of embarking advanced students in a given grade onto completely new outputs taken from an upper grade, it might be better for both students and teachers to help those students cover the same outputs (standards) as their peers, but deeper in depth and wider in breadth, especially in a cross-disciplinary approach. Otherwise, when they move to the upper grade, advanced students might lose interest in the materials previously covered, and/or the gap with their peers would widen further, and perhaps to the extent that might not be afforded by teachers in this grade.

Various activities in a given unit are listed episodically in a very traditional fashion, just like the standards they correspond to. Students can develop various standards more systematically, with a paradigmatic perspective, if learning takes place through structured learning cycles with well-defined peer interaction dynamics, and with the purpose of developing coherent scientific models rather than isolated outputs.

The idea of a learning cycle began in the late 1960s with the works of Robert Karplus and colleagues at the University of California at Berkeley (Karplus, 1977). It evolved with time to the extent that all major science textbooks are nowadays being developed around this idea. The education literature around the globe abounds with research showing that the more instruction, especially science instruction, guides students through the same systematic learning stages in every lesson, and the more the end of a given lesson provides a smooth transition, or even an opening to the following lesson, the more efficient and meaningful learning becomes. That is exactly what learning cycles are meant to do.

A variant of Karplus learning cycle is adopted in the Qatari EYFC, but not in the science curriculum documents. In science, a learning cycle is, for many, a modelling cycle, a cycle for model construction, evaluation and deployment. Each learning cycle (whether modelling or not) begins with an exploration phase whereby students discover the potentials and limitations of specific outputs that they have developed so far, and realise the need to develop new outputs. In a modelling cycle, all outputs would pertain to a model that represents a given pattern in specific respects. Students may then be directed, in an adduction phase, to propose appropriate hypotheses about the desired pattern, i.e. to propose a candidate model, and an appropriate strategy for testing their hypotheses. The strategy, subsequently implemented in a formulation phase, would take students into a process of gradual corroboration and progressive refinement of the proposed model. At certain points during the process and afterwards (deployment phase), students would deploy the model in order to consolidate it and relate it to other models within the context of the theory and paradigm which all these models belong to (Halloun, 2001; 2004/2006; 2007; 2011b).

When learning and instruction are done following a learning cycle, and especially a modelling cycle, changes would be necessary in the structure and content of units in the *Scheme of Work*. Some of these changes are necessary even if no particular learning cycle is adopted. For instance, students cannot realise the importance of any conception, or any other output, unless introduced when needed (exploration phase in a learning cycle). Thus, no standard should be introduced in any unit unless needed to complete the big paradigmatic picture pertaining to a given system or phenomenon discussed in the unit (or model, in the proposed approach). For example, units like the one on 'handling physical quantities' in Grade 10 physics would be better not existing independently, and each standard in this unit would need to be moved to a more appropriate unit where students can meaningfully realise its importance.

To illustrate this point, take the foundational key standard 21.4 and the advanced key standard 25.4 in Grade 10 physics. These two standards are identical and state that students should 'distinguish between vector and scalar quantities, manipulate them appropriately and interpret their meaning'. Activities are proposed to accomplish this in the unit on 'handling physical quantities' (e.g. 147 in the scheme of Grade 10 advanced) from a pure mathematical perspective, with secondary applications from mechanics. Students can meaningfully and efficiently develop the standards in question only when they 'need' to deal with vectorial quantities such as velocity in contrast with scalar quantities such as speed in real world situations, and in the context of more involved conceptions such as Galilean state laws of kinematics or Newton's law of dynamics. 'Learning' of the two identical standards in question would then be better deferred until these laws or similar conceptions are discussed (preferably in the context of Galilean particle models of translation).

Learning cycles are structured well enough to lead students consistently in productive paths, and flexible enough to allow individual students to follow their preferred learning style and afforded pace. A variety of teacher mediation protocols may be prescribed in a learning cycle (Halloun, 2004/2006) that would suit the call in the Qatari standards for 'differentiated activities', and for overall flexible student-centred instruction. Such protocols would be a valuable addition to the *Scheme of Work*.

Assessment and evaluation

Authentic assessment is often called for in the educational community whereby teacher and students are allowed to reliably: (a) ascertain the extent to which individual students meaningfully achieve various outputs at specific points of instruction, (b) identify progress or evolution paths of individual students' profiles throughout the course of instruction, (c) track and efficiently regulate the evolution of student profile along these paths in meaningful ways, and (d) evaluate and efficiently regulate course content and teacher practice, and subsequently the curriculum. In short, authentic assessment is meant to be assessment for learning and not of learning (Halloun, 2011a).

The Qatari science curriculum acknowledges to a certain extent some of these aspects of authentic assessment. However, 'there are no pre-scribed methods of assessing and recording students' progress' (Education Institute, 2004: 11). The *Scheme of Work* provides some 'examples of assessment tasks and questions' with every unit, sometimes with some helpful 'notes'. However, it does not prescribe specific mechanisms for various types and forms of assessment. Teachers are then left to figure out on their own when and how they should administer various types of assessment (diagnostic, formative, summative), what outputs any assessment should cover and according to what taxonomy and specifi-cations, what item format should be used (open, multiple-choice, case study, essay, etc.), in what medium assessments should be produced and delivered (oral, written, online, etc.), how they should be marked or graded, how to record, analyse and interpret data, what feedback to pro-vide to students and how, etc. Failure to address these issues would leave teachers to wander in dark labyrinths. At best, different teachers would end up using different assessment philosophy and approach, and subse-quently different instructional methodology, which would lead the students to be torn apart while working to satisfy various teachers' requirements that may be at odds with each other, and thus learn things by rote rather than meaningfully.

Authentic assessment does not consist only of tests and exams. Various activities, interactions, and even spontaneous thoughts contrib-ute to assessment, and subsequently to student regulation of their own conceptions, habits of mind and dexterities. Scientific enquiry and other experiential activities provide students with the opportunity for continuous self-evaluation, and especially for minds-on, insightful reg-ulation of their profiles. Group work provides the opportunity for individual students to think aloud and thus proceed consciously and more efficiently in the self-evaluation and self-regulation processes. The same goes for even when students recapitulate on their own what they have learned in a given lesson. The rules of engagement in all these opportunities need to be laid out and implemented explicitly through teacher mediation.

The *Scheme of Work* recognises the need to 'summarize lessons and round them off', and suggests that the 'last lesson of each unit will require a more extended review or summary of the unit as a whole ... This is the time to draw out the key learning points and what students need to remember [and prepare themselves for] what they will go on to learn next. Where relevant, links can be made to work in other units and to real world applications' (Education Institute, 2005: 36, in Grades 10 to 12). Such 'summary' should not be made by teachers, but by students in the form of a self-assessment exercise. The teacher may assign a class-room or homework activity for students to work on individually, or in groups, whereby they would recapitulate the major outputs in a given lesson, and then in a given unit, and to set the grounds to extrapolate what they have learned so far to novel contexts within and outside the scope of the studied field(s). The teacher may provide students with appropriate mechanisms (e.g. a template and a protocol or guidelines) for recapitulation or synthesis, and for extrapolation to novel domains, along with necessary criteria for evaluating the viability of their work.

'The only requirement on Independent Schools is that every student participates in the national tests based on the standards' (Education Institute, 2004: 11). This requirement may lead teachers to teach to the test and thus to defeat the very purpose of the Qatari curricula. For this not to happen, appropriate regulations and monitoring mechanisms need to be put in place, state tests need to be carefully structured and weighted by comparison to school assessments, a preventive awareness campaign needs to properly target students, parents and various stakeholders.

Curriculum viability

In his acceptance speech for the 1989 Oersted Medal presented to him by the American Association of Physics Teachers, A.P. French (1989) noted:

> When it comes to curriculum, anyone who studies such matters must, I think, be struck by two things. One is the enormous amount of dedicated effort that has gone into the design of new curricula. The other is the way in which the results of such efforts tend to disappear from the scene.

The impact of a curriculum on the state of education is determined, to a large extent, by its internal and external viability as indicated in Table 5.1 on p. 55. Internal or structural viability pertains to the coherence, con-tinuity, practicality, plasticity, suitability and universality of various facets of the curriculum. External or systemic viability pertains to the sustainability of the curriculum, and the extent to which various imme-diate stakeholders, especially teachers, take ownership of the curriculum and the community at large provides necessary support.

In Table 5.1, viability is addressed to two different ends. First, the extent to which each of the six structural viability facets is explicitly addressed in the curriculum documents at hand is ascertained in three respects: (a) explicit formulation of criteria pertaining to each facet ('constituents' column), (b) explicit proposition of adequate facet mechanisms for curriculum evaluation and monitoring ('mechanisms' column), and (c) the structural viability of the facet's criteria and mechanisms ('structural viability' column). Second, each facet of the curriculum is ascertained with respect to the six structural viability facets as outlined in the previous chapter.

Criteria and related mechanisms are not spelled out explicitly for any of the six structural viability facets in the science curriculum documents at hand. There is a sporadic mention of some aspects pertaining to viability, mostly in the introduction sections of various documents, and during the discussion of certain curriculum design or deployment facets. The ratings in Table 5.1 of the six structural viability facets are based on such discussion.

There might be other documents where such viability criteria and mechanisms have been actually spelled out explicitly by the concerned authorities in the State of Qatar. However, having no access to such documents, the ratings in Table 5.1 of the various curriculum facets had to be made based on the outline provided in the previous chapter for the six structural viability facets. Whether the Qatari curriculum writers followed or adopted different viability facets and related criteria and mechanisms, or whether they worked in the absence of such facets and related criteria, it is normal to end up with the viability ratings indicated in Table 5.1 for various facets of the curriculum.

It is worth noting at this point that the science curriculum documents at hand sometimes duly point to certain problems or threats that may impede proper curriculum deployment. For example, it is recognised that 'a teacher who is not completely fluent in English may have difficulty explaining a science concept' and may confuse students (Education Institute, 2005: 39 in Grades 10–12). Such a situation leads to practicality and sustainability issues. Proper contingency plans need to be envisaged in the curriculum and/or in the educational system to counter such situations. Curriculum writers have to warn concerned authorities of potential threats to a curriculum, like the one just mentioned about English proficiency of science teachers. Those authorities could also benefit from some hints on how to efficiently address such situations.

Early Years Foundation Curriculum: Case Specific

Chapter summary

Case study review of the Early Years Foundation Curriculum.

The Early Years Foundation Curriculum (EYFC) (SEC, 2010) consists of five booklets: Communication, Exploration, Creative Expression, Managing Self – Developing Identity, and Physical Development. Table 6.1 shows the overall rating of various curricular dimensions, using the template discussed in the previous chapters. Detailed findings in the booklets in question are discussed in the following about the design, deployment and viability of the EYFC.

Curriculum design

The EYFC states that it is 'based on a programme of active learning, spontaneous and structured play' (SEC, 2010: 1). As such, it is well intentioned and it does incorporate an understanding that there needs to be an underpinning philosophy of play-based curriculum/pedagogy to properly empower the child to learn (Isaacs, 1971; Vygotsky, 1978; Froebel, 1997; Goouch, 2008; Siraj-Blatchford, 2009). The EYFC is also unique in its inclusive use of a play-based philosophy which embraces older children's learning needs (i.e. beyond KG and into Grades 1 and 2).

In practice, a play-based pedagogy needs to address a certain number of questions, for example: Who is doing the leading in the play activities? Why? Where will the activity lead to in learning terms for the child?

Such questions are partially addressed in the EYFC. Another related issue pertains to how well the concept of 'play' is developed within the curriculum progressions: (a) in accordance with a well-defined taxonomy of play such as the one proposed by Hutt (1997), among others, and (b) in relating particular kinds of material provision (the home area, natural materials, a messy area, a computer, construction kits, clay, paint, etc.) to different aspects of the child's development (symbolic play, superhero play, investigative play, ludic play, heuristic play, epistemic play, physical play, socio-dramatic play). Most importantly, how systematically the EYFC adheres to a clearly defined 'play theory' such as, say, 'chaos theory', which posits that play, is most fruitful when in a 'free-flow' situation for the children (Bruce, 1997).

Bruce (2001) appreciates the value of structured play and games with rules being operationalised with children, but critiques their dominance. Her research evidences that this dominant pedagogy is created by teachers not fully appreciating the value of 'free-flow' play and being tentative about using it. For Bruce, 'free-flow' play is an active process without a product; is intrinsically motivated; the teacher should exert no external pressure on the child to conform to rules, goals or tasks, nor definite direction. 'Free-flow' play takes the child into an exploration of possible alternative worlds. These involve 'supposing' and 'as if', involving being imaginative, original, innovative and creative. The teacher is actively enabling the use of the child's previous first-hand experiences, including discovery, exploration, struggle, manipulation and practice. 'Free-flow' play can be initiated by a child or an adult (judicious sensitive teacher intervention); it can be solitary, it can be in partnership, or with groups of adults and/or children who will be sensitive to each other in an integrating mechanism which brings together learning, knowing, feeling and understanding.

The EYFC may have fallen short of explicitly addressing the issues just discussed. However, it shows numerous points of strength in its design. For instance, the EYFC promotes learning progressions – although we feel that some of those progressions are mis-calibrated or mis-located, and require a finer granularisation of specificity to enable differentiation to take place. It is also laudable that it does not encourage an emphasis on memorisation of facts by the child, and therefore rejects the reductionism of the curriculum to a 'recitation script' (Brown et al., 1998; Tharp and Gallimore, 1988; Alexander, 2008).

The EYFC aims to focus on the child as an active, competent learner and provides Qatari teachers with a structure to achieve this. However, philosophically the document should emphasise clearly the importance of 'sustained shared thinking' as a strategy leading to the development of the child as self-regulated learner (Siraj-Blatchford, 2009). The interim steps in this journey are the self-generation by the child of his/her own learning themes, topics, experiments, investigations, stories, etc., rather

Table 6.1   EYFC ratings

Dimension	Facet	Constituents	Mechanisms	Structural viability	Notes
Curriculum design	Architecture	P	P	P	
	Philosophy	P	P	P	
	Framework	S	P	P	
	Scope	P	P	P	
	Outputs	P	P	P	
	Hierarchy & progression	P	P	P	
	Integration	P	P	P	
Curriculum deployment	Programme of study	P	P	P	
	Learning & instruction	P	P	P	
	Assessment	P	P	P	
	Resources	P	P	S	
	Environment	P	P	S	
	Evaluation	P	P	P	
Structural viability	Coherence	P	P	P	
	Continuity	P	P	P	
	Practicality	P	P	P	
	Flexibility	P	P	P	
	Suitability	S	P	S	
	Universality	N	N	P	
Systemic viability	Sustainability	S	P	S	
	Ownership	P	P	P	
	Community support	N	N	N	

than these being imposed by the teacher. Vygotsky (1978) warns against the dangers of learning a pedagogy of 'teaching from without'. The EYFC often appears as teacher-centred, although it espouses an active learning, participatory, play-based curriculum.

The 'Questions for reflection' section at the end of each strand is a good idea. However, these questions focus more on the teacher than on the child. Although the questions are appropriate in a professional development capacity, their focus is on self-evaluation for the teacher rather than on how the teacher encourages the child to self-generate questions/activities.

The format of the EYFC reinforces the deviation from the adopted philosophy. Each page is structured as follows: teaching strategies, curriculum references and assessment strategies and evidence. There is no column for child initiated/led learning activities, which leads the reviewer to this conclusion. As stated at the beginning of this review, the EYFC needs to be more flexible with less concern about packaging content in neat steps in grade by grade definitions and compartments. It is important that a well-conceptualised, structured and progressive framework is in place, but the necessity of reiteration, recursiveness and spirality of learning requires non-compartmentalisation of a curriculum by 'annual coverage of content' (Early Years Foundation Stage, 2008, UK). 'In a structured curriculum in annual steps, it is difficult to diversify [learning] routes' (Perrenoud, 2001). Such a dominant concern with pedagogy driven by 'coverage' and pace', and proceeding by 'steps', produces an impoverished curriculum model dominated by 'coverage and elicitation of facts rather than the creation and co-construction of inter-connected learning' (Myhill, 2006).

International paradigms such as the New Zealand (Te Whāriki) model envisage the curriculum as a web rather than a set of stairs. The step or staircase model conjures up the image of a series of independent steps that lead to a platform from which the child exits, and at which point measurable outcomes can be identified. By contrast, Te Whāriki emphasises a model of 'knowledge and understanding for young children as a tapestry of increasing complexity and richness'. The New Zealand model recognises the intricacies and complexities of children developing in a non-linear way. The metaphors represented in both models of how children learn, i.e. the 'woven mat/spider web' represent the ever expanding development of children's learning in a horizontal rather than a vertical stepped way. In Northern Italy, Reggio Emilia has many similarities to the Te Whāriki model, but the main difference is that Reggio Emilia is not a compromise between a national curriculum framework and a learner-centred curriculum. What is particularly unique about the Reggio Emilia model is that its core philosophy of child-centredness has been accepted, maintained and strengthened since its 1967 inception. A criticism levelled at Reggio Emilia is based on the absence of a written curriculum, leading to a perception of a lack of measureable accountability. Reggio Emilio's philosophy is based on opposition to a focus on standardisation and outcomes. Its authenticity has enabled it to retain its child-centred philosophy because of this absence of rigid accountability as experienced in many other countries.

Curriculum deployment

Four guiding principles underlie mainstream international pre-school education (UK, Finland, Denmark, Italy, New Zealand, Sweden, UK and USA). Similar principles may have guided the writers of the EYFC in their work, but they are nowhere stated explicitly. In the DfES (2008) document on Early Years Foundation Stages, the four principles are stated as follows:

1. A unique child: recognises that every child is a competent learner from birth who can be resilient, capable, confident and self-assured.
2. Positive relationships: describes how children learn to be strong and independent from a base of loving and secure relationships with parents and/or a key person.
3. Enabling environment: explains that the environment plays a key role in supporting and extending children's development and learning.
4. Learning development: recognises that children develop and learn in different ways and at different rates and that all areas of learning and development are equally important and interconnected.

The UK conceptual framework for the pre-school curriculum is structured around the following concepts: child development; inclusive practices; keeping safe; health and well-being; respecting each other; parents as partners; supporting learning; positive relationships supporting every child; the learning environment; the wider context; play and exploration; active learning; creativity and critical thinking; areas of learning and development; communication, language and literacy; problem solving, reasoning and numeracy; knowledge and understanding of the world; physical development; creative development.

To compare the Qatari EYFC to the UK framework in question, take the example of the last concept above, creative development. The UK Early Years document sets out creative development around four themes or goals as follows:

1. Being creative: responding to experiences and expressing and communicating ideas.
2. Exploring media and materials.
3. Creating music and dance.
4. Developing imagination and imaginative play.

By contrast in the Qatar EYFC, 'creative expression' is organised under three goals:

1. Children experience an environment in which they explore different forms of creative expression (drama, movement, music, art and media, creative play).
2. Children respond positively to diverse creative opportunities.
3. Children develop their creative skills in expressing themselves through art, music, movement and dramatic performances.

Each of the three goals is packed with information about: (a) curriculum standard (what is achieved), (b) curriculum experience (what the child is exposed to), and (c) curriculum presentation (conceptual applicability to learning needs). The format in which information is presented leads sometimes to confusion, especially for teachers with no appropriate pedagogical background.

The EYFC offers an advantage to the K–12 science and mathematics curricula by adopting a four-phase, closed 'learning cycle'. The four phases are 'plan', 'teach', 'assess' and 'reflect'. The cycle is laid out in the form of a diagram with little guidance. The outline of each phase addresses the role of the teacher and not the student. The language used thus seems to defeat the very purpose of a learning cycle as a student-centred learning and not teaching methodology.

Because of the nature of the five EYFC booklets pertaining to the 'five key areas of young children's development', findings are discussed in the following for each booklet separately and not, for the various curriculum deployment facets as revealed in all booklets together, as done in the previous two chapters. Furthermore, explicit recommendations are made, whenever necessary, for specific goals in each of the five key areas. These recommendations may be considered during the revision of the EYFC.

Book 1: Communication

The opening statement to this key area of the EYFC provides a positive rationale to the importance of developing a child's language skills, and this is also recognised within a supportive structure of bilingualism. However, a wider, more comprehensive description of what communication, language and literacy means for children would enhance this section:

- As children develop speaking and listening skills they build the foundations for literacy, for making sense of visual and verbal signs and ultimately for reading and writing. Children need lots of opportunities to interact with others as they develop these skills, and to use a wide variety of resources for expressing their understanding, including mark making, drawing, modelling, reading and writing. (Depree and Iverson, 1994; Berninger et al., 2006; Nilsson, 2010)
- Research suggests the positive relationship between bilingualism and a wide range of other cognitive measures including the enhanced ability to restructure perceptual solutions (Balkan, 1970), stronger performances in rule discovery tasks (Bain, 1975), greater verbal ability and verbal originality and precocious levels of divergent thinking and creativity (Cummins and Gulutsan, 1974). Vygotsky (1978; 1986) suggests that the bilingual child is able to see a language as one particular system among many, to view its phenomena under more general categories, and this leads to awareness of his/her linguistic operation. 'Experience with two language systems may enable bilinguals to have a precocious understanding of the arbitrariness of language' (Lee, 1996: 510).

The five goals presented in the Qatar EYFC are set out in great detail in an attempt to create a very comprehensive literacy programme. However, this at times results in a mismatch of layered goals stemming from the overarching goal creating and affects coherence and progression.

The following are recommendations regarding the five goals in the Communication key area, and a suggested additional goal.

Goal 1: Children gain confidence and competence in the use of their first and second languages.
   It is recommended to rename this goal as 'Language for communication', and to do the following with the listed sub-goals:

1.1 To remain in Goal 1
1.2 To move to Reading goal
1.3 To move to Linking sounds and letters goal
1.4 To move to Handwriting goal
1.5 To move to Writing goal

It is also recommended to include the following in this goal:

- Sensitively demonstrate pronunciation and ordering of words in response to what children say, rather than correcting them.
- Plan to talk through and comment on some activities to highlight specific vocabulary or language structures.
- Provide books with repetitive stories and phrases to read aloud to children to support specific vocabulary and language structures.
- Introduce 'rhyme bags' containing books to take home and involve parents in rhymes and signing games, ask parents to record regional variations of songs and rhymes in other languages.

Goal 2: Children use verbal interactions effectively for different purposes to express ideas, inquire, gain information, achieve social purposes, and to solve problems.
   It is recommended to rename this goal as 'Language for thinking', and to do the following with the listed sub-goals:

2.1 To move to Language for communication goal
2.2 To move to Language for communication goal
2.3 To remain in Language for thinking goal

It is also recommended to include the following in this goal:

- Use talk to describe what children are doing by providing a commentary, e.g. 'I can see what you are doing, you have put the milk in the cup first'.
- Ask children to think in advance as to how they will accomplish a task. Talk through and sequence the stages together.
- Help children to identify patterns, e.g. 'What generally happens to good and wicked characters at the end of stories?'; to draw conclusions, e.g. 'The sky has gone dark, it must be going to rain'; to explain effect, e.g. 'It sank because it was too heavy'; to predict, e.g. 'It might not grow in there if it is too dark'; to speculate, e.g. 'What if the bridge falls down?'.

Goal 3: Children take turns, listen attentively and respond appropriately to other speakers.

It is recommended to replace this goal completely with a new goal, 'Linking Sounds and Letters', and to do the following with the existing sub-goals:

3.1 To move to Language for Communication goal
3.2 To move to Language for Communication goal
3.3 To subsume within 3.2 (Repetition)

It is also recommended to include the following in the revised goal:

- Encourage young children to explore and imitate sound. Talk about the different sounds they hear such as a car, 'brrrmm, brrrmm'.
- Encourage repetition, rhythm and rhyme by using tone and intonation as you tell, recite or sing stories, poems and rhymes from books.
- Talk to children about the letters that represent the sounds they hear at the beginning of their own names and other familiar words and incorporate these into games.
- When making up alliterative jingles draw attention to the similarities in sounds at the beginnings of words and emphasise the initial sound, for example 'mmmm' mummy; 'shshsh' shadow; 'kkkkk' Kalum.

Goal 4: Children increase their knowledge and skills in using pronunciation, vocabulary and grammar through natural conversation in Arabic and English.

(Continued)

(Continued)

It is recommended to rename this goal as 'Reading', and to do the following with the listed sub-goals:

4.1 To remain in Reading goal
4.2 To subsume within 4.1
4.3 To remain in Reading goal

It is also recommended to include the following in this goal:

- Provide stories, pictures and puppets which allow children to experience and talk about how characters feel.
- Provide dual language books to raise awareness of different scripts. Try to match dual language books to languages spoken in the setting/class.
- Remember that not all languages have written forms and not all families are literate either in English or a different home language.
- Develop children's familiarity with the way that books work, e.g. turning the pages, telling the story using pictures, using phrases such as 'once upon a time'.
- Discuss with children the characters in books being read. Encourage them to predict outcomes, to think of alternative outcomes and to compare plots and feelings of characters with their own experiences.

Goal 5: Children engage in and enjoy reading and writing Arabic and English.
It is recommended to rename this goal as 'Writing', and to do the following with the listed sub-goals:

5.1 To move to Reading goal
5.2 To move to Reading goal
5.3 To remain in Writing goal

It is also recommended to include the following in this goal:

- Draw attention to marks, signs and symbols in the environment and talk about what they represent. Ensure this involves recognition of English and other relevant scripts.
- Write poems and short stories with children, scribing for them. After they say a sentence, repeat the first part of it, say each word as you write and include some punctuation.
- Make books with children of activities that they have been doing using photographs of them as illustrations.
- Provide word banks and other resources for segmenting and blending to support children to use their phonic knowledge.

Goal 6: This is an additional new goal recommended for 'Handwriting' with the following sub-goals:

6.1 Formation of letters
6.2 Fine motor skills development
6.3 Hand–eye co-ordination
6.4 Developing a range of tools for handwriting

It is also recommended to include the following in this new goal:

- Help young children to develop their manipulative skills by engaging them in activities such as tearing (paper), scribbling, rolling and printing.
- Vary the range of tools and equipment located with familiar activities, for example, put small scoops, rakes or sticks with the sand.
- Provide opportunities for large shoulder movements, for example, swirling ribbons in the air, batting balls suspended on rope and painting.
- Teach children to form letters correctly, for example, when they label their paintings.
- Continue writing practice in imaginative contexts, joining some letters if appropriate, for example, 'at, in, on'.

Book 2: Exploration

The introduction to this key area outlines the positive attributes of enquiry-based learning but omits to identify the existence of mathematics as a subject within the book despite references to related aspects such as to 'create and solve problems', to 'develop conceptual knowledge', and to 'test theories'. Mathematics and science at least (although there are other subjects interwoven throughout the book, such as geography, ICT, history) need to be identified, disaggregated and separated with subject identities within this book. The current approach does not preserve the integrity of the individual subject and makes it very difficult to ascertain subject-relationship within each discrete activity.

The intention of cross-disciplinarity is laudable in the EYFC. However, there is sometimes an over-emphasis on cross-subjectivity in this approach which inevitably leads to a misrepresentation of progression in pupil learning trajectories. Take, for example, Goal 3 (below): 'Children manipulate; group and regroup; observe and describe; identify differences and similarities in people and objects; compare qualities regarding length, mass and capacity'. This goal is far too dense, too concept laden and compounds the fusion between mathematics and science, a misunderstanding of cross-disciplinarity.

Other examples of over-emphasis on cross-disciplinarity can be found in Goal 3.1 of Grade 2, and in Goal 3.3 of Pre-K. The former goal asks to 'provide a 100 square for children to count and make number patterns in pairs'. This activity is located within the section on 2D and 3D Exploration. The latter goal asks to 'provide pictures of places, animals and birds in Qatar for the children to sort and look at, e.g. "What lives in the sea and what lives in the desert?"' However in the next suggested activity, for Kindergarten, the EYFC states: 'provide opportunities to learn names of body parts through singing'. How will the child see the progression from physical geography to the science of the human body?

The document sometimes even misrepresents how concepts are built, named and classified by children as learners. In the pre-K section, it states: 'provide children with a range of 2D and 3D shapes'. However, according to the literature, children should first be exposed to and experience 3D shapes: 'children are concerned from babyhood with feeling, observing and arranging solid shapes. They are interested in properties of solid shapes long before they are ready to consider plane shapes' (Liebeck, 1984: 54).

The following are recommendations regarding the five goals in the Exploration key area.

Goal 1: Children show curiosity and ask questions; evaluate information and seek understanding.

Recommendation: Rename this goal as 'Exploration and investigation' and subsume Goal 2. The focus on science to include scientific enquiry; life processes and living things; materials and their properties; physical processes. It is also recommended to include the following in this goal:

- Recognise and name external parts of plants.
- Communicate observations of a range of animals and plants in terms of features.
- Recognise and identify a range of common animals.
- Know about a range of properties, e.g. texture and appearance, and communicate those observations.
- Communicate observation of changes in movements that result from actions, e.g. pushing and pulling objects.

Goal 2: Children initiate and undertake inquiry projects; experiment and persevere to find solutions.

Recommendation: This goal is subsumed within Goal 1 (see revised Goal 1 above).

Goal 3: Children manipulate; group and regroup; observe and describe; identify differences and similarities in people and objects; compare qualities regarding length, mass and capacity.

Recommendation: Rename the goal as 'Numbers, calculating, shape and space'. It is also recommended to include the following in this goal:

- Say and use numbers in order in familiar contexts.
- Know that numbers identify how many objects are in a set.
- Estimate how many objects they can see and check by counting.
- In practical activities and discussion begin to use the vocabulary involved in adding and subtracting.
- Use familiar objects and common shapes to create and recreate patterns and build models.
- Use language such as 'greater', 'smaller', 'heavier' and 'lighter' to compare quantities.

Goal 4: Children develop concepts and are encouraged to theorise about objects, living things and the environment.

Recommendation: Rename the goal as 'Using technology to explore the environment' and subsume Goal 5.

It is also recommended to include the following in this goal:

- Become familiar with simple equipment such as twisting or turning a knob or using a mouse.
- Use the control technology of toys, e.g. toy electronic keyboard.
- Use pieces of ICT equipment, e.g. computer, mobile phone, interactive white board.
- Click on icons to cause things to happen in a computer program.
- Comment and ask questions about where they live and the natural world.
- Respond to sights, sounds and smells in the environment and what they like about playing outdoors.

Goal 5: Children develop a sense of responsibility for helping to care for the environment.

Recommendation: The goal is subsumed within Goal 4.

Book 3: Creative Expression

In the Qatar EYFC model, Creative Expression is organised under three goals. These goals are too dense, need unpacking and are sometimes confusing to the practitioner. Sometimes there is some overlap between goals or sub-goals. Take for example Goals 2.1 and 3.1. Goal 2.1 is about 'enjoyment' and 'appreciation', whereas Goal 3.1 is mainly about dexterities or 'performance skills'. Yet Goal 3.1 also talks about 'confidence' as a consequence of skill development, a disposition that relates to Goal 2.1, which is purely about dispositions.

In the Art and Media section (Goal 1), the EYFC's treatment of the development of a concept at Kindergarten level such as 'painting' simply requires that children 'are encouraged to paint using a variety of ways, including their fingers and toes'. In Grade 1, they are encouraged to mix colours, and in Grade 2, painting has disappeared from the curriculum. Painting is therefore not seen as a developmental process in the Qatari EYFC. By contrast, a progressive international Early Years Framework, as in the UK, would be more structured and precise in its examples for the teachers in the continuum from Kindergarten onwards as follows: 'Explores making marks on a variety of papers. Uses a variety of tools to spread paint – straws, matchsticks as well as brushes. Explores mark-making using thick brushes, foam and sponge brushes. Experiments with and enjoys colour. Creates pattern using different tools and colours. Uses colours and marks to express mood ...'.

This booklet as it stands reflects some problems with assessment in the EYFC. For example, Goal 1 of Art and Media asks the Grade 2 teacher to assess children's understanding of secondary colours. However, the teaching of secondary colours does not take place at all in the curriculum as printed. This kind of mismatch between learning and assessment activities figures in other places in the same and other key areas, and needs to be attended to.

The following recommendations may further be considered:

Goal 1: Children experience an environment in which they explore different forms of creative expression (drama, movement, music, art and media, creative play).

Recommendation: Rename the goal as 'Exploring media and materials', and include the following under sub-goal 1.4 ('Children gain an understanding of different forms of expression'):

- Encourage professional musicians to model play and perform throughout the grades.
- Encourage children to compose/devise their own songs and creative language expression.
- Ensure that there is enough time for children to express their thoughts, ideas and feelings in a variety of ways such as in role play, painting and responding to music.

Goal 2: Children respond positively to diverse creative opportunities.

Recommendation: Rename the goal as 'Being creative – responding to experiences, expressing and communicating ideas', and include the following:

- Introduce language that enables children to talk about their experiences in greater depth and detail.
- Be sensitive to the needs of children who may not be able to express themselves easily in English, using interpreter support from known adults, or strategies such as picture cards to enable children to express preferences.
- Be alert to children's changing interest and the way they respond to experiences differently when they are in a happy, sad or reflective mood.

Goal 3: Children develop their creative skills in expressing themselves through art, music, movement and dramatic performances.

Recommendation: Rename the goal as 'Creating music and dance – developing imagination and imaginative play', and include the following:

- Listen with children to a variety of sounds, talking about favourite sounds, songs and music.
- Introduce children to language to describe sounds and rhythm, for example, 'loud' and 'soft', 'fast' and 'slow'.
- Draw on a wide range of musicians and storytellers from a variety of cultural backgrounds to extend children's experiences and to reflect their cultural heritages.
- Make materials accessible so that children are able to imagine and bring to fruition their projects and ideas while they are still fresh in their minds and are important to them.
- Provide opportunities indoors and outdoors and support the different interests of children, for example, a building yard encourages narratives to do with building and mending.

Book 4: Managing Self – Developing Identity

The opening statement to this section of the curriculum is well presented and inclusive of the developing child. However, one suggestion would be to have a clear underpinning philosophy of development for the better of each child's attitude and disposition (outlook on life). Another strong suggestion is to widen the rationale to include a more comprehensive description as to what personal, social and emotional development means for children as follows (DeVries and Kohlberg 1990; Bruce, 1997; Barger, 2000; Tobias, 2000; DCSF, 2007; Siraj-Blatchford 2009):

- For children, being special to someone and well cared for is vital for their physical, social and emotional health and well-being.
- Being acknowledged and affirmed by important people in their lives leads to children gaining confidence and inner strength through secure attachments with these people.
- Exploration within close relationships leads to growth of self-assurance, promoting a sense of belonging which allows children to explore the world from a secure base.
- Children need adults to set a good example and give them opportunities for interaction with others so that they can develop positive ideas about themselves and others.
- Children who are encouraged to feel free to express their ideas and their feelings, such as joy, sadness, frustration and fear, can develop strategies to cope with new, challenging or stressful situations.

The four goals presented in this area of learning have many positive aspects. These include the importance of a child's affective domain development. The document recognises that: 'most human beings operate in an integrated way when making decisions and emotion plays a considerable part in the interactions in which social and moral rules are articulated' (Tobias, 2000: 2).

The following are recommendations regarding the four goals in the Managing Self key area.

Goal 1: Children develop an appreciation of their [Qatari] identity and awareness of belonging to different groups (family, Kindergarten, school, community, religion).

Recommendation: Rename the goal as 'Sense of community', and include the following:

- Help children to learn the names of each of the other children in the group, for example, through songs and rhymes.
- Strengthen the positive image which children have of their own cultures and faiths and those of others by sharing and celebrating a range of practices and events.
- Support children's understanding of difference and of empathy by using props such as PERSONA dolls to tell stories about diverse experiences, ensuring that negative stereotyping is avoided.
- Develop strategies to combat negative bias and where necessary support children and adults to unlearn discriminatory attitudes.

Goal 2: Children make friends, build and practice respectful relationships and resolve conflict peacefully.

Recommendation: Rename the goal as 'Making relationships', and include the following:

- Provide books which represent children's diverse backgrounds and which avoid negative stereotyping. Make photographic books about children in the setting and encourage parents to contribute to these.
- Provide real contexts in which children are encouraged to listen and wait for others' contributions. Discuss the value of this skill in developing and maintaining friendships.
- Help young children to label emotions such as sadness or happiness by talking to them about their own feelings and those of others.
- Create areas in which children can sit and chat with friends.

Goal 3: Children accept rules and procedures to function successfully.
Recommendation: Rename the goal as 'Behaviour and self-control', and include the following:

- Encourage children to be involved in the creation of class rules. Collaborate with children in creating explicit rules for the care of the environment.
- Reduce incidents of frustration and conflict by keeping routines flexible so that very young children can pursue their interests.
- Help children to understand their rights to be kept safe by others and encourage them to talk about ways to avoid harming or hurting others.
- Provide books with stories about characters that follow or break rules and the effects of their behaviour on others.
- Be alert to injustices and let children see that these are addressed and resolved. Make time to listen to children respectfully when injustices are being discussed and resolved in the best fit solution.

Goal 4: Children develop self-esteem along with an increasing ability to make choices, ask for support when they need it, express feelings and adapt to change.
Recommendation: Rename the goal as 'Self-confidence, self-esteem and self-care', and include the following:

- Help children and parents to see the ways in which their cultures and beliefs are similar, encouraging them to contribute to everyone's knowledge and understanding by sharing and discussing practices, resources, celebrations and experiences.

(Continued)

(Continued)

- Plan extra time for helping children in transition such as when they move from one setting/class to another or between different groups in the same setting/class.
- Explain carefully why some children may need extra help or support for some things and why some children feel upset by a particular thing. This helps children understand that when it is required their individual needs will be met.
- Collect information that helps children to understand why people do things differently from each other and encourage children to talk about these differences.

Book 5: Physical Development

All of the five goals in this key area are somewhat repetitive. Goals 2 and 3 and similarly Goals 1 and 4 are obvious examples of this. Furthermore, under the section called 'Examples of teaching strategies', strategies are simply listed without any structural progression. All this jeopardises the cohesion, precision and progression of the document.

It might be better if the five physical development goals were combined and reorganised (see below) under more concise definitions, such as Movement and Space; Using Equipment and Materials; Health and Body Awareness. In addition, planning is needed for the Dance, Gymnastics, Games and Athletics components of the curriculum. In the present format, a teacher cannot confirm if they are developing and teaching the appropriate skill sets for each area.

The five goals may be redesigned under, say, three simple discrete headings: Knowledge, Skills, Attitudes, with the four components (Dance, Gymnastics, Games and Athletics) layered within this reorganised framework in each case. The key area would then naturally develop into higher order skill development. This is crucial because the EYFC framework supplies a baseline and developmental learning into Grades 2/3. As the document currently stands the strands of progression are simply not developmentally appropriate.

The following are recommended revisions to the document to make it more comprehensive.

Goal 1: Children develop loco-motor skills, such as walking, running, jumping, climbing, galloping and skipping, and non-loco-motor skills such as balancing, swaying, turning, swinging, twisting.

Goal 2: Children develop hand–eye co-ordination, using gross motor and fine motor skills.

Goal 3: Children develop skills for using manipulative materials, such as hand strength, pencil grip, precision with spatial awareness.

Recommendation: Combine Goals 2 and 3, and rename as 'Using equipment and materials', with the following additional teaching examples:

- Talk to children about what they are doing, how they plan to do it, what worked well and what they would change next time.
- Encourage children to use the vocabulary of manipulation, e.g. 'squeeze' and 'prod'; the language of description, e.g. 'spiky', 'silky' 'lumpy' and 'tall'.
- Justify and explain why safety is an important factor in handling tools, equipment and materials and have sensible rules for everybody to follow.
- Provide activities that give children the opportunity and motivation to practise manipulative skills, e.g. cooking, painting and playing instruments.

Goal 4: Children develop spatial and perceptual awareness through exploration of visual and sensory experiences.

Recommendation: Combine Goals 1 and 4, and rename as 'Movement and space' with the following as additional teaching examples:

- Plan for relaxation and rest periods as children can be very energetic for short bursts.
- Encourage children to move with controlled effort and use associated vocabulary such as 'strong', 'firm', 'gentle', 'heavy', 'stretch', 'reach', 'tense' and 'floppy'
- Lead imaginative movement sessions based on children's current interests such as space, travel, zoo animals or shadows.
- Help children to communicate through their bodies by encouraging expressive movement linked to their imaginative ideas.
- Talk to children about their movements and help them to explore new ways of moving such as 'squirming', 'slithering' and twisting on the ground like a snake.
- Plan to respect individual progress and preoccupations. Allow time for exploration and for children to plan for movements they choose.

(Continued)

(Continued)

- Pose challenging questions such as 'Can you get all the way round the climbing frame without your knees touching it?' Encourage the children to devise their own questions/tasks to create a PE bank of challenges.
- Provide opportunities for children to repeat and change their actions so that they can think about, refine and improve them.
- Provide CDs and voice recorders, scarves, streamers and musical instruments so that children can respond spontaneously to music.
- Undertake risk assessment and provide safe places where children can move freely. Create 'zones' for some activities and explain safety to children and parents.
- Observe children's skill development, if it is exploratory and experimental or repetitive and whether they are ready for a new challenge (assessment).
- Encourage the ideas that children suggest to make things 'fair'.

Goal 5: Children develop knowledge of health, safety and nutrition and enjoy being physically active.

Recommendation: Rename the goal as 'Health and body awareness', and include the following:

- Establish routines that enable children to look after themselves, for example, putting their clothes and aprons on hooks, washing themselves.
- Create time to discuss options so that young children have choices between healthy options such as whether they will drink water, juice or milk.
- Be aware of eating habits at home and of the different ways that people eat their food. For example, some families use hands to eat and some cultures strongly discourage the use of the left hand for eating.
- Be aware that physical activity is important in maintaining good health and in guarding against children becoming over-weight or obese in later life.
- Encourage children to notice the changes in their bodies after exercise such as their heart beating faster.

Curriculum viability

At this first stage of the process, the reviewer felt it to be of extreme importance to micro-edit the Qatari EYFC document so that across the five books and their respective sub-goals there was a consistency, continuity and coherence of both approach and mechanisms throughout the Framework. For the EYFC to have structural viability as a curriculum for

Early Years education those three elements are paramount and essential. The other elements of viability, such as plasticity (flexibility/differentiation), suitability and practicality, can only flourish within the secure framework supplied by coherence, continuity and consistency.

However it is crucial that the desire for consistency, continuity and coherence are not interpreted or indeed misinterpreted as simply packaging content in neat 'steps'. As already stated at the beginning of this review but worthy of repetition, the EYFC needs to be more flexible with less concern about packaging content in neat steps in grade by grade definitions and compartments. For curriculum viability it is important that a well-conceptualised, structured and progressive framework is in place but not at the expense of producing compartmentalisation and 'coverage' of content. There is a necessity for reiteration, recursiveness, and spirality in learning. This requires abandoning the model of a straitjacket compartmentalisation of a curriculum by 'annual coverage of content' (Early Years Foundation Stage, UK). 'In a structured curriculum in annual steps, it is difficult to diversify [learning] routes' (Perrenoud, 2001). Such a dominant concern with pedagogy driven by 'coverage' and pace', and proceeding by 'steps', produces an impoverished curriculum model dominated by 'coverage and elicitation of facts rather than the creation and co-construction of inter-connected learning' (Myhill, 2006). Such a curriculum may present itself as neat and tidy and pay lip service to curriculum viability but in actuality it is exactly the opposite.

7

Balancing Raising Standards with a Well-designed and Broad Curriculum

Chapter summary

The tensions between the intention of a 'broad and balanced' curriculum and the conflicting pressures of a political rather than educational definition of 'raising standards'.

As part of its 'raising standards' agenda, the Department for Education and Skills (DfES) set performance targets for the results of the statutory end of key stage 2 tests in English and mathematics for the academic year 2005–6 (end of key stage 1 testing was no longer statutory by 2006). The targets were that 85% of the school population of 11 year olds (Year 6 pupils) would achieve Level 4 (or above) in English and in mathematics. The results of the 2006 end of key stage 2 tests (well before 2006, the term assessments had been replaced by 'testing' both in policy documents and in the minds of teachers, parents and pupils) were that 79% of pupils achieved Level 4 in English while 76% achieved that level in mathematics.

This development posed several worrying issues for schools, teachers, pupils and parents, all related to the importance or status which the government had attached to these 'targets' for its own publicity value in electioneering. The Education Secretary at the time, Alan Johnson, stated that 'Nothing is more important than the 3Rs and no government has done more to improve attainment in these basic skills … the attainment of young people at the end of their primary years has vastly improved on what it was in 1997 [the year New Labour was elected as the government]' (BBC News Education, 2006b).

The biggest of the issues of concern is that, whether those targets were achieved or not, do those results (test outcomes) justify the wholesale change in the balance of the primary curriculum that had (and still is, based on a government obsession with concentrating teaching and inspections on the outcomes of 'high stakes' testing of 11-year-old pupils) taken place? When the National Curriculum was first legislated and introduced in 1988, the intention of the Education Reform Act which instituted that National Curriculum was for breadth and balance in the school curriculum (DES, 1988). In 2004 the DfES's *Five Year Strategy for Children and Learners* stated it (DfES) would 'make sure that every subject is taught well in primary schools and that every child gets the benefit of a rich, well-designed and broad curriculum' (DfES, 2004). However from our research it appears that the opposite has happened.

Since 1997 the authors have been collecting a range of curriculum data for the government's education agencies (principally for the QCA) as part of the Education Department's school curriculum and assessment monitoring role. The survey question used for these research data was one which asked the primary school headteacher: 'In your school what is the teaching time for the following subjects over one year? Please give an approximate percentage of time spent on each subject'. The additional guidance supplied to the schools requested that 'where subjects are taught together in a topic, please estimate the percentage of time spent on the individual subjects within the topic'. This enabled the research team to establish accurate percentages of teaching time allocated to core (English, mathematics, science) and foundation (the remainder of the statutory) subjects. The analysis of the data illustrated and evidenced how at key stage 1, science and all the foundation subjects (apart from a small percentage gain in teaching time allocated to physical education), and at key stage 2, science and all the foundation subjects without exception, suffered reductions in their teaching time over the research period 1997 to 2005 (Boyle and Bragg, 2006).

For most of the period under review, two subjects, English and mathematics, were allocated over 50% of the available teaching time, reducing the other ten statutory subjects to divide up the remaining 45% (approximately) of available teaching time between them (Boyle and Bragg, 2006). There has been evident a 'science-effect': science was nominated as a 'core' subject in the original legislation decreeing the National Curriculum. However, science, although a core subject, was not set a DfES performance target level. Science is always high profile in government pronouncements about shortages of science graduates and more scientists being needed, and is also 'tested' at the end of key stage 2 alongside English and mathematics. Therefore one would have anticipated that, like English and mathematics, it would retain its 'elite' role in teaching time allocation. In fact, evidenced by the research data, science has been reduced in primary teaching time by more than any of the foundation subjects. Hence the power of government prioritisation of English and mathematics 'scores' has trickled down to the classroom reduction in science teaching in the primary phase.

Therefore a 'raising the standards' agenda, in government terms, only concerns the standards of the two subjects of English and mathematics, a fact coldly emphasised by the media coverage of education which focuses, following government lead, on success or failure narratives about pupil performance in those two subjects. 'What gets measured gets taught. What gets reported gets taught twice as well' (Rothman, 2001).

A second issue follows on from that. If education 'standards' are to be measured and publicly reported, shouldn't those standards be measured across a broader set of subject domains than the tested or testable curriculum sub-domains of two, or at most three, subjects which are judged (by policy makers, not classroom professionals) suitable for national testing formats on 'national test day'? Continuous classroom assessment, valued in the TGAT report (TGAT, 1988a) on which national curriculum assessment was based, has long since ignominiously vacated any place in the 'standards' debate.

The reduced model of standards is restricted to the subjects of English and mathematics; in fact, even more narrowly the standards are based on the measurement and public reporting of performance testing of (the testable) elements of those two subjects. Teachers (of the tested year groups) have been made aware that it is on their 'performance' (coaching skills) that the reputation of their school depends and it is necessary for them to produce not learners who understand and are involved in reflection, deep learning, co-construction, self-regulated autonomous learning – but to produce 'test-wise' pupils who will have been coached not to be phased by the testing situation and will produce acceptable outcomes on those tests and ensure that the school's cohort's performance will group around and preferably above the DfES's required percentage target 'bar'. This will be ensured by their teachers teaching (coaching) the two 'performance measured' subjects (and usually the predicted 'testable items') for a disproportionate amount of classroom time. So this is what, in 2006, Education Secretary Johnson meant by claiming that 'no government has done more to improve attainment in these basic skills' (BBC News Education, 2006b). At publication, we are nine years further on, and the situation has remained in that stasis, with pupils being exposed to 'one size fits all' curricula and the pedagogical narrowness that goes with it – required only to factory-like regurgitate the 'ideal learner' (Bradbury, 2013) acceptable responses to the end of key stage tests. Therefore the claim of 'raising standards' is shallow, hugely contrived as a contortion and restriction of the curriculum and bears no resemblance to anything connected to a school's role in developing teaching and learning matched to individual needs or offering children the opportunities to experience an involvement in a 'broad and balanced' curriculum.

Integrating Subjects and Themes

Chapter summary

The dominant role of subjects in a national curriculum and the attempts at flexibility and cross-curricularity to ensure a 'balanced' curriculum offering.

Introduction

As detailed earlier in this book, from 1996 until 2007 Bill Boyle was funded by the UK government's Qualifications and Curriculum Authority (QCA) to carry out longitudinal curriculum data collection and analysis from a nationally representative sample of primary and secondary phase schools. This survey supplied data for the QCA's annual curriculum monitoring reports for schools. One of the annual questions in the survey asked schools to detail the use they make of 'combining' subjects for teaching. Using analysis of the survey data produced by this question alongside other sources of evidence, this chapter reflects on changes in primary school curriculum planning and design in that period. We contextualise the origination of a subject-discrete National Curriculum (which for political reasons in the years preceding and post-ERA, side-stepped the cross-curricular issue) and then supply a descriptive analysis of the period covered by the data survey, a period influenced by the introduction of the national strategies in English (literacy) and mathematics (numeracy) (Boyle and Bragg, 2006).

An imposed curriculum

The first version of the National Curriculum in 1988 was criticised for its rigidly subject-structured model (White, 2004). Rather than taking the opportunity to at least consult about a reformed 'aims and values' based model, the 'curriculum model presented was locked into socio-historical precedent, traditional and academic' (Crawford, 2000) and 'the 8–10 subject timetable has as academic a look to it as anything Sir Robert Morant could have dreamed up' (*TES*, 1987). Aldrich drew attention to the similarity between the subjects list and the one prescribed for the newly introduced state schools in 1904 (Aldrich, 1988: 22). Recent retrospective commentaries such as that by White (2004: 2) go further by stating: 'The National Curriculum gives every appearance of having been lifted from what was originally traditional grammar school practice'. Brehony (2005: 31) asserts that 'The National Curriculum adopted, in opposition to the primary schools' adoption of projects, the time-hallowed conception of the organisation of school knowledge into subjects'.

Among practitioners there was a common perception that the original National Curriculum (DES, 1987; TGAT, 1988a) and its subsequent amendment following the Dearing Review (SCAA, 1993) were devised by sets of subject specialists working at the government's direction within the isolation of subject parameters and without a clear view of the aims and purposes of the curriculum as a whole (SCAA, 1997).

> The construction of a subject-based curriculum seemed to suggest that the policy battle had been won by supporters of tradition rather than the advocates of a utilitarian and pedagogic tradition. (Crawford, 2000)

Better Schools (DES, 1985) provided a stronger rationale for the subject-based structure of the National Curriculum than other succeeding documents. However, it also stated that the curriculum is described in subject terms for the sake of convenience and that it is not in dispute that the purposes of education at school go beyond learning the traditional subjects (DES, 1985, para 53). The *National Curriculum 5–16* consultation document (DES, 1987) did not ignore whole curriculum issues and there is a clearly discernible direct line from *Better Schools*:

> there are a number of subjects or themes ... which can be taught through other subjects ... It is proposed that such subjects or themes should be taught through the foundation subjects. (DES, 1987: 8)

The consultation document clarified 'the description of the National Curriculum in terms of how the school day should be organised and the curriculum delivered' (DES, 1987: 9) and that programmes of study should 'reflect cross-curricular themes' (DES, 1987: Annex A, para. 3). Subsequent commentators have reported that behind the scenes there had been complex manoeuvrings based upon the DfES's objective of 'getting teachers to accept, understand and implement a National Curriculum free from the distraction provided' (Crawford, 2000: 629) by the cross-curricular debate, while managing 'conflict between the curriculum endorsed by Baker (Minister of Education) and the DES and that supported by Thatcher, her policy advisers and right wing pressure groups' (Crawford, 2000: 625). The Thatcherite view of a National Curriculum was a 'basic syllabus' with the pupils' knowledge and skills being assessed by 'simple tests' (Thatcher, 1993: 53), a view echoed in 1991 by her successor John Major's call for a return to basics in education. This 'nostalgic' view of education (Ball, 1994: 44) extended into the Blunkett years of tenure of the Department and there is an interesting current parallel in that 'with the National Literacy and National Numeracy Strategies, New Labour went much further in the direction of a "teacher proof" curriculum that indicated that teachers could not be trusted to implement its top down, standards agenda' (Brehony, 2005: 33). Oblivious to this political in-fighting, the absence of any formal 'cross-curricular' guidance, however, was noted by teachers and commentators alike with dismay – as this to them seemed to emphasise the rigidity of the new curriculum structure. 'Some of the teachers I have spoken to over the past year maintain that the only way to meet the large number of attainment targets in the core and foundation subjects is to continue the tradition of cross-curricular themes' (Tyler, 1992: 564). 'These teachers further support this view by pointing to the large overlaps between the various subject documents – the only effective way to teach when there are so many common themes is by using a cross-curricular approach – the overlaps with English, mathematics, geography and design and technology are probably the most obvious' (Tyler, 1992: 564). It was not as if the 'cross-curriculum debate' was not alive during the development period for the original National Curriculum. Shoemaker (1989: 5) described an integrated curriculum as 'education that is organised in such a way that it cuts across subject-matter lines, bringing together various aspects of the curriculum into meaningful association … it views learning and teaching in a holistic way and reflects the real world which is interactive'. Humphreys et al. (1981: 11) described 'links among the humanities, communication arts, natural sciences, mathematics, social studies, music and art. Skills and knowledge are developed and applied in more than one area of study'. Palmer (1991: 59) described 'developing cross-curriculum sub-objectives within a given curriculum guide; developing model lessons that include cross-curricular activities and assessments and including sample planning wheels in all curriculum guides'.

However, Tyler also presented the contradictory opinion of other teachers who argue that the discrete subject approach is best as 'the National Curriculum documents are quite complicated enough as they are and to try to develop a cross-curricular approach on such a basis is virtually impossible' and can 'only lead to a rather vague and ineffective implementation of the various programmes of study' (Tyler, 1992: 564). Tyler reported the early 1990s debate between 'the teachers who support the cross-curricular approach' and their belief that creating artificial divisions between different areas of the curriculum will not help children to learn' and 'those who prefer to consider the curriculum in terms of discrete subjects' who believe that their approach will make it 'easier to teach the National Curriculum' (Tyler, 1992: 565).

For those primary schools in the early and mid-1990s coming to terms for the first time with a National Curriculum and which many viewed (see Tyler above) as a refocusing of their whole teaching strategy onto 'teaching the National Curriculum', there seemed to be emerging three styles of curriculum planning: (a) individual subject teaching; (b) subject-led or subject-specific topics and (c) thematic planning (Goodson, 1989; Tyler, 1992). In 1993 the National Curriculum Council (then chaired by Ron Dearing) produced *Planning the National Curriculum at Key Stage 2* which advised on the organisation of the curriculum within the National Curriculum framework and recommended units of work divided into 'continuing' units and 'blocked' units which contained a progressive sequence of learning activities either within or across subjects. The development of thematic planning focused on a cross-curricular approach with subjects embedded within thematic units which were stimulating and retained the child's interest through their active involvement with the theme.

A nationally representative sample (by region, school type and size) of state maintained primary schools that participated in the primary curriculum survey form the basis of this study. As an example, Table 8.1 shows the 2005 sample (41% response rate) by geographical distribution against the national statistics. The number of schools in each sample year was as follows: 1997 N=297, 1998 N=362, 1999 N=339, 2000 no survey, 2001 N=367, 2002 N=348, 2003 N=463, 2004 N=802, 2005 N=677.

A range of key themes was embedded in the longitudinal questionnaire, one in particular focused on trends in teaching approach, i.e. whether subjects were taught separately or the degree to which they were combined. Questions also investigated the number and range of subjects combined into topic planning and issues concerning curriculum balance and breadth.

The authors are aware that there are methodological issues with the instrument, for example, changes over time in the wording of question

Table 8.1   Sample by regional distribution (2005)

	Invited Sample		Returned Sample		National Statistics*	
	N	%	N	%	N	%
East Midlands	156	9.5	70	10.3	1,729	9.7
Eastern	193	11.7	69	10.2	2,085	11.7
Inner London	65	3.9	18	2.7	702	4.0
North East	87	5.3	42	6.2	949	5.3
North West and Merseyside	247	15.0	91	13.4	2,639	14.9
Outer London	106	6.4	43	6.4	1,147	6.5
South East	267	16.2	118	17.4	2,717	15.3
South West	179	10.8	71	10.5	1,981	11.2
West Midlands	176	10.7	73	10.8	1,892	10.7
Yorkshire and Humber	174	10.5	82	12.1	1,921	10.8
Total	**1,650**	*100*	**677**	*100*	**17,762**	*100.1*

* DfES January 2004.

stems and in the style of a question. These witness to the constraints which emerge in publicly funded policy research. The key longitudinal question probed the profile of separate and combined teaching implementation across all subjects by year group. In the years 1997–2001 the sub-categories of the question were: nearly always separate, separate half the time and never/hardly ever taught separately. For 2002 and 2003 the sub-categories were: hardly ever/never combined, combined half the time and nearly always combined. The same information was collected but the categories were labelled differently in those two years. For 2004 and 2005 the question addressed English, mathematics and ICT only and looked at key stage rather than year group.

The reliability and limitations of 'self-report' data should also be considered. Despite the random selection of a representative sample and the healthy response rate (e.g. 41% return in 2005, see Table 8.1), completion of the survey was not compulsory, therefore a percentage of schools chose not to respond. One might therefore expect a certain bias in the output, for example, do rather more 'successful' schools tend to participate and therefore 'skew' the resultant data? The findings of this study are reliable to the extent that the self-reported information is accurate. In the context of this survey, in which all reporting of responses is anonymised, one would hope that there is little or no reason for respondents to give inaccurate responses. In order to enrich this study through deeper understanding of practice at the classroom level, a sub-sample of case study schools was selected to reflect examples of different approaches to achieving curriculum balance. It was anticipated that data generated in these studies would triangulate with evidence from the quantitative survey.

The data

In presenting the school response data we look at a chronological year by year profile for each subject across each teaching year group and at patterns of subject combinations. We illustrate the findings with qualitative data generated through the case study interviews and from supplementary survey data where appropriate.

Teaching by single subject or combination of subjects

Table 8.2 shows the percentage of time that each subject was taught separately across each primary year group in 1997, indicating that the only subject at key stage 1 (years 1 and 2) which 75% of the respondents reported as being 'nearly always taught separately' was mathematics. Apart from the timetabling of physical education and music for administrative and resource reasons, all the other subjects at key stage 1 were in some form of combination for up to or more than half their taught time.

At key stage 2 (Years 3 to 6), especially in the year prior to key stage testing, the profile of separate and combined subjects was different from that at key stage 1. Mathematics was reported by over 90% of the schools (91% Y3 – 93% Y6) to be taught as a separate subject. Science (not tested at key stage 1, but tested at key stage 2) increased from 44% single subject teaching in year 2 to 77% single subject teaching in year 6. English similarly increased from 38% single subject teaching in year 2 to 56% single subject teaching in both years 5 and 6. Quite how much of that increase of single subject teaching is due to test preparation we can only speculate. However, our most recent survey data (2007) indicated that test preparation (basically a euphemism for 'coaching' or 'teaching to the test') in year 6 in the second half of the spring term, accounted for three or more hours per week in two thirds of schools (66%) and two hours per week in about a quarter of the schools returning data (22%). Over three quarters of the sample (77%) indicated that the amount of time devoted to test preparation had increased over the past ten years. Data from the 2003 survey illustrate that in the month of April in year 6 classrooms, an average of almost 14 hours per week (56% of the available teaching time) was spent on test preparation across the three tested subjects. Over 10 hours per week of 'teaching time' was spent on test preparation in January in year 6.

Table 8.2 Percentage of time a subject is taught separately, 1997

(%)	Y1	Y2	Y3	Y4	Y5	Y6
English	36.8	37.9	48.3	50.6	55.8	55.8
Mathematics	74.1	78.2	91.2	92.4	93.8	93.3
Science	37.9	43.8	68.2	69.1	74.7	77.3
D&T	24.1	27.7	38.7	37.4	41.1	47.3
ICT	11.6	12.6	14.3	15.8	15.2	16.5
History	15.1	24.0	52.7	55.1	57.8	61.3
Geography	16.5	23.7	50.4	52.3	53.8	58.3
Art & design	19.6	21.6	36.1	38.7	41.7	44.6
Music	73.0	73.6	84.2	87.3	88.3	88.8
PE	91.3	91.5	96.7	97.0	98.2	97.8
RE	64.4	67.2	78.4	80.2	81.0	82.1

There was an interesting non-test but cross-key stage effect apparent from the reported data for both geography and history – clearly not prioritised as discrete subjects at key stage 1 (geography 23% and history 24% taught as separate subjects in year 2) but becoming timetabled as 'separate' subjects at key stage 2 (geography 50% in Y3 to 58% in Y6; history 53% in Y3 to 61% in Y6).

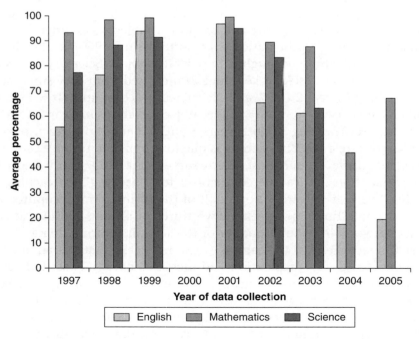

Figure 8.1 Percentage of time core subjects are taught separately in year 6 (1997–2005)

As illustrated by Table 8.2, the teaching profile of each subject was relatively consistent across the year groups within each key stage, so for the sake of simplicity and also because of the 'high stakes' associated with end of key stage 2 testing, the following discussion focuses on the trends in year 6.

The introduction of the National Literacy Strategy (NLS) (1998) and the piloting of a National Numeracy Strategy (NNS) (full strategy introduced 1999) would, from the data, seem to have had a marked and immediate effect on the teaching models across all core subjects in year 6. Figure 8.1 shows that all the core subjects (English 93.9%, mathematics 99.2% and science 91.4%) largely became 'separate subjects' by 1999 and almost entirely separate by 2001 (English 96.8%, mathematics 99.5%, science 95.0%).

The foundation subjects also followed a trend towards increased separate subject teaching which peaked in 2001 (Figure 8.2). With the introduction of the revised National Curriculum in September 2000 there was no curriculum data collection funded by QCA in 2000, so data are missing for one year when key implementation changes of a revised curriculum were happening. Subjects such as history and geography, which are well suited to a combined topic-based teaching approach, reported

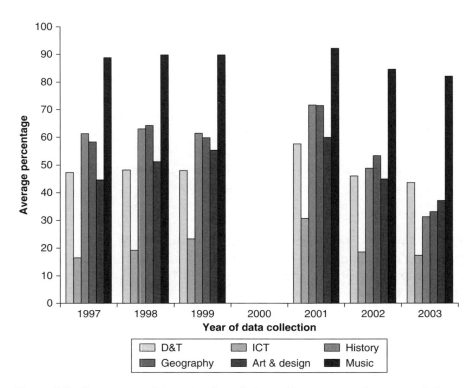

Figure 8.2   Percentage of time that foundation subjects are taught separately in year 6 (1997–2003)

increases of respectively 11% and 13% in separate subject teaching from 1997 to 2001. The political message crudely interpreted as 'single subject teaching good, combined subjects bad' had now reached its peak, for all of the foundation subjects were now following the model based on their reported increased percentages (D&T 48% 1999 – 58% 2001; history 61% 1999 – 72% 2001; geography 60% 1999 – 71% 2001). ICT, which had traditionally been regarded as either cross-curricular or as a facilitating agent of other subjects, increased from 23% in 1999 to 31% in 2001.

Curriculum 'balance'

In the 2001 survey, over two thirds (69%) of the sample schools reported having made changes to the balance of their curriculum and a further 21% indicated that they were currently implementing changes. Just over a quarter (26%) stated that they were not able to maintain a balanced curriculum; of those, 93% offered reasons for this; their main comments referring to the fact that time had been reduced for the foundation subjects (40%), and that this reduction was due to the national emphasis on core subjects as school performance indicators (37%). Time constraints were mentioned by 30% of respondents and 14% stated that they would have to combine the teaching of certain subjects in order to cover more subject content.

> 'We try to make it as balanced as possible but often feel non-core subjects are squeezed out'.
>
> 'Same argument as in the past – too much content not enough time, pressure on school to continue to improve reading, writing and maths'.
>
> 'Priority given to raising standards in order to meet targets, non-core subjects are not given a great deal of emphasis'.

Of the 74% of schools who indicated that they could still maintain a balanced curriculum, 7% stated that this was 'with difficulty', others offered explanations of the strategies they had adopted in order to maintain balance.

> 'We have extended the school day to fit everything in'.
>
> 'Time restraints – subject areas are blocked together to enable us to cover more'.

'Overwhelming pressure from LA on behalf of government to improve SATS results in core subjects, can only maintain balanced curriculum because our SATS are good and therefore able to resist pressure'.

'It is difficult, as demands increase something has to give usually a reduction in time allocated to non-core subjects'.

'Curriculum was more balanced five years ago, strong emphasis on literacy/numeracy has created imbalance between practical/academic subjects, try to give pupils as many practical skills as possible but this has reduced with revised curriculum'.

In 1998 the detailed statutory requirements in the programmes of study at key stages 1 and 2 in the six foundation subjects had been lifted in order to enable schools to concentrate more on targets for literacy and numeracy. Primary schools were told that they could reduce time spent on subjects such as art, PE and music (Brehony, 2005: 35). A trend in increased teaching time allocation in the core subjects and subsequent decreases in teaching time for foundation subjects is clearly evident from other longitudinal data collected as part of this survey (Boyle and Bragg, 2006). Teaching time allocated to English (+4%) and mathematics (+2%) increased at key stage 2 between 1997 and 1999 resulting in these two subjects accounting for over half (51%) of the timetable. One of the sample schools interviewed by the authors reported that the Strategies 'squeezed the time for everything else, when the numeracy hour came in it was very discrete and everybody was getting used to the structure of it and nothing (i.e. no subjects) did cross over then'.

There is evidence from the comments to suggest that some schools planned to return to a more integrated approach or to create more cross-curricular opportunities in order to accommodate the required emphasis on literacy and numeracy and still provide a balanced curriculum.

'Still over emphasis on NLS/NNS requirements in timed format, integrated approach to day would better suit the majority of the classes but having the courage to buck the requirements is too high'.

'Some subjects have limited time available due to priority of core subjects, imbalance will be addressed next academic year as improvement in effectiveness of policies creates more cross-curricular opportunities and releases time for these subjects'.

(Continued)

(Continued)

'Pressure on time squeezes out humanities to an extent, although we are working at organising topics so that they overlap especially into literacy and art'.

'Determined to maintain balanced curriculum, to do this need to regain autonomy over school day, reject structure of literacy/numeracy framework, want pupils to follow line of enquiry in depth using curriculum as analytical/planning tool not straitjacket'.

'Literacy and numeracy account for majority of time, this year have also prioritised foundation subjects – planning and delivery much of which we try to deliver cross-curricular, but staff still nervous of diverting from the NLS and NNS'.

It seems that necessity encouraged schools to return to the combined teaching approaches that were common practice prior to the NLS and NNS. The longitudinal data (Figure 8.2) show a return to combination subject teaching from 2002. It is unclear whether this change happened spontaneously in schools, i.e. prompted by an over-crowded curriculum and government imposed strategies to focus on the core subjects and the conflicting natural desire to provide a broad and balanced experience in the best interests of the pupils. The 2001 Ofsted annual report highlighted the pressure on the primary curriculum that some schools said was emanating from the demands of the national strategies for literacy and numeracy (Ofsted, 2001). In 2002, HMI carried out a survey of the effect of the national strategies on the primary school curriculum (Ofsted, 2002b: 11) and published the news that 'while a majority of headteachers report a continuing squeeze on the curriculum, just one in three feel that the pressure is beginning to ease … they take a more flexible approach to the timetabling of subjects and they establish productive links between English and mathematics and other subjects. Headteachers reported that this flexibility provides further opportunities for their teachers to strengthen links between subjects.'

In 2002 Galton and MacBeath reported that the concentration on literacy and numeracy was reducing teaching time for other areas of the curriculum, 'art, drama, music and ICT are being squeezed and are only partially covered by lunchtime and after-school clubs' (Galton and MacBeath, 2002). The disparity between the current emphasis on literacy and numeracy and the broad and balanced curriculum outlined in the original National Curriculum was raised in David Bell's (the Chief Inspector of Schools) annual report of 2002: 'The strong focus on raising standards in English and mathematics and on meeting targets exerts considerable pressure on the time devoted to the teaching of other subjects' (Ofsted, 2002a: 3). The report reinforced the link between the strategies and the beneficial effects on the teaching of English and mathematics: 'English and mathematics, strongly influenced by the two national strategies, remain the best-taught subjects' but lamented that 'the strongest features of this teaching too seldom carry over into other subjects' (Ofsted, 2002a: 3). Bell then reinforced the point even more strongly: 'the gulf between what pupils achieve in the core subjects and in the rest of the curriculum remains a concern' (Ofsted, 2002a: 5). This statement was not lost on other commentators: 'In what was a departure from Ofsted's previous commitment to the standards agenda, the report referred to the amount of time taken up by the drive to raise standards in English and mathematics and by the national tests' (Brehony, 2005: 36). As Alexander phrased it: 'Ofsted discovered a link between breadth, balance and standards ... Ofsted found that of the 3,508 primary schools inspected in 2000–1 under 6% achieved both high test marks in English and mathematics and consistently excellent teaching and learning across the full range of the National Curriculum' (Alexander, 2004: 25). Ofsted posited that it was the breadth and richness of the wider curriculum which gave teachers and pupils a meaningful context in which to apply, reinforce and extend the basics (Ofsted, 2002a). However, it is interesting to note that in 2007 Christine Gilbert, HMCI, laments the worrying existence of the 'two tier curriculum' in her annual report (Ofsted, 2007).

One of our survey samples summarised this need:

> 'We are still in the mind-set of each subject having an allocated time, feel numeracy and literacy are fantastic but we need to adapt a different approach to afternoons or the other 50% of the timetable. I think it should be holistic, a more topic-based approach, skills based rather than fact based, D&T as such is not a serious contender for time in primary but 'making' – art and craft should be. Blocking things like arts (literacy, music, art) is really rewarding. I feel we need more artists, writers, etc. in school in the primary phase while focusing on maths/English. Vital that some knock-on effect be realised at key stage 3 or why bust our collective guts?'

Alexander contests that New Labour took the opposite view that 'the rest of the curriculum was a distraction to the (annual performance) targets' (Alexander, 2004: 25) and transmitted to schools the unspoken threat that 'reducing the time spent on literacy and numeracy in order to free time for the rest of the curriculum, knowing as they do how much hangs on the next round of literacy and numeracy targets' (Alexander, 2004: 15) could have serious implications. One of our case study schools, situated in challenging circumstances, explained how using a skills-based rather than subject-focused approach to teaching, in which subject content was covered in the form of blocked two-week topics, had resulted in a marked improvement to their key stage 2 test results.

Adapting, combining and embedding: modelling a flexible curriculum

In 2002 QCA published *Designing and Timetabling the Primary Curriculum* which advocated a return to broad and balanced planning and exemplified to schools models of a more flexible form of subject timetabling introducing the notions of adapting, combining and embedding aspects of subjects within other subjects. In 2003, 75%, and in 2004, 68%, of the schools surveyed reported that they found this guidance booklet useful. Data illustrating further integration of both core subjects in 2004 followed the publication of *Excellence and Enjoyment: A Strategy for Primary Schools* (DfES, 2003), 72% of the sample in this year indicated that the document would have implications for their school. An open-response question requested schools to detail those implications. Almost a third (31%) of the respondents stated that it would enable greater flexibility in curriculum design, 29% reported that it would lead to reorganisation of the curriculum and 17% that it would mean a return to a cross curricular/topic-based approach to teaching. One of the sample schools responded that 'We were thinking in that way prior to the document because we had done all the creativity work already'. All subject areas (Figure 8.2) recorded a return towards more combination teaching in 2002, indicating that the restrictions on breadth imposed by the strategies were beginning to be challenged at school planning level – prior to the publication of the Primary Strategy in the following year which legitimised the change.

More integrated core subject teaching, particularly evident in English, and a desire to move in this direction exemplified by the qualitative comments corresponds with QCA's encouragement to embed literacy and numeracy (QCA, 2002; 2004). In 2002, over four out of five schools (84%) stated that their schemes of work in the foundation subjects identified opportunities for pupils to apply their literacy skills and three quarters of schools (75%) opportunities for numeracy skills. In 2005, QCA's new website 'Customise your curriculum' supplied support materials for: 'adapting and combining the original schemes' and 'embedding English and mathematics across the curriculum'. One of the interviewed schools offered the following description of how staff training is provided 'to highlight speaking and listening in the classroom and teaching the skills that children need for speaking and listening, and actually teaching those skills through other subjects. We did them, initially as discrete activities where we had to work with each other and make eye contact and ask a question then waiting for a question to be asked before responding. Now we build that into our lessons', in order to embed literacy across the curriculum.

Our 2005 survey data illustrate further changes that were happening to the school curriculum. Most schools (over 90% for science, design and technology, ICT, history and geography) were using the QCA/DfES schemes of work and of those, almost two thirds were adapting the units to suit their school (61% key stage 2) and around a quarter of schools were selecting activities from units to 'fit' their own scheme (23% key stage 2). At key stage 2, nearly half (45%) of the sample schools were combining units from different subjects. Figure 8.3 shows that those subjects perhaps most often associated with the traditional topic-based model, i.e. design and technology, history, geography and art and design, are most often combined.

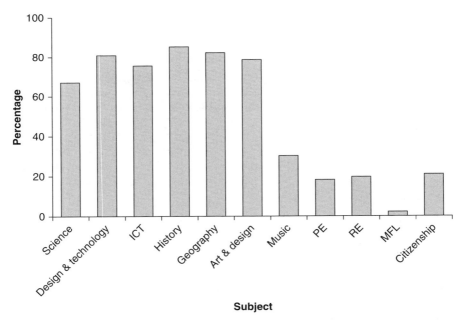

Figure 8.3   If you combine units from different subject schemes, in which subjects are units combined? (QCA, 2005)

Modelling subject combinations over time

We analysed survey data in order to gain insight into how schools construct their topics and how this may have changed over time. There were methodological issues (outside our control) about the way that the data were collected and the fact that in some years schools were asked to list 'the subject combinations that you usually teach together' (1997) and in other years 'which subjects are most often linked in topics? Please give three typical examples' (2005). Due to the many permutations of subject combinations and generic topic titles it was difficult to draw any firm conclusions. However, the data do illustrate issues which have emerged in earlier discussion.

Table 8.3 looks at subject combinations at key stage 2 from 1997 to 2003 because for these years the question stem remained consistent. In 1997 English was taught in a cross-curricular context by 11% of the sample and taught with at least one other subject by 16% of surveyed schools. With the introduction of the NLS these percentages fell to 4% in 1998 and to 2% in 2002 and 2003 for the cross-curricular model, and to 12% in 1998 and to 9% in 2002 for English taught with at least one other subject. However, in 2003 after the introduction of the Primary Strategy (DfES, 2003) there was an increase to 30% for English taught with at least one other subject. It is interesting that in 2003 cross-curricular

Table 8.3   Single subject most frequently combined at key stage 2**

	1997		1998		2002		2003	
	N=242	%	N=286	%	N=314	%	N=200	%
English cross curricular	27	11.2	10	3.5	7	2.2	8	1.7
ICT cross curricular	60	24.8	56	19.6	22	7.0	66	14.3
D&T cross curricular	1	0.4	3	1.0	-	-	10	2.2
PSHE cross curricular	2	0.8	2	0.7	5	1.6	33	7.1
Art cross curricular	-	-	4	1.4	-	-	5	1.1
Maths cross curricular	3	1.2	-	-	3	1.0	-	-
History and geography	-	-	43	15.0	41	13.1	39	8.4
English and at least one other subject*	39	16.1	35	12.2	28	8.9	59	29.5
Maths and at least one other subject*	13	5.4	19	6.6	15	4.8	19	9.5
Science and at least one other subject*	36	14.9	42	14.7	89	28.3	67	33.5
History & geography and at least one other subject*	2	0.8	12	4.2	7	2.2	30	15.0
PSHE and at least one other subject*	6	2.5	7	2.4	71	22.6	78	39.0

* note some overlap between these categories as the subjects identified can occur in the same topic group.

** The QCA did not ask questions on these themes 1999–2001

English did not report an increase but English combined with one other subject substantially increased. This perhaps illustrates the complexity of fully integrating English while still meeting the requirements of the NLS. No longer can the writing of an essay in history be defined as integrated English, i.e. the aspects of literacy must be more precisely accounted for. Mathematics was reported as taught 100% as a separate subject at key stage 2 apart from 1% (1997) and 1% (2002) cross-curricular teaching and in the range 5% (1997) to 9% (2003) taught with at least one other subject.

At key stage 2 ICT was the subject reported with the highest percentage for being taught in a cross-curricular context (25% in 1997 – 14% in 2003), a model largely sustained throughout the course of the survey to-date. Art was minimally evidenced as a cross-curricular subject at key stage 2 with 1% of schools reporting that model in both 1998 and 2003.

What did we discover?

The longitudinal data supplied by the sample schools have proved important in chronicling and supplying a detailed primary phase subject-level picture of changes in curriculum planning for the period 1997 to 2007. However, while reflecting on the reported data, it is important to keep in mind the political nature of the 'curriculum reforms' of the last 19 years. The original political concept of a National Curriculum circa 1988 was very much a discrete subject-based model. The unchanging nature of this model was confirmed by the Dearing revisions (SCAA, 1993). When the authors' curriculum survey started to collect national sample data in 1997, the evidenced profile from the schools which supplied data was one of teaching discrete subjects but with a medium to high level of cross-subject teaching especially in key stage 1 and throughout both key stages in certain subjects, e.g. geography and history – with the exception of mathematics which retained its 100% exclusivity even at key stage 1.

The introduction of the National Literacy and National Numeracy Strategies and the high level of external auditing and accountability of the implementation of those strategies resulted in a pronounced reduction in cross-subject planning, linkage and teaching alongside an increased concentration of teaching time on English and mathematics which reduced time allocated to the foundation subjects (Boyle and Bragg, 2006). The introduction of the revised curriculum in 2000 did not initially redress the balance (despite suggesting that opportunities for connections could be planned between subjects, DfEE, 1999a). The survey data for 2001 evidence that the emphasis on single separate subject teaching is as strong as it had been prior to the revised curriculum.

Gradually, supported by QCA's *Designing and Timetabling the Primary Curriculum* booklet (2002) and *A Strategy for Primary Schools* (DfES, 2003) and a more supportive attitude from Ofsted (2002) towards planning for subject teaching, schools began to demonstrate flexibility in their timetabling of subjects.

There is still some way to go because while English is now reported by schools as being taught through a blend of separate subject and in combination with other subjects, mathematics is still firmly located in a separate subject teaching model. The political imperative still prevails. 'The literacy and numeracy strategies worked' (Blair, 2005) – to some level but at what cost? (Fullan, 2003; Alexander, 2004; Boyle and Bragg, 2006). 'With that recent history in mind, with the Literacy and Numeracy Strategies firmly in place, and with a continuing commitment to targets who can possibly believe the primary strategy's avowed commitment to a broad and balanced set of learning experiences' (Alexander, 2004: 25)

To conclude on a note of optimism, subsequent to our review of the data, in curriculum design terms, the QCA (now replaced by the Standards and Testing Agency) stated: 'the national curriculum subjects are only part of the curriculum ... the real curriculum is the entire planned learning experience ... this is about looking at how the curriculum can meet the needs of children now and in the future' (Waters, 2006), a view that was (temporarily) heartening. This conceptualisation seemed to sit well with existing initiatives such as *Opening Minds* (RSA, 2005), the International Primary Curriculum (www.greatlearning.com/ipc/), Building Learning Power (www.buildinglearningpower.co.uk) among others, and linked to school clusters and networks exploring practically issues such as how an effective curriculum can be negotiated with learners, how learning can be created by learners and not simply 'mandated' to them, and how teachers could feel liberated from a curriculum which is presented as a high pressure chase to 'cover content' within prescribed time limits. That had to be the way forward. Sadly, the evidence, the data and our reporting was ignored. The fruits can be seen in the 'accountability dominated' curriculum models which pass for teaching and learning in our schools in 2015 and the replacement by a Standards and Testing Agency of the national agency (QCA) which monitored and reviewed the curriculum.

Curriculum Construction

Chapter summary

The determining elements in content selection and prioritisation to ensure a progressive, achievable but challenging curriculum.

Selection of the content of the curriculum

The fundamental question to be addressed is: What is the basic structure of the content that is necessary for an understanding of this theme/ sub-domain/subject for a group of learners?

Content is the basis by which learning activities are linked to each other, to goals and to the theoretical rationale. Meaningful selection of content will involve variations from one learning situation to another because selection must take into account the strengths and weaknesses of the teachers and of the learners. Content is the core organising factor in curriculum design. The most common elements of curriculum organisation are:

- concepts: such as culture, growth, number, space, etc.
- generalisations: conclusions drawn from careful observations
- skills: proficiency plans for building continuity in programmes
- values: beliefs taken as directives of behaviour.

Methods for selecting content

Content can be developed through research into the literature of that field or domain, usually through the input of expert(s) in that content area, through the growth of the participants into a group of new experts as a result of their own intensive study and through a needs assessment.

Practical example: Science curriculum, theme of solar energy

The curriculum working group took expert advice in selecting the content of the curriculum for that theme. As a result of that input from the experts the participants in the working group identified key concepts required for an understanding of solar energy. They began with a collaborative 'brainstorming' session to list crucial concept areas. They listed fundamental questions: What is the sun? How does it work? What is energy? Why is there an energy crisis?

Logical background concepts were easily identified but others were more difficult to grasp or assimilate into planning. Some participants felt that identifying different kinds of energy would be important while others felt that modes of technological solutions to energy problems should take precedence in the conceptual framework. Other members of the working group stressed that 'quality of life' issues should take precedence.

The experts showed the group how all the expressed concerns could fit compatibly within a conceptual framework. They all agreed that the concepts of 'sun' and 'energy' were the foundation but that solar energy itself needed to be identified as a content area. Within that concept was the question: How can solar energy be used effectively? Then the technological possibilities became concept areas of their own, e.g. passive modes, active modes and indirect modes. All of these then naturally created implications for the last concept area in this theme plan: the quality of life issues. The final model emerged with seven key areas for content development (see Boyle, 2005–6).

Identifying content through needs assessment

Steps proposed for curriculum needs assessment are:

- identify student-oriented goals (content areas)
- rank the importance of these goals without regard to performance levels
- assess the level of performance for each of the goals
- establish a priority for each student goal, considering both importance and performance.

The technique used for displaying the data is based on the following premises:

- findings of a needs assessment, in order to be useful, must establish priorities
- performance level and importance of a goal share equally in determining priorities
- data are not useful unless the users understand, accept and can act upon the information.

For a full description, see Boyle (2005–6).

Learning goals

A goal can be defined as a statement of broad intent which is general and timeless and not concerned with a particular achievement within a specified time period.

Educational goals should describe the desired product. The teaching units, the instructional methodologies and environmental conditions for learning will be determined later in the development/ training process. Educational goals should be stated as desirable characteristics attributable to learning. Goals should define what an individual is expected to achieve. The scope of educational goals is important. Goals should not be so wide that they give purpose and justification to everything. Conversely goals should not be as narrow as behavioural objectives.

Practical example: Goal statements for solar energy

A1 Students understand that the sun is essential to all life on earth.

A2 Students learn the physical properties of the sun.

A3 Students learn the astronomical relationships of the sun to the earth.

A4 Students learn that all of our sources of energy on earth are traceable to the sun.

B1 Students learn to recognise various forms of energy.

B2 Students evolve a concept of energy.

B3 Students understand the difference between renewable and non-renewable energy sources.

B4 Students learn about energy measurements.

(Continued)

(Continued)

B5 Students understand how the 'energy crisis' relates to the ways in which we use energy.

B6 Students know about alternative energy sources.

B7 Students understand energy conservation.

C1 Students understand basic issues/problems involved in using solar energy.

D1 Students learn some of the ways of using solar energy.

D2 Students understand some of the technical problems involved in using solar energy; collection (and non-collection-passive) conversion, utilisation, storage.

E1 Students recognise how political issues affect solar energy technology.

E2 Students understand how economic issues affect solar energy.

E3 Students understand the environmental impact of solar energy.

E4 Students understand the sociological constraints on using solar energy.

E5 Students understand the institutional constraints on using solar energy.

Checklist for evaluating programme goals

Each goal should be stated:

- at a level of generality that clearly indicates the expected learning outcome and that is definable by specific types of student behaviour
- so that it includes only one general learning outcome rather than a combination of several outcomes
- in terms of student performance rather than through teacher performance
- as a learning product rather than in terms of the learning process.

Instructional objectives

The purpose of instructional objectives

Every teacher plans to objectives. How do instructional objectives fit into curriculum development? How can they be used more effectively?

Early curriculum models were written from instructional objectives and were criticised as being simply a list of objectives and accompanying tests of mastery of those objectives. Let us assume that curriculum never emerges directly – instead the objective is a logical outcome of the structural framework and of the stated goals. Instructional objectives therefore are a process by which goals are translated into appropriate teaching plans and state a consequence of learning.

Characteristics of instructional objectives

- Objectives graphically describe the terminal behaviour – this is what the pupil will be doing at the time that he or she has achieved the objective.
- Objectives state the criteria of an acceptable performance: time limits, productivity levels, quality control standards, minimum essentials, thresholds, etc.
- Objectives include any qualifying conditions or restrictions that must exist for the terminal behaviour to be acceptable.

Command words

It is very important when writing instructional objectives that 'command words' are carefully chosen. It is desirable to select verbs that are open to limited interpretations.

- Verbs open to many interpretations: to know; to understand; to enjoy; to believe; to appreciate; to trust.
- Verbs open to limited interpretations: to write; to identify; to differentiate; to solve; to contrast; to compare; to list; to construct.

Scope

The term 'scope' can be loosely defined as 'what the curriculum will include'. It has been discussed as the 'breadth' of the curriculum content. For example in the UK in 1988 when the first National Curriculum was introduced, the legislation described the curriculum to be 'broad and balanced' in its content, range of experiences and demand. This 'scope' includes the subjects, the topics, learning experiences, activities and organisation of the curriculum.

Opinion on the 'scope' of the curriculum varies by country. Four countries that have introduced a statutory curriculum within the past 20 years (the Netherlands, New Zealand, England, Wales) have recently reduced the level of prescription in favour of 'frameworks'. Within these frameworks, schools can design a curriculum to suit local circumstances.

In Italy, however, central control has been tightened while in Scotland there are non-statutory curriculum guidelines which tend to be followed by most schools.

Sample frameworks

In the Netherlands (Holland) integrated objectives are grouped around six themes: attitude to work, working according to a plan, use of a diversity of learning strategies, self-image, social behaviour, and finally, the use of a new media.

In Singapore, project work and inter-disciplinary learning offer children opportunities to bring together the knowledge and skills they have acquired from different areas of learning. Similarly, the revised primary science syllabus is based on a thematic approach (diversity, cycles, systems, interactions, energy) which allows for the integration of scientific ideas and encourages pupils to see how topics are linked across the scientific disciplines.

Modelling the curriculum

In modelling the curriculum, once the conceptual framework, the goals and objectives have been stated, many of the focal points of the curriculum have been identified. The curriculum developers know what they want to emphasise. Unit and lesson planning can then be built around these organising centres.

Organisational issues

What shall I teach? Why shall I teach it? How shall I organise my teaching? How shall I differentiate my teaching? What resources do I have access to?

If it is established that subjects will be the organisational structure, then it is possible to recognise that the variety of links between those subjects can be described in the form of a taxonomy. At one extreme some subjects may disappear entirely as autonomous elements from the curriculum either permanently or for a period of two or three years (see Boyle and Bragg, 2006). Their place may be taken by a single integrated study which may be labelled 'humanities' or 'environmental studies' or 'people and society' or a combination of these or other titles. At the opposite end of the spectrum subjects may continue to exist as separate subjects after an analysis of each subject's contribution at each stage of the pupil's school life.

Example organisational structures

- The continued existence of subjects separately and in their own right, side by side with their participation in integrated programmes on a long- or short-term basis.
- Planned combinations of subjects on an occasional basis, e.g. for the common exploration of a theme. Different subjects may be grouped together at different times and the themes and thus the groupings of subjects may be planned after successive terms according to an overall curricular policy.
- General studies programmes which are genuinely planned to relate the different contributions of a range of subjects to a single scheme.
- Occasional or episodic consequences of interest in two or more subjects; these may be in response to a local issue or an event of wider significance and may result in joint thematic work over a long/short period.
- The identification of shared objectives leading to parallel work in two or more subjects (e.g. mathematics and art in work on symmetry).
- New areas of the curriculum, e.g. health, personal social development, moral education.
- Expansion in the field of interest of one subject which calls upon 'servicing' elements of other subjects (music may enlist the help of design technology for the making of musical instruments).

Sequence

If 'scope' is the 'what' of the curriculum, then sequence is the 'when' (Oliva, 1982). Sequencing a curriculum refers to the optimum order of presenting materials, lessons and activities. There are several successful methods of establishing an effective sequence to a curriculum programme. Sequence should effect and reinforce continuity in progression of the individual pupil's learning.

A sample intermediate science curriculum sequence emphasising continuity in progression

Year/Grade 7

- Term/Semester 1:

    o 7C Environment and feeding relationships
    o 7D Variation and classification

(Continued)

(Continued)

- o 7L The solar system and beyond
- o 7G Particle model of solids, liquids and gases

- Term/Semester 2:

  - o 7H Solutions
  - o 7K Forces and their effects
  - o 7A Cells
  - o 7B Reproduction

- Term/Semester 3:

  - o 7E Acids and alkalis
  - o 7F Simple chemical reactions
  - o 7I Energy resources
  - o 7J Electrical circuits

Year/Grade 8

- Term/Semester 1:

  - o 8E Atoms and elements
  - o 8F Compounds and mixtures
  - o 8J Magnets and electromagnets
  - o 8I Heating and cooling

- Term/Semester 2:

  - o 8A Food and digestion
  - o 8B Respiration
  - o 8G Rocks and weathering
  - o 8H The rock cycle

- Term/Semester 3:

  - o 8K Light
  - o 8L Sound and hearing
  - o 8C Microbes and disease
  - o 8D Ecological relationships

Year/Grade 9

- Term/Semester 1:

  - o 9I Energy and electricity
  - o 9A Inheritance and selection
  - o 9E Reactions of metals and metal compounds
  - o 9F Patterns of reactivity

- Term/Semester 2:

  - o 9J Gravity and space
  - o 9B Fit and healthy

- o 9G Environmental chemistry
- o 9H Using chemistry

- Term/Semester 3:

- o 9K Speeding up
- o 9L Pressure and moments
- o 9C Plants and photosynthesis
- o 9D Plants for food

Curriculum organisation

Organising and labelling the curriculum

Although a national curriculum is usually specified in separate subjects, aspects of one subject can be combined with aspects of another subject and aspects of one subject can be planned into the teaching of other subjects.

New or revised planning or 'packaging' can make a difference to some pupils' interests and therefore their motivation for learning. Where subjects or aspects of subjects are grouped, care is needed to retain the distinctiveness of each subject and its knowledge and skills base.

To achieve these goals, curriculum and assessments will be organised around a well-defined set of learning progressions along multiple dimensions within subject areas. The following criteria should be used to develop and organise the curriculum:

- It is aligned with future performance expectations.
- It includes rigorous content and application of knowledge through high-order skills.
- It builds upon strengths and lessons of current national curriculum standards.
- It is informed by top-performing countries, so that all students are prepared to succeed in global economy.
- It is evidence-based.

In addition, formative and interim assessments and instructional supports will be conceptualised in tandem with summative assessments – all of them linked to the curriculum standards and supported by a unified evidence-centred design.

Curriculum learning standards

The standards will define the rigorous skills and knowledge in academic subjects that need to be effectively taught and learned for students to be ready to succeed academically. These standards will be developed with the following characteristics:

Fewer, clearer, higher: One of the goals of this process will be to produce a set of fewer, clearer and higher standards. It is critical that any standards document be translatable to and teachable in the classroom. As such, the standards must cover only those areas that are critical for student success. This means making tough decisions about what to include in the standards; however, these choices are important to ensure the standards are useable by teachers.

Evidence-based: Evidence will be used in deciding what to include – or not include – in the standards. Rather than focusing on the opinions of experts exclusively, evidence to guide the decisions about what to include in the standards will be used. This is a key difference between this updated process and the processes that have come before.

Internationally benchmarked: These standards will be informed by the content, rigour and organisation of standards of high-performing countries so that all students are prepared to succeed in a global economy and society.

Special populations: In the development of these standards, the inclusion of all types of learners will be a priority. Standards writers will select language intended to make the standards documents accessible to different learners.

Assessment: The standards will ultimately be the basis for an assessment system that will include multiple measures of student performance. Once the final standards are agreed, attention will be focused on creating a high quality system of measurement that will include proper motivation, training and professional incentives for teachers to teach to these standards, and a variety of assessments that will reinforce teaching and learning tied to the agreed pupil learning expectations.

Twenty-first-century skills: The curriculum and standards will incorporate twenty-first-century skills where possible. They are not inclusive of all the skills students need for success in the twenty-first century, but many of these skills will be required across disciplines.

The revised curriculum intends to set forward-thinking goals for student performance based on evidence about what is required for success. The curriculum and standards will set the stage for education for the next decade, and they will ensure that all students are prepared within an expectation to contribute to and access the global economic workplace.

Furthermore, the standards created will raise learning outcomes for all students.

The standards as a whole must be essential, rigorous, clear and specific, coherent, and internationally benchmarked.

Essential: will be reasonable in scope in defining the knowledge and skills students should have to succeed in entry-level or baseline assessment.

Rigorous: will include high-level cognitive demands by asking students to demonstrate deep conceptual understanding through the application of content knowledge and skills to new situations. High-level cognitive demand includes reasoning, justification, synthesis, analysis and problem solving.

Clear and specific: will provide sufficient guidance and clarity so that they are teachable, learnable and measurable.

Teachable and learnable: will provide sufficient guidance for the design of instructional materials.

Measureable: student attainment will be observable and verifiable and the standards and curriculum will be used to develop broader assessment frameworks.

Coherent: the standards and curriculum will convey a unified vision of the 'big ideas' (main learning themes) and supporting concepts within a discipline and reflect a progression of learning that is meaningful and appropriate.

Grade-by-grade: the standards and curriculum will have limited repetition across the grades or grade spans to help educators align instruction to the standards.

Internationally benchmarked: the standards and curriculum will be informed by the content, rigour, and organisation of standards of high-performing countries so that all students are prepared for succeeding in the global economy and society.

Such curriculum and standards will require three major shifts from the traditional approach:

Focus: indicate strongly where the standards focus.

Coherence: think across grades and link to major topics within grades.

Rigor: in major topics, pursue conceptual understanding, procedural skill and fluency, and application with equal intensity.

Shift 1: Focus

Example: Mathematics traditional approach

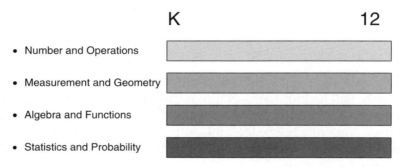

Figure 9.1   New focus approach

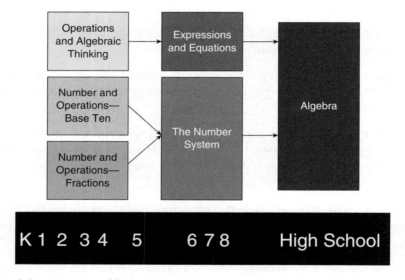

Figure 9.2   Key areas of focus in mathematics

Table 9.1   Content emphases by cluster

Grade	Focus Areas in Support of Rich Instruction and Expectations of Fluency and Conceptual Understanding
K–2	Addition and subtraction – concepts, skills and problem solving and place value
3–5	Multiplication and division of whole numbers and fractions – concepts, skills and problem solving
6	Ratios and proportional reasoning, early expressions and equations
7	Ratios and proportional reasoning, arithmetic of rational numbers
8	Linear algebra and linear functions

The first shift helps support focus by identifying the content emphasis by cluster. The curriculum and standards will indicate content that is major (m), and content that is additional or supporting (a/s).

For example, Grade 4 mathematics cluster emphases:

Table 9.2

Operations and Algebraic Thinking Cluster
[m] Use for operations – addition, subtraction, multiplication and division – with whole numbers to solve problems
[a/s] Get familiarity with factors and multiples
…

Shift 2: Coherence

Connect the learning within and across grades so that students can build new understanding on foundations built in previous years.

Begin to count on solid conceptual understanding of core content and build on it.

Each standard is not a new event, but an extension of previous learning.

Example:

Table 9.3 Coherence alignment in context: neighbouring grades and progressions – the staircase design

Grade	Curriculum standard
4	1. Apply and extend previous understandings of multiplication to multiply a fraction by a whole number
5	1. Apply and extend previous understandings of multiplication to multiply a fraction or whole number by a fraction
	2. Apply and extend previous understandings of division to divide unit fractions by whole numbers and whole numbers by unit fractions
6	2. Apply and extend previous understandings of multiplication and division to divide fractions by fractions
	3. Interpret and compute quotients of fractions, and solve word problems involving division of fractions by fractions, e.g. by using visual fraction models and equations to represent the problem

Shift 3: Rigour

The new curriculum and standards, for example, in mathematics will require a balance of:

- conceptual understanding
- procedural skill and fluency
- application of skills in problem solving situations.

Table 9.4

Grade			
1	Operation and algebraic thinking: *If 5+2=7 known then 2+5=7 known*		
2		Operation and algebraic thinking: *If 6x2=12 known then 2x6=12 known*	
3			Operation and algebraic thinking: *Express 3 add 7 and multiply the result by 2 as (3+7)x2*
4			Operation and algebraic thinking: *Express 2(3+x) as 3 + 2x*

Pursuit of all three requires equal intensity in time, activities and resources.

- Teach more than 'how to get the answer' and instead support students' ability to access concepts from a number of perspectives.
- Students are able to see maths as more than a set of mnemonics or discrete procedures.
- Conceptual understanding supports the other aspects of rigour (fluency and application).
- The standards require speed and accuracy in calculation.
- Teachers structure class time and/or homework time for students to practice core functions such as single-digit multiplication so that they are more able to understand and manipulate more complex concepts.

Table 9.5   Required fluencies for K–6

Grade	Standard	Required Fluency
K		Add/subtract within 5
1	1	Add/subtract within 10
2	2	Add/subtract within 20 (know single-digit sums from memory) Add/subtract within 100
3	3	Multiply/divide within 100 (know single-digit products from memory) Add/subtract within 1000
4	4	Add/subtract within 1,000,000
5	5	Multi-digit multiplication
6	6	Multi-digit division Multi-digit decimal operations

Linking aspects of subjects

Different subjects require different amounts of overall teaching time for adequate coverage of the study programme. Some schools also like their overall time allocations to be blocked together to allow occasional cross-subject working, for example, in language, science and mathematics or the across the creative arts.

Schools should be encouraged to make links across subjects where there are related skills and knowledge. They should look for these links between subjects so that pupils can reinforce their learning by applying it in different contexts. Subject leaders should work together to organise aspects of the programmes of study for different subjects into blocks of learning. They should consider how coverage and progression can be built. Which aspects of each programme of study need to be taught separately? Which aspects can be linked with other subjects? They can then plan units of work that link together some aspects of art and design, dance, drama and music as 'the arts' and some aspects of science, design and technology and information technology as 'science and technology'.

When links across subjects are effective, they enable pupils to apply the knowledge and skills learned in one subject to others. Linking aspects of subjects brings coherence to learning when complementary aspects across subjects are brought together.

- Are some subjects best taught as separate subjects rather than cross-curricular?

Languages and mathematics usually tend to be taught as separate subjects. However, our planning models (models for training programme/

workshops) show how explicit links can be made between those subjects and the blocks of learning in other subjects. Through these linked experiences pupils' skills, knowledge and understanding can be applied in a range of contexts. The school should value the varied learning experiences offered in this way to the pupils and build on the fact that they are helping pupils' learning through making connections across subjects.

- Which aspects of subjects can be combined?

An audit of the subjects in the national curriculum programme will identify opportunities to combine aspects of subjects across the curriculum (see example of audit rigour in the Appendix).

Strengthening curriculum coherence

By combining aspects of one subject with aspects of one or more subjects in their planning, the teacher will strengthen curriculum coherence. Pupils will then gain insights into and an understanding of the relationships between aspects of subjects and between subjects themselves. This will develop for the pupils a growing understanding of the interdependence of knowledge areas and a knowledge of the relationships between subjects.

In most countries the curriculum is still organised mainly in separate subjects. However, good teachers have developed skills at making the best use of links between subjects to strengthen and reinforce learning. They recognise that where links are effective, they enable pupils to apply the knowledge and skills learnt in one subject to the knowledge and skills of other subjects. It also brings coherence to learning when complementary aspects of subjects are brought together.

Where subjects are grouped under the heading of a theme such as 'where we live' or 'food and healthy living', the number of subjects is rarely more than three and the links between those three subjects are strong.

Curriculum development at the national level for teaching, learning and assessment

Decisions needing to be made by the curriculum developers at the national level to focus planning:

- *Values and aims*: how will these inform decisions about the curriculum?
- *Curriculum priorities and emphasis*: how much importance should be given to each subject and which aspects within them need to be emphasised?

- *Organising and labelling the curriculum*: which subjects or aspects within subjects will be taught separately and which will be combined with other subjects?
- *Opportunities for development*: what opportunities will be offered to apply and develop children's skills, knowledge and understanding across the curriculum?
- *Distributing the curriculum by stages or phases*: when will subjects, units of work, topics or themes be taught? Daily, weekly, how many times a term/semester?
- *Curriculum inclusion and differentiation*: how will the curriculum be adapted for children with different abilities or needs?
- *Curriculum continuity*: how will the design of the curriculum help children to make a smooth transition from one stage or phase to the next one?

Selecting learning objectives

Teachers should select their learning objectives from either the content of the national curriculum syllabus, the study programme or the school's teaching programme. In planning for the teaching and learning activities for a lesson with pupils at a range of different levels of understanding, these objectives may be separated into small discrete learning steps. It is important that the teacher is trained to explain to the pupils at the start of the lesson:

- what they would like to see/know from each stage of a pupil's outcomes
- the purpose of each of the learning tasks.

Forms of assessment

Assessment should form a natural and wholly integrated aspect of teaching and learning activities in the classroom. Each use of assessment information by the teacher is aimed at the improvement of pupil learning through the adjustment of teaching to meet the identified (through ongoing classroom assessment) learning needs.

- Teachers need to reflect upon and have practical guidance on how to use assessment effectively for improving learning outcomes.

Within the teaching and learning process, assessment is *not* to be planned at the end of the unit or lesson. The teaching, learning and assessment process is a coherent whole. When the teacher selects the learning objectives for the lesson, they are planning for the pupils to achieve specific learning outcomes. The teacher plans for different levels of performance to be demonstrated by the pupils against tasks which are differentiated to meet the pupils' abilities. Because of this process of matching objectives and outcomes, the teacher is able to report with great specificity on individual pupil learning and plan for next steps required in learning for that pupil. The teacher is building up a very accurate profile of pupil performance.

Reporting to stakeholders

Assessment must provide an effective communication of information with parents and other stakeholders in the learning partnership so that all partners can support learning in an informed way.

There are three main audiences for reporting assessment information:

Pupils: Reporting to pupils takes place all the time, both orally and in writing. In reporting to pupils the teacher/school communicates with them on their progress, their strengths and weaknesses and what will be their next learning steps. Reporting in this factual and specific method to pupils is at the centre of the formative assessment process.

Parents: Parents need to know how their children are progressing. Parents need to understand the reports, the language used and the measurement of performance information supplied. If teachers make their reports accessible to parents, the parents can understand how they can share in and support the development of their child by and with the school.

Educational professionals: These include Department of Education officers, local and national policy makers, Ofsted, local authority school improvement partners, next school or a professional whose role it is to support a pupil in some way, perhaps an educational psychologist.

10

Curriculum and Assessment

Chapter summary

Assessment of the teaching and learning within a taught national curriculum programme should enable analysis of effective progression of pupils; once the political imperative seizes the assessment system, the curriculum becomes meaningless.

Defining assessment in the context of a national assessment system in the twenty first century therefore always seems to indicate a form of testing to provide outcomes that are acceptable to governments for their purposes of monitoring and accountability. (Boyle and Charles, 2015)

What is a national curriculum assessment system?

While the proponents of a national curriculum may see it as a means to provide social cohesion and to give all of us the capacity to improve our schools by measuring them against 'objective' criteria, the effects will be the opposite. Rather than leading to cultural and social cohesion, differences between 'we' and 'the others' will be produced even more strongly, and the attendant social antagonisms and cultural and economic destruction will worsen. (Apple 1996: 33)

A national assessment is designed to describe the achievement of pupils in a curriculum area aggregated to provide an estimate of the achievement level in the education system as a whole for a particular age or grade. It provides data for a type of national education audit carried out to inform policy makers about key aspects of the system. In the majority of countries it involves administration of achievement tests either to a sample or to a whole population of pupils at a specific age or grade; in some countries, teachers' own assessments of their pupils are used to support these achievement test outcomes (e.g. UK Year 2 children).

The original intention of UK National Curriculum assessment was that externally designed and standardised tests and the classroom teachers' own assessments should have parity (TGAT, 1988a). However, government policy (see earlier background on the political context of the national curriculum) almost immediately changed that potential balance and by 1991 the public reporting was solely of the outcomes tests (Reeves et al., 2001).

National assessment systems in various parts of the world tend to have common features. All include an assessment of pupils' language or literacy and of students' mathematics abilities usually focusing on numeracy. In the majority of countries pupils at primary school level are assessed and in many systems assessments are carried out in secondary schools. Teachers are often asked to supply background data either about the pupils (gender, first language, special educational needs) or the school context (type of school, selection, funding type, state or independent).

Differences also exist in national assessment systems from country to country:

> *Frequency*: in some countries, an assessment is carried out every year, although the curriculum area (domain) that is assessed may vary. In other systems, assessments are less frequent.

> *Agency*: in some systems the ministry of education carries out the assessment; in others the assessment is by a national research centre, a consortium of educational bodies, a university or an examinations board.

> *Participation*: may be voluntary or statutory and mandated. When it is voluntary, non-participation of some schools will certainly bias the results and lead to an inaccurate profile of educational achievement across the system.

Although most industrial countries have had systems of national assessment for some time, it was not until the 1990s that the capacity to administer assessments became more widely available in other parts of the world. For example, rapid development in the establishment of national assessments took place during the 1990s in Latin America and the Caribbean countries, often to provide baseline data for educational reforms. These developments represented a shift from the assessment of inputs to the assessment of outcomes. Focus of basic education should be 'on actual learning acquisition and outcome, rather than exclusively upon enrolment, continued participation in organized programmes and completion of certification requirements' (UNESCO, 1990: 5)

The Dakar Framework for Action (UNESCO, 2000) highlighted the importance of learning outcomes: 'to improve all aspects of the quality of education ... so that recognised and measurable outcomes are achieved by all, especially in literacy, numeracy and essential life skills' (UNESCO 2000: iv, 7). As a result national governments have greatly increased support for monitoring pupil achievement through national assessments. The assumption is made that not only will national assessments provide information on the state of a nation's education system (against international competitors) but the use of that information will lead to improvement in teacher training, teaching and hence pupil achievements.

Whether this desired improvement happens is not proven and in many cases does not happen: this failure to improve may be due to the fact that larger numbers attending schools were not matched by increased resources (principally, professionally or even adequately trained teachers); also the information obtained from assessments has often been of poor quality or has not been factored systematically into decision making. Of course, there are dichotomous views as to what the word 'improvement' means within education systems that are, in the main, dominated by politicians and by short-term political aims.

A 'model' for national curriculum assessment?

In 2003 the USA introduced the No Child Left Behind (NCLB) legislation as the federal educational means of assessment. The data accumulated over those 12 years indicate three clear issues:

1. NCLB has severely damaged educational quality and equity with its narrowing and limiting effects falling most severely on the poor.
2. NCLB has failed to significantly increase average academic performance and significantly narrow achievement gaps.
3. 'Reform' attempts for NCLB (Obama Administration waivers; Senate Education Committee's Elementary and Secondary Education Act (ESEA) reauthorisation bill) failed to address NCLB's fundamental flaws. NCLB demanded results (to measure improvements in education) in the form of test data – bottom line results have fallen.

The NCLB law, however, has succeeded in transforming many schools into data-driven environments. Testing and test preparation have proliferated – the amount of time spent on testing in some schools has doubled. A study for Congress by the Government Accountability Office (GAO) estimated states would have to create more than 433 tests (at a huge cost) to satisfy NCLB mandates (GAO, 2003). In Massachusetts there were 33 state test sessions in one school year (2011) while in Wisconsin teachers spent an average (per district) of 976 hours administrating tests. Cheating in the tests has become an epidemic: in Atlanta where cheating was confirmed in 44 public schools (involving 78 teachers and principals), a Georgia Bureau of Investigation (GBI) Report described 'a culture of fear, intimidation and retaliation throughout the district' (GBI, 2011a). Incidents of cheating have been confirmed in 30 states.

NCLB has resulted in the omission by schools of low-scoring pupils to improve a school's test score bottom line. Nichols and Berliner (2007) compiled substantial evidence of this in their book *Collateral Damage*, including in Birmingham Alabama where 500 students were dropped from high school before test time, and New York City where a law suit exposed policies that pushed out thousands of low-scoring students.

NCLB had the effect of encouraging low-performing schools to meet benchmarks by narrowing curriculum and instruction.

National assessments often focus on one or more of the following questions:

- How well are students learning in the education system (with reference to general expectations, aims of the curriculum, preparation for further learning, or preparation for life)?
- Does evidence indicate particular strengths or weaknesses in pupils' knowledge and skills?
- Do particular sub-groups in the population perform badly? Do disparities exist, for example, between the achievements of (a) boys and girls, (b) pupils in urban and non-urban situations; (c) pupils from different language and ethnic groups, (d) pupils in different regions of a country?
- What factors are associated with pupil achievement? To what extent does achievement vary with characteristics of the learning environment (e.g. school resources, teacher training and competence, type of school) or with pupils' home and community circumstances?
- Are government standards being met in the provision of resources (e.g. textbooks, teacher qualifications, other quality inputs)?
- Do the achievements of pupils change over time? This requires carrying out assessments that produce comparable data over periods of time.

International example: Ethiopia

National assessment objectives

- To determine the level of student academic achievement and attitude development in Ethiopian primary education.
- To analyse variations in student achievement by region, gender, location and language of instruction.
- To explore factors that influence student achievement in primary education.

- To monitor the improvement of student learning achievement from the first baseline study in 1999/2000.
- To build the capacity of the education system in national assessment.
- To create reliable baseline data for the future.
- To generate recommendations for policy making to improve educational quality.

International example: Vietnam

Examples of questions addressed by Vietnam's National Assessment

Questions related to inputs:

- What are the characteristics of Grade 5 pupils?
- What are the teaching conditions in Grade 5 classrooms and in primary schools?
- What are the general conditions of the school buildings?

Questions related to standards of educational provision:

- Were Education Ministry standards met regarding:
  - o Class sizes?
  - o Classroom furniture?
  - o Qualifications of teaching staff?

Questions related to equity of school inputs:

- Was there equity of resources among provinces and among schools within provinces in terms of:
  - o Material resource inputs?
  - o Human resource inputs?

Questions related to achievement:

- What percentage of pupils reached the different levels of skills in reading and mathematics?
- What was the level of Grade 5 teachers in reading and mathematics?

Questions related to influences on achievement:

- What were the major factors accounting for the variance in reading and mathematics achievement?
- What were the major variables that differentiated between the most and least effective schools?

What are the main elements of a National Assessment?

In the majority of cases, the ministry of education (MoE) appoints either an implementing agency within the ministry or an independent external body (for example, a university department or a research organisation) and the MoE provides funding for the work. The MoE then determines the policy imperatives which need to be addressed in the assessment; usually in (some form of, or a pretence at) consultation with key education stakeholders (e.g. teachers' representatives, curriculum specialists, business people and parents).

The MoE, or a steering committee nominated by the MoE, identifies the population to be assessed (e.g. whole population at an age group, for example fifth grade pupils). The MoE determines the area(s) of achievement to be assessed (most commonly, literacy or numeracy). The implementing agency defines the area to be assessed and defines it in terms of domain content and cognitive skills. The implementing agency prepares achievement tests and supporting questionnaires and administration manuals and takes steps to ensure their validity and reliability. These draft tests and supporting documents are pilot-tested by the implementing agency and the data including samples of scripts are subsequently reviewed by the steering committee and other competent bodies to (a) determine curriculum and pupil appropriateness and (b) ensure that items are effective discriminators and reflect gender, ethnic and cultural sensitivities.

In parallel with these technical issues, the implementing agency selects the targeted sample (or population) of schools or pupils, arranges for printing of materials and establishes communication with selected schools. The implementing agency trains test administrators (e.g. classroom teachers, school inspectors or graduate university students) and marking teams. The assessment instruments (test and/or questionnaires) are administered in schools on a specified date or dates under the overall direction of the implementing agency. Post-assessment, the implementing agency takes responsibility for collecting survey instruments, for scoring the test items, for cleaning and preparing the test scores data for analysis.

The implementing agency carries out the data analysis and produces draft reports at a range of levels, e.g. pupil outcomes, item performance, school or region, etc. The draft reports are prepared by the implementing agency and reviewed by the steering committee. The final reports are prepared by the implementing agency and are disseminated by the appropriate authority. The MoE and other relevant stakeholders review the results matched to the policy needs they have been targeted against and determine an appropriate course of action.

Teaching, learning and assessment

Integration of teaching, learning and assessment into pedagogy

To take a simple definition of differentiation as 'a teaching philosophy based on the premise that teachers should adapt instruction to student differences, rather than marching the students through the curriculum in "lock-step", teachers should modify their instruction to meet students' varying readiness levels, learning preferences, and interests' (Willis and Mann, 2000: 1). At a glance this definition is comprehensive and perhaps even inspirational; however, closer analysis reveals assumptions and assertions which require some critique. Firstly teachers, classrooms, students and schools are treated as one homogenised organ, separate, disconnected and uninfluenced from society as a whole. It presupposes that these 'student differences' are free from bias and 'adapted instruction' is free-flowing, equitable and unproblematic. According to Anyan (2006), 'the education system does not take up its role as the great equaliser' (cited in Clycq et al., 2014: 3). Furthermore, Bourdieu (1990) suggests 'the education system [its schools, its policy, its staff and its curriculum] would favour those whose home-environment, world views and habitus correspond most with the system'. In short, policy makers, leaders and teachers need to be cogniscent of the reasons and their rationale for differentiating pedagogical aspects of their practice and how students are organised for learning. The 'why' and 'how' of differentiation must not only concern itself with important features such as the 'modifying of content, process and product' (Willis and Mann, 2000: 1) alongside the focused staff development of curriculum planning and learning evaluation, because these are just slices of an incomplete whole. Therefore the implication is to 'minimise the effects of systemic socio-ethnic inequalities. In these hegemonic discourses on "success" and the privileges of those pupils the dominant background are disguised ... while the cultural and ethnic bias in the system remains implicit and unproblematic' (Frankenberg, 2001; DiAngelo, 2011).

Campbell (2013) argues that 'teacher judgements of their pupils can relate to the groups of which children are members – groups which bear little or no relationship to a child's ability or potential (Harlen, 2004). Recent studies have suggested that this bias is apparent, for example, in relation to pupil ethnic grouping (Burgess and Greaves 2009), gender (Hansen and Jones, 2011), special educational status (Reeves et al., 2001).

Has the hidden curriculum first popularised by Philip Jackson (1968) almost five decades ago become so embedded in our educational system and practices that these norms go unquestioned or worst still defended with statements such as 'we treat all our children the same here' as a statement of rhetoric? Jackson's seminal text entitled *Life in Classrooms* identified features of classroom life which were inherent in the social relations of schooling. He observed that there were values, dispositions and social and behavioural expectations that brought rewards in school for students and that learning expected along these lines was a feature of the hidden curriculum (Margolis, 2001: 5). The work of Michael Apple during this period reasserted curriculum as a political text linked to hegemony:

> the hidden curriculum in schools serves to reinforce basic rules surrounding the nature of conflict and its uses. It posits a network of assumptions that, when internalised by students establishes the boundaries of legitimacy. This process is accomplished not so much by explicit instances showing the negative value of conflict, but by merely the total absence of instances showing the importance of intellectual and normative conflict in subject areas. The fact is that these assumptions are obligatory for the students, since at no time are the assumptions articulated or questioned. (Apple, 1975: 99)

Assessment of learning and assessment for learning

Teaching, learning and assessment are inter-related and assessment should always be planned and integrated seamlessly into teaching and learning activity. The assessment activity (using a pedagogical strategic model such as 'guided group') should arise from what is going on in the pupil's current learning activity. The need for the teacher to understand 'when' and 'how' to make an individual assessment intervention should be one of the focal points of a pre-service training programme. An assessment task must scaffold from a pupil's previous or current experience. It must be clearly and specifically introduced to the pupil – the need to understand what is required is critical. Teacher assessment is not based on a traditional testing model. Teacher assessment is continuous and classroom life for the pupil goes on as usual. From the assessment information (observation, dialogue, outputs) then the teacher modifies teaching and learning for the individual who has been assessed. There has to be a change in (learning) behaviour by both teacher and pupil for assessment to be effective.

Teacher assessment has to be criterion-referenced: a pupil is assessed in relation to a criterion (based on the concept or domain of the learning objective being taught) and not in relation to the other pupils in the class or group. The teacher then shares responsibility for the learning with the pupil by prompt analysis and 'feeding back' specific support information (scaffolding) to enable that pupil (or pupils if a shared task) to progress through the required learning steps or sequence.

There are a number of methods for teachers to obtain assessment information: these include systematic planned observation; differentiated task setting; encouraging a culture of dialogue (not teacher-dominated Q&A) in the classroom; 'guided group' pedagogy.

What is 'formative' assessment?

If the above principles are followed, the teacher is using formative assessment to support pupil involvement and therefore more effective learning. Formative assessment can also be described as the best method to develop 'self-regulated learning' for the pupil. Formative assessment is summarised by Perrenoud as 'pupils do not have the same abilities nor the same needs nor the same way of working, an optimal situation for one pupil will not be optimal for another. One can write a simple equation: diversity in people + appropriate treatment for each = diversity in approach' (Perrenoud, 1998: 86). Pryor and Crossouard (2008) extend Perrenoud's definition by incorporating Perrenoud's vision of a 'change' in the relationship or 'regulation' between teacher and pupil in the classroom workplace. 'The educator teaches different definitions of him/herself to the pupils and develops different relationships with the pupils through them ... to become teacher, assessor, subject expert and learner, all involving different division of labour and rules shaping their interaction with pupils' (Pryor and Croussouard, 2008: 10). This 'change' in relationship has been shown to be impenetrable or, at best, problematic to some teachers either through poor pedagogical training with minimal exposure to research literature or through a stubborn adherence to a transmission teaching model. Those teachers have become 'normalised', too used to the neatly planned rigidity and conformity of whole class teaching (transmission) and its preparation of pupils to solve problems, to answer questions in specific ways (to obtain test credits). Unfortunately what they are doing is not teaching for learning because 'learning is messy' (Martin et al., 2005: 235) because it involves complex pupil minds. Complexity takes time, dialogue, detail, flexibility and involvement of the learner. It requires transaction rather than transmission, the changing of that traditional role of the teacher.

For formative assessment to be effective in supporting and improving teaching and learning, both the teacher and the pupil must understand what they are doing and why they are doing 'it'. This raises the implication of how well or how shallowly teachers are trained pedagogically as teaching, learning and assessment is a very demanding but requisite professional strategy and requires specific methodological awareness and facility. Changes to classroom practice are central to the effectiveness of formative assessment. One of the focal points of teacher training must be an awareness of the changing role for teacher and pupil in the learning context. Teachers need to understand the important role that the pupil has in learning taking place. Far too much transmission of information (the recitation script; Alexander, 2005) and too little transaction takes place in many classrooms. Formative assessment implies empowering the pupil to have more control over his/her learning to understand the adjustments to his/her learning behaviours required for learning to take place in different learning situations; and that learning is a continuous process, not a summative measure.

Perrenoud states that 'in the absolute an ideal teaching approach would do without all (formative) assessment. All the feedback necessary for learning would be incorporated in the (teaching and learning) situation, without it being necessary for the teacher to observe and intervene in order to bring about learning progress (dialogic?). In other words it would be absurd to proceed with formative assessment without first calling into question the teaching methods and without seeking as a priority, to make the teaching situations more interactive and richer in spontaneous feedback' (Perrenoud, 1991: 94). That says it all!!! But is hard work!

> When one is thinking in terms of formative assessment, it is necessary to break with this egalitarian approach. There is no need to give all the pupils the same dose of assessment. The differentiation begins with the amount that goes into the observation and interpretation of the processes and acquisitions of each pupil. There is an analogy with medical diagnosis: it is not a case of carrying out the same tests, analyses and examinations on all patients. The important thing is to make a correct diagnosis and identify a disease and, if possible, its causes. In some cases, the diagnosis is glaringly obvious and no particular analysis is required. In others, it requires a succession of hypotheses and checks which require specialists. Like medical diagnosis, formative assessment requires differential investment. (Perrenoud, 1991: 96)

Perrenoud's thinking leads us directly into the concept of the learner as autonomous, developing 'self-regulation' on his/her learning journey. This is a model of teaching which recognises that the pupil (of any age) is developing as an autonomous learner and therefore should be involved actively in sharing the construction of his/her own learning path. For Zimmerman (2000: 14), self-regulation refers to 'self-generated thoughts, feelings and actions that are planned and cyclically adapted to the attainment of personal goals'. While Paris and Paris (2001: 1) emphasise its 'autonomy and control by the individual who monitors, directs and regulates actions towards goals of information acquisition, expanding expertise and self-improvement'. The research of Perry et al. (2007: 29), found that pupils develop the process of self-regulation through 'instrumental support from teachers and peers through forms of modelling and scaffolding attitudes and actions'. These three definitions, while not totally congruent, all include an understanding that the pupil, as part of developing as a self-regulated learner, has to be supported to systematically monitor his/her own learning.

11

Assessment and Testing

> Chapter summary
>
> Assessment paradigms and their implications for teaching and learning.

Assessment is synonymous with testing ... [and] ... testing success is the main driver for the models of pupildom available. (Hall et al., 2004)

Assessment judges and labels and levels, creating hierarchies across schools and in classrooms. Assessment has traditionally been defined by two methodologies: summative and formative (TGAT, 1988a). Both summative and formative approaches to assessment are important. Summative assessments are 'an efficient way to identify students' skills at key transition points such as entry into the world of work or for further education' (OECD, 2005: 6). Tests and examinations are the traditional ways of measuring student progress and have become integral to accountability of schools and the education system. However, internationally, assessment has become almost universally equated with high stakes scoring and testing (Shepard, 2000; Hall et al., 2004; Shepard, 2005; Twing et al., 2010) and teaching is reduced to servicing that metric (Guinier, 2003). This is a minimum competency accountancy model (Karsten et al., 2001; Wiggins and Tymms, 2002; Tymms, 2004) which does assessment a disservice but has grown in status and has dominated both internationally (PISA, TIMMS) and nationally (SATs, NCLB testing)[1] since at least the millennium. In England the introduction of National Curriculum

---

[1]SATs (Standard Assessment Tasks) were introduced as annual tests for pupils aged 7, 11 and 14 in England during the 1990s; NCLB tests: No Child Left Behind legislation (2002) introduced federal tests to rate all 91,000 US schools.

Assessment in the Education Reform Act of 1988 led, by the early 1990s, to the supremacy of summative forms of assessment. This was despite the fact that the National Curriculum Task Group on Assessment and Testing stipulated clearly that the 'system will rest on the levels and criteria alone, through which different pupils may progress at different paces' (TGAT, 1988b: 1). Similarly in the United States of America school funding decisions became dependent on the summative outcomes from No Child Left Behind legislation.

Assessment paradigms

The outcome of this has been the restriction of pedagogy to a 'banking model' (Freire, 1970) and a 'delivery model' designed to service a 'one size fits all', 'testing what is taught' agenda (Alexander, 2005; 2008) for accountability purposes. Governmental interventions have produced an international 'testocracy' (Guinier and Torres, 2003) in which limited domain testing has been used to benchmark 'national standards' and has reduced breadth and balance within the taught curriculum to support the pupil performance outputs (modelled on a factory production-line) of a small core of elite subjects – or more accurately the testable aspects or domains of those subjects. In England, despite a raft of government interventions (Booster classes, Catch Up programmes, Excellence in Cities, Optional tests) there is evidenced (Boyle and Bragg, 2009) a national league table of school performance which profiles the socio-economic 'haves' doing well and the 'have-nots' doing poorly. Consequently the schools habituated by the 'have-nots' are judged and criticised for their 'underperformance' (Gray, 2001; Lupton, 2004; Gorard and Smith, 2004; Gray, 2004; Brehony, 2005; Boyle and Charles, 2010a; Gorard, 2010).

The competition for comparability in dubious (in terms of validity, contextually misaligned, reliability, 'standards over time', item consistency) international testing programmes whose data are used to produce international league tables has spawned test domain-dominated curriculum-cloning (England, Russia, Singapore, USA, etc.) in countries aspiring to gain promotion up the Champions League table. It has also promoted a blatant commercial market place developing publishing empires procuring vast profits from this misunderstanding of the role of assessment in education by promulgating that 'purchasing our products will improve your school performance data'.

The purpose of assessment in its current definition is reduced to measurement. The psychometricians have become the twenty-first century's alchemists turning base data into … into what? The notion of the child at the centre of education or the development of the whole child through a teaching programme which integrates the affective, conative and cognitive domains (Allal and Ducrey, 2000) as part of a formative teaching, learning and assessment cycle is ignored or seen as superfluous. Teachers no longer believe that they need a philosophy to support their actions in teaching and learning. 'Why do I need a philosophy while we have the SATs?' has been a common response from our classroom research (Boyle and Charles, 2010b). Observed lessons (Alexander, 2005; 2008; Boyle and Charles, 2010b) have become 'one size fits all' (Alexander, 2004) with no differentiation to address learning needs (Boyle and Charles, 2010b) – note that is differentiation, not setting (Boaler, 2005) – or to identify and supply the micro-support required to scaffold learning. The teaching menu is not modelled on the use of pedagogical strategies such as the guided group to enable optimum assessment opportunities to feed directly into learning but on coaching and preparing for the type of questions anticipated in the test. Longitudinal national school data evidence and illustrate that the primary curriculum in England has become skewed, narrowed and unbalanced in favour of time allocated to the two tested subjects, mathematics and English (Boyle, 2006). By 2002 the combined teaching time of English and mathematics had totalled exactly 50% of the available teaching time per week – so that the remaining ten statutory subjects had to scramble to divide the remaining 50% available teaching time as equitably as possible between them (Boyle and Bragg, 2006: 577).

Assessment now has three paradigms and one result. Paradigm one is the accountancy model, beloved of policy makers and at the core of the school effectiveness debate (Gorard, 2010). It is best defined as 'teach to be measured', in which the sole purpose of teaching is to deliver or cover material that will later be tested; there is no involvement of the pupil in that learning process. Paradigm two is the banking model (Freire, 1970) in which the teacher teaches and the pupils are taught, those are the fixed and immutable roles; there is no deregulation of the role (Perrenoud, 1998; Allal and Ducrey, 2000; Zimmerman, 2000). In 'olden days' this was known as the 'topping up' model in which the child was the empty vessel and was topped up or filled up with knowledge, which they 'recited back to the teacher to prove that learning had taken place (Tharp and Gallimore, 1991, in Smith et al., 2004; Alexander 2005; 2008). Paradigm three is the 'testocracy' in which the metric is laid down and the teaching and learning process conforms to that testing metric. Its limitations and the humanistic and social implications (as follows) are not even considered as flaws in the system: 'test scores correlate with parental income (and even grandparents' socio-economic status) rather than actual student performance' (Guinier and Torres, 2003: 68). The fact that the testocracy reduces merit and a meritocracy to a meaningless pre-destined ordination is ignored. 'Test-centred techniques are used to ration access to elite higher education as appropriate measures of merit' and '... at no point was any attempt made to reconcile this with an elitist rationing process' (Guinier and Torres, 2003: 69). Guinier and Torres assert that alongside the testocracy even the vagaries and lack of standardisation of teacher assessment stand out like a beacon of fairness and equity: 'reliance on teacher ratings excludes fewer people from lower socio-economic backgrounds than does reliance on test scores' (Guinier and Torres, 2003: 71). The testocracy knows no boundaries but income, it even, as Guinier and Torres found in their research in the USA, redefines merit: 'it moved from an assumption that tests are meritocratic for everyone except people of colour to a larger critique of the way in which the conventional testocracy denies opportunity to many deserving white applicants as well. It changed the definition of merit' (Guinier and Torres, 2003: 72).

The three paradigms of assessment as outlined above have contrived to produce one result: a reduced pedagogy so that the complexity of the individual learner is ignored through the insistence of the system that the learner conforms to the (narrow) norms of the metric (Guinier and Torres, 2003) as defined by political intervention which soon became centralised control of a minimum competency standards-based accountancy and accountability system.

Implications for pedagogy

What was all this doing to pedagogy? 'Education can either socialise students into critical thought or into dependence on authority', that is, according to Shor (1992: 153), 'into autonomous habits of mind or into passive habits of following authority, waiting to be told what to do and what things mean. Unfortunately in traditional schooling, the latter most often occurs'. According to this definition, the teacher's pedagogical positioning is at the centre of the 'how' and the 'what' of teaching and learning. In short pedagogy is dichotomous: it can encourage and support growth for children, locate and empower children at the centre of learning or it can stultify and reduce the process to following externally prescribed schema (Edwards, 2001; Dunphy, 2008).

Within this accountability-compliant model there was no place for 'teachers shifting from control of knowledge to creation of processes whereby students take ownership of their learning and take risks to understand and apply their knowledge' (Graziano, 2008: 157). And there was certainly no way that the factory-product technicians would understand 'teachers and children are partners in teaching and learning transactions. We need to find ways of interacting with children to co-construct shared meanings in ways we cannot do if the children themselves are not active participants in exploring the situation' (Makin and Whiteman, 2006: 35).

And there was even less understanding that 'child-centred teaching includes behaviours that actively involve children in guiding the learning process, such as offering choices, encouraging activity and suggesting solutions' (Hayes, 2008: 433).

Researchers (Edwards 2001; Patrick et al., 2003; Alexander 2005; Wyse et al., 2007; Alexander, 2008; Dunphy, 2008; Boyle and Charles, 2010b) have chronicled the sterility of the pedagogy that has emanated in England from 14 years of central government imposed strategies designed to improve test scores under a minimum competency model and restricted definition of the term 'standards'. 'Pedagogy is so palpably the missing ingredient ... and it is so obviously vital to (pupils') progress and to learning outcomes that we have no alternative but to find ways of remedying the deficiency' (Alexander, 2008: 22). So teachers and their trainers have to rethink the basis of pedagogy: synonymous with this process is an understanding that a pupil as an autonomous learner should be involved in sharing the construction of his/her own learning, i.e. self-regulated learning. For Schunk and Zimmerman (1997: 14), 'self-regulation refers to self-generated thoughts, feelings and actions that are planned and cyclically adapted to the attainment of personal [learning] goals'. For Perry et al. (2007: 29) pupils 'develop the process of self-regulation through instrumental support from teachers and peers through the forms of modelling and scaffolding attitudes and actions'; note the focus across both definitions on allowing the pupils to systematically monitor their own learning. The importance of Perrenoud's thinking is evident as he states that 'the roles of teacher and pupil have to be deregulated from the traditional transmission and passive reception model' (1998); so as a minimum requirement for teaching, teacher training should stress avoidance of the 'recitation script' style of pedagogy so criticised by Alexander (2005). The current summative metric model and didactic pedagogical style are producing pupils who cannot self-regulate (because they are not offered the experience of working that way) and teachers who are still located in the traditional model of whole class teaching and didactism. Ruttle (2004: 75) warns the didacts to reflect whether their 'preconceived learning objectives, however well-intentioned and metacognitively "pure" get in the way of actually working with how some children think about their own writing'. Ruttle is cautioning teachers (and the teacher-trainers) against both the rigidity of the pre-planned package version of teaching and the dangers of ignoring individual learning needs to keep the majority moving at pace through the weekly objectives.

In England the influence of the government's national strategies which listed learning outcomes by term and by year encouraged teachers to believe that there was a requirement for strong pacing. The Office for Standards in Education (Ofsted), the government's school monitoring force, exacerbated this situation through its 'concern to sharpen pace in teaching which led to the pursuit of pace at all costs, regardless of the fact that pace without attention to [children's] understanding leaves all but the fastest learners stranded' (Alexander, 2008: 18).

In practical terms one step which would demonstrate a critical movement from the 'one size fits all' didacticism (Alexander, 2008: 18) is that of the teacher engaging in systemic guided group methodologies. The guided group is a pedagogical strategy which enables the teacher to focus on small size (four–six pupils maximum) differentiated groups of pupils. The teacher still makes managerial decisions about the differentiated learning objectives, teaches and interacts with the whole class, but the notable difference is that the teacher then teaches the targeted group. She has specific aims and objectives for a 20–30 minutes maximum session of focused, uninterrupted teaching, having planned high level, challenging, self-supporting activities from the lesson's theme for the rest of the class to engage with. This formative teaching and learning approach optimises the teacher's insights and understanding of the pupils' location and learning needs, e.g. the levels of language that a child has such as complex/non-complex sentence structure, use and breadth of vocabulary, etc. It enables each pupil to have the necessary time and space to explore and internalise rather than being rushed through a 'coverage' model. The teacher, through the structure and formality of the guided group approach, can support each pupil's affective domain which consequently develops both conation and cognition (Allal and Ducrey, 2000). Conation (Huitt, 1999) is in the 'work domain' of learning. Pupils will engage or disengage their will to learn based on whether the topic or subject matter has some personal or 'real life' meaning for them. 'Conation can be thought of as an "internal engine" that drives the external tasks and desires ... The drive shaft links "what I want to know" to "how I feel about the task" and subsequently "how I will ultimately respond to the task"' (Riggs, 2004: 3).

Pupils will not arrive at this self-regulated position overnight nor by accident nor will the trainee teacher understand self-regulated learning without tutoring and support, both theoretical and empirical. Meyer and Turner (2002: 23) recognise the pupil's achievement of self-regulation as a learner by describing the process as 'assuming responsibility, this becomes contingent not only on the classroom climate and growing competence but also on the opportunities afforded to demonstrate that competence'.

Taking the development of writing competence as an example, in that writing is more complex than a discrete linear staged process, and with the added variable of ESL (ESL = English is not the child's first language) it becomes even more complex (Flower et al., 1986). Flower's metaphor of writers as switchboard operators, juggling a number of different demands on their attention and various constraints on their behaviour captures a learning model which, although pedagogically sound, has been made redundant. This failure to engage with such a rich and relevant teaching and learning model has been caused by a generation of teachers who feel no need to have this level of complexity in their pedagogy as they follow the outcomes-oriented demands imposed by the English government's national strategies. Like a distant voice from history, Piazza (2003) recommends referring to content features which are divided into four critical components: the writer, the process, the text and the context. Examples of the writer factor include background, interests, self-efficacy, learning style, knowledge base in writing and developmental level. Piazza is demonstrating the relationship between the affective and cognitive domains essential for the development of automaticity in the writer. However, it is important to understand the contextual contrast between Piazza's findings and the current standards agenda for literacy in England. Teachers here are being told 'many schools are finding difficulty in raising standards in writing' (Ofsted, 2006: 55) and that 'improving standards of writing at the end of Key Stage 2 [age of 11] is a national priority' (DCSF, 2007: 5).

Conclusion

We have attempted to draw the distinction between one inclusive model of teaching which has the child at the centre of a learning agenda and the complex pedagogy required for that process to be supported and to compare it with the present situation in which the child is reduced to a provider of statistical data within the minimum competency model of teaching (Perrenoud, 1996). The current pre-service teacher training model in England is based on short-term training (a one year PGCE, an even shorter Teach First model and an in-school School Direct model) and the formal 'surface' accretion of 33 standards (TDA, 2008). These standards are based on process competencies rather than on the development of teacher professionalism through a focus on understanding and using differentiated formative teaching practices, developing an active pedagogy and engaging in innovative approaches to involve both teacher and pupil in self-regulated learning (Perrenoud, 1996). Rowsell et al. (2008: 115) suggest that 'pedagogy refers to an educational position or approach that includes both theory and practice'. This definition focuses on the strength or weakness of the connection between theory and practice in the teacher's pedagogical development. There should be no end point in the teacher's development as a practitioner and for that development to produce a truly reflective formative practitioner there has to be a synthesis between theory and practice.

The issue requires a reconstruction of the conceptual field which controls our understanding, our values of an educational system dominated by a model of metrics which demands conformity from the learner. This current (last 20 years) definition of assessment has reduced teaching and learning (pedagogy) so that the complexity of the learner is ignored but which, dictated by political intervention and centralised control, insists that the learner conforms to the norms of the metric. Teaching has become the 'banking model' (Freire, 1970): the teacher teaches and the pupils are taught in a delivery model. What is taught has to be measured in a summative definition of assessment and its judgemental role. Future models of training the next generation of teachers have to redefine assessment so that 'the more the evaluation is integrated into situations, becomes interactive and lasts, the further it distances itself from normative or summative evaluation, the province of tests and exams and their consequences' (Perrenoud, 1998: 100). In conclusion it is important to remind ourselves what the introduction of this testocracy was meant to provide for the community: standardised tests and other objective measures of excellence were to enable administrators to compare individuals from different demographic, geographic and social cohorts and to strategies equitable policies accordingly. In a comparatively short time, the system and its attendant testing industry have become established as the 'primary gatekeeper to upward mobility' (Guinier, 2003: 71).

'Under pressure from bureaucrats to demonstrate achievement, schools which desperately need to cater to their pupils' diverse learning requirements are having to tailor teaching to the test' (de Waal, 2006: 19). To enable a change to take place from an auditing to a teaching and learning culture in our schools 'we need to accept that a rigorous model of professional development in "understanding and using assessment to support learning" will have to take place – basically because after almost two decades in which summative assessment (testing) has dominated pedagogy, teachers have either forgotten how to or lost confidence to incorporate rigorous teacher assessment into their planning for teaching and learning' (Boyle, 2008).

12

National Curriculum and Summative Testing

Chapter summary

The narrative ends with a bleak situation in 2015 of a National Curriculum dominated by a summative testing system which has successfully established a seemingly immoveable 'testocracy' that has stultified and reduced pedagogy in classrooms and restricted learner autonomy.

Contextual background

Summative assessment is carried out for the purpose of reporting achievement of individual pupils at a particular time. The aggregated results of National Curriculum end of key stage tests in England 'are used for (i) accountability, i.e. for evaluation of teachers, schools and local authorities and (ii) for monitoring, i.e. to compare results for pupils of certain ages and stages, year on year, to identify changes in standards' (Harlen, 2007: 2). National Curriculum end of key stage tests in contradiction of the intention of the TGAT (TGAT, 1988a) soon became 'high stakes' in England when aggregated results were used to set targets which schools are held accountable for meeting (DfES cohort percentage success at fixed level targets for English and mathematics at KS2 and KS3 introduced in 1997) and to form the basis of 'league table' style performance indicators (Harlen and Deakin Crick, 2003).

In the autumn of 1988, the government's newly instituted organisation with responsibility for national assessment, the Schools Examinations and Assessment Council (SEAC) issued a specification for the development of Standard Assessment Tasks (SATs) for seven year olds. CFAS, nationally profiled through the involvement of Tom Christie as technical consultant to TGAT (TGAT, 1988a), put in a bid for developing the assessment materials based on the assumption that the intention of the process was 'seeking and interpreting evidence for use by learners and their teachers to decide where the learners are in their learning, where they need to go and how best to get there' (ARG, 2002). CFAS assumed that these evidences would be collected through themed units of teaching materials with integrated assessment which supported as well as measured children's learning and which the teacher could administer individually or in small groups when the time was judged right. SEAC funded three development groups, one of which was CFAS (the other two were the National Foundation for Education Research (NFER) and the Consortium for Assessment and Testing in Schools (CATS), a group based round the London Institute of Education). The CFAS conceptualisation of an assessment task (the CFAS management group consisted of Christie[1], Harlen[2], Russell[3], Boyle and Qualter[4]) was based on the thinking that the materials should support teachers' understandings of pupil learning and misconceptions at point of use and if teachers were going to make decisions on entry levels and administer the 'assessment materials' then teachers primarily should devise and write those materials with support from higher educationists. So five local education authorities (LEAs – Bradford, Kent, Lancashire and Salford from England and Clwyd from Wales[5]) seconded teachers to provide classroom experience and 'task' writing expertise to materials development workshops and subsequently to mount classroom-based trials of the materials; the Assessment Research Centres at the Schools of Education of both Manchester (CFAS) and Liverpool (CRIPSAT) assisted in the development and writing of the materials so that they had assessment validity, reliability and rigour. The CFAS Standard Assessment Task, which was piloted across a national sample of seven year olds in 1990, represented a holistic approach to assessment while demanding explicit demonstration and enabling analysis

---

[1]Professor Tom Christie, founding Director of CFAS, Dean of the School of Education, University of Manchester; now Director, National Examinations Reform, Aga Khan University, Pakistan.

[2]Professor Wynne Harlen, Head of the School of Education, University of Liverpool; Director of the Scottish Council for Research in Education; now Visiting Professor of Education at the University of Bristol.

[3]Professor Terry Russell, Director of the Centre for Research in Primary Science and Technology (CRIPSAT), University of Liverpool.

[4]Anne Qualter, Senior Research Fellow, CRIPSAT, University of Liverpool.

[5]Wales was involved with England in joint national test development at that stage.

of achievement. The unit of assessment was the statement of attainment (SoA) and each SoA was embedded in its own purpose built task. Each task contained a 'confirmatory' phase and an 'exploratory' phase. In the confirmatory phase each task was associated with a general cross-curricular class-based activity. This set of materials was to be used to confirm teacher assessment (TA), i.e. pupils only attempted tasks which, according to their TA judgements, they should attain. The exploratory phase was packaged as task strings each covering all the SoA in an attainment target (AT). These were intended to be used to 'explore' children's conceptual understandings with more depth or to put more detail on the profile of their attainments. For ease of reference and access they were packaged by AT and subject. They allowed teachers to take individual or groups of children through a number of related tasks at an appropriate level (STAIR, 1990: 3–4). The decision to use the exploratory material with a child depended on whether or not that individual child had attained the 'teacher-expected' level in the confirmatory phase. Teachers had a task menu which was tailored to their TA and enabled them to plan their assessments and manage their time (did they need to observe an assessment or was there a tangible product/outcome which allowed for deferred assessment?). We recognised the tensions inherent in a national 'test as assessment' programme development, e.g. breadth of curriculum coverage versus the restrictions of test item writing, but within the constraints of the specification as issued by the SEAC on behalf of the government, we felt that the assessments were embedded in current classroom activity and empowered teacher and child by being matched to their current estimations of ability. In 1990 it was impossible to predict the enculturation of 'teaching to the test' and the resultant skewing of the primary curriculum which resulted from the government policies of league tables and the standards agenda.

The Department for Education and Science's (DES) view of national assessment swiftly emerged as rather different from the CFAS concept and after consuming vast amounts of public money (£3.8 million was Manchester's share of the development pot gifted to the three contracted agencies) on large scale materials production and trialling necessitating the destruction of several forests, the NFER was awarded the contract for the 'live' paper and pencil tests. These soon became known as the 'SATs' to which every seven-year-old cohort from 1991 onwards has since been subjected in the first week of the month of May.[6] We suppose most observers of the politico-educational scene during the late 1980s/early 1990s under the crude accountancy/accountability policy of the central

---

[6]Since 2004 the end of key stage 1 tests have been used to 'confirm' teachers' summative level judgements; since that date these have been based on cumulative TA over the year's teaching.

government then in power were unsurprised by the decision. For example, Kenneth Baker, then Secretary of State for Education and Science, outlined the government's intention as 'raising the quality of education in our schools is the most important task for this Parliament' (*Hansard*, 1987). This device of control has never been far beneath the surface of this or subsequent National Curriculum legislation, a legislation which was badly designed and intended to increase England's status in the arena of international competitiveness. At the time the specification for the assessment materials development had seemed an opportunity to develop some meaningful and valid (in teacher, face validity terms and in academic, construct validity and reliability terms) materials which would support teaching and learning and also 'measure' the first steps on the ladder of progression for young children. Instead of which we got the imposed sterility of the 'which bits of the (mathematics and English) curriculum can I write a paper and pencil test for' and the beginning of the 20 year cycle which has led us to primary classrooms being test-prepared and tested to the limit to the detriment of the rest of the curriculum (Boyle and Bragg, 2005; 2006).

Since that initial involvement in national assessment (summative test) development we have been involved in 22 further national assessment projects (see the Appendix): three of these have been materials development for the English national assessment system; five have been materials developments for the Northern Ireland Council for Curriculum and Assessment and one materials development project for the Welsh national assessment system (ACCAC); eleven have been evaluations of English national assessment systems. The most rewarding of these projects was our involvement in the conceptualisation of the key stage 3 e-assessments for ICT for which Bill Boyle acted as assessment consultant to QCA and Research Machines (2004–6). The project aimed to innovatively create a model of assessment and to assess pupils' levels of ICT ability not through the traditional route of a finite set of discrete items to be judged as answered correctly or incorrectly, nor through a scheme or algorithm for aggregating the responses into a mark, nor through a straightforward relationship between 'mark' and overall level award. We conceptualised and developed a measurement model called the 'sufficient evidence' model in which each taken opportunity (i.e. pupil opportunity to demonstrate by key stroke his/her actions in resolving an ICT contextualised task) was regarded as a piece of evidence to be considered in making an overall judgement as to the performance level of the pupil. The tasks had been constructed (designed) in such a way that this was the function that the opportunities were conceived to do. The evidence model provided a means of combining these pieces of evidence in a reasoned and defensible way. This approach brings together the requirements for machine scored methodology and the desire that the outcomes should reasonably mirror the broadly based professional judgements which teachers currently make in determining the national curriculum level of an individual pupil.

The expectation was that there would also be some formative aspect to the research and development in that the evidences collected would provide a profile of a pupil's performance in aspects of ICT and those evidences would enable the teacher to enter the child for more/less challenging tasks on the next sitting. The whole development collapsed in some acrimony between the Department of Education and the QCA after small scale national piloting – more on grounds of level awarding than on merits of the material informing and supporting teaching and learning.

Teacher assessment strategies

Policy context

In 1988, the TGAT recommended that formative assessment should be an 'integral part of the education process, continually providing both "feedback" and "feedforward". It therefore needs to be incorporated systematically into teaching strategies and practices at all levels' (TGAT, 1988a: 1). The intention was neither negatively judgemental nor accountability inclined but rather 'so that the positive achievements of a pupil may be recognised and discussed and the appropriate next steps planned' (TGAT, 1988a: paras 3 and 4). This definition has worn well. In 2002 the Assessment Reform Group (ARG) defined formative assessment (and its alternate, assessment for learning) as: 'the process of seeking and interpreting evidence for use by learners and their teachers to decide where the learners are in their learning, where they need to go and how best to get there' (ARG, 2002: 3). In 2007 Harlen further fine-grained the definition: 'this is detailed evidence interpreted by the teacher and pupil to decide where the pupil has reached and so what next steps are needed to help achievement of the goals or to move on' (Harlen, 2007: 2). Unfortunately the role of 'formative assessment' has not figured large in policymakers' vision (and hence in practitioners' views of its prioritisation) in the 20 years since TGAT.

In 1990 Tom Christie, Bill Boyle and several other 'assessment experts' associated with the CFAS key stage 1 national test development group were commissioned by the SEAC to develop and produce a national primary teacher's manual for classroom based assessment. This was mainly to address the fact that there now was a National Curriculum which had to be assessed summatively both by a national test and through ongoing cumulative teacher assessment – but there was no authorised non-technical guide on how to conduct formalised teacher assessment for the primary teacher. In brief this was central government's attempt at standardising Teacher Assessment (TA) judgements (authors' initialising capitals to denote that the government in 1989 saw this TA process as a *summative teacher assessment judgement* on a pupil rather than the gathering and using of *ongoing formative learning support information*) across the nation's primary classrooms. This was because despite the flood of funding which was allocated to the test development process there was an absence of any substantive funding for understanding and sharing the principles of moderation across schools and LEAs. The vast bulk of the 'national assessment' budget was being devolved to test development agencies, printing and marking. The manual was hastily compiled, was rough and many of the activities were not rigorously enough exposed to classroom trialling and subsequent redesigning but it was duly published later that year with ourselves as the authors under the anonymity of SEAC with the title, *A Guide to Teacher Assessment* (SEAC, 1989).[7] It was sent by the SEAC to every primary school in England and the pack consisted of three publications: one was a slim booklet of activities for the teacher in the classroom to support professional development of assessment skills, a second booklet contained group activities for teachers, curriculum or key stage co-ordinators to support in the development of a whole school policy on assessment, with a third bulkier output designed as a source book of information, exemplars, questions, etc. The whole package was planned to support the dialogue envisaged by the authors (predicting a current modern or 'reform' model of professional development) that teachers would be 'sharing learning collaboratively' about teaching, learning and assessment in the (then) new National Curriculum climate (Boyle et al., 2005). The materials were to serve as focal points for and to support in-school 'conversations about teaching and learning' in the current New Labour education policy terminology. They sank without trace to no little ridicule from contributors to the TES on the grounds of 'yet more things for primary teachers to be required to do and record' (Wragg, 1990). The guide was accused of contributing to the increased teachers' workload mantra which was gaining in volume subsequent to the introduction of a complex and unwieldy national assessment system of statements of attainment, attainment targets and profile components which were then 'weighted' to produce aggregated pupil assessment levels. All this while teachers were feeling insecure through struggling to master the planning of the new National Curriculum programmes of study into their teaching. Wynne Harlen (then Director of the Scottish Research Council) writing

---

[7]Main contributing authors were Christie, Harlen, Russell, Boyle and Qualter; Boyle also served as editor.

in *Issues in Setting Standards* (Boyle and Christie, 1996) pointed out the prevailing belief that the government valued state school teachers as good for nothing and that as the national assessment stakes are raised, 'quality control takes precedence over quality assurance' so that 'the argument that the most appropriate ways to make teachers' assessments more dependable is through in-school and inter-school in-service and the provision of support materials seems to be losing ground' (Boyle and Christie, 1996: 22).

The government of the day had already signified its priorities for pupil assessment with the production of paper and pencil tests for seven year olds, with more of the same promised for 11 and 14 year olds; the tests to be 'sat' on given days and to supply all the assessment information that any norm-referenced-inclined stakeholder could surely want to know to label a child and to rank his/her school on the promised national performance (league) tables. That government prioritisation signalled the end of classroom assessment in all but name – teachers decided that all they had to do was report their summative national test level in the teacher assessment column of the record and this ensured that test and TA score agreed so every base was covered for accountability and auditing purposes. The QCA's view consistently reiterated was: 'Teacher assessment is an essential part of the national curriculum assessment arrangements. The results of end of key stage teacher assessments are reported alongside the test results. Both have equal status and provide complementary information about pupils' attainment' (QCA, 1999: 7). Reeves, Boyle and Christie explored this statement in a piece for the *British Educational Research Journal* (Reeves et al., 2001):

> the relationship between test results and TAs is also of considerable research interest. Comparison of the outcomes from the two methods can tell us something about how well teacher expectations of their pupils match up to performance on an 'objective' test. The global extent of concordance between the tests and TA is also of interest. If the methods agree completely in nearly every case there would be a strong argument that one or the other was redundant, while on the other hand, if they frequently yield quite different results, this would raise serious concerns that the system contained a fundamental flaw. (Reeves et al., 2001: 142)

Our data revealed 'overall levels of agreement were very high' (Reeves et al., 2001: 153), and 'the proportion of exact agreement between TAs and test results remained consistently around 75% and that less than 0.5% of disagreements exceeded one level on the rating scales. Thus the teacher and the test were in complete concordance for the large majority of pupils' (Reeves et al., 2001: 158), findings which echoed that of Tymms (1996). There was therefore little discrepancy between test and TA so the national curriculum was being taught and its assessment was working! As Harlen writing in the Primary Review report reflected retrospectively in 2007: 'When schools are held accountable for meeting targets set solely on the basis of results of pupils' performance in external tests there is evidence that this becomes associated with teachers' own classroom assessment becoming focused on achievement rather than on learning' (Harlen, 2007: 20).

Therefore from the introduction of the national test regime in 1992 until the appearance of 'assessment for learning' (an accessible synonym for its historically TGAT-endorsed antecedent, 'formative assessment') in the concluding years of the last millennium, which provided a focal point for the resistance movement against the pervasive embrace of summative testing (Harlen and Deakin Crick, 2003; Hall et al., 2004; NUT, 2006), England[8] had tests, test-wise teachers and their test-wise pupils, test preparation sessions in Y2 and Y6 which gobbled up vast tracts of (at best) the annual spring term and reduced foundation subjects and any notion of exposing children to creativity to a ghostlike existence in percentage teaching time terms (see Figures 12.1–12.4 below).[9]

	English	Maths	Science	D&T	ICT	History	Geography	Art	Music	PE	RE	PSHE
1997	26.6	19.8	10.1	4.9	3.9	4.8	4.8	5.9	4.8	6.7	4.9	5.1
1998	28.3	20.8	9.8	4.7	3.9	4.5	4.6	5.5	4.7	6.6	4.4	4.1
1999	28.8	21.8	9.6	4.2	4.6	4.2	4.2	5.0	4.3	6.4	4.7	4.5
2000	.	.	.	.	.	.	.	.	.	.	.	.
2001	28.7	21.7	9.3	4.1	4.9	3.9	3.9	4.9	4.2	6.7	4.7	3.9
2002	29.2	22.0	8.5	4.0	4.7	3.7	3.7	4.7	4.1	6.8	4.8	3.1
2003	29.3	22.2	8.5	4.1	4.8	3.8	3.9	4.7	4.0	6.8	4.6	3.5
2004	28.7	21.7	8.6	4.1	5.0	3.8	3.8	4.7	4.0	6.8	4.6	3.6
% change	+2.1	+1.9	(−1.5)	−0.8	+1.1	(−1.0)	(−1.0)	(−1.2)	−0.8	+0.1	−0.3	−1.5

Figure 12.1   Key stage 1: average percentage teaching time

---

[8]Wales was quietly shedding national tests throughout the late 1990s, Scotland had never participated, and Northern Ireland had a 'supported assessment' system.

[9]Figures taken from Boyle and Bragg (2006).

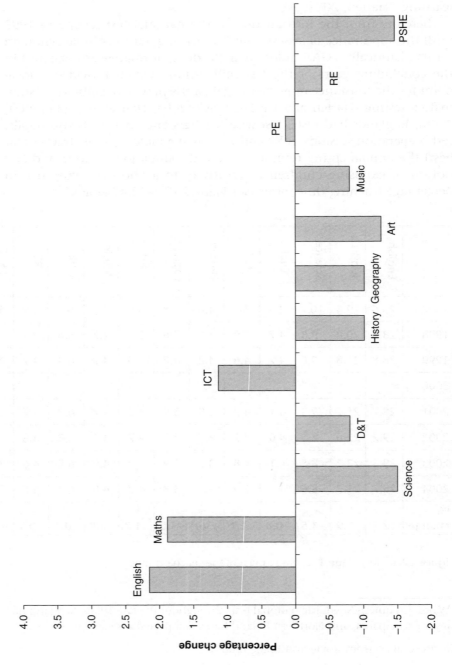

Figure 12.2 Key stage 1: percentage change 1997–2004

	English	Maths	Science	D&T	ICT	History	Geography	Art	Music	PE	RE	PSHE
1997	23.0	19.3	11.4	5.1	4.1	5.7	5.6	5.5	4.7	7.2	5.1	4.4
1998	24.6	20.6	11.1	4.9	4.1	5.2	5.2	5.2	4.6	7.2	4.6	4.0
1999	26.7	21.6	11.2	4.2	4.6	4.6	4.5	4.6	4.1	6.8	4.8	4.1
2000	.	.	.	.	.	.	.	.	.	.	.	.
2001	26.9	22.0	10.3	3.9	5.0	4.2	4.1	4.4	3.9	7.1	4.5	3.4
2002	27.2	22.1	9.8	3.9	5.0	4.1	4.1	4.3	3.9	6.8	4.7	2.9
2003	27.1	22.2	9.7	4.0	5.0	4.2	4.2	4.3	4.0	7.0	4.7	3.2
2004	26.7	21.9	9.8	3.9	5.1	4.1	4.1	4.3	4.0	7.0	4.6	3.2
% change	+3.7	+2.6	−1.6	−1.2	+1.0	−1.6	−1.5	−1.2	−0.7	−0.2	−0.5	−1.2

Figure 12.3 Key stage 2: average percentage teaching time

In 1993 Ron Dearing (SCAA, 1993) in his report which presaged National Curriculum version two, nodded at equity between test and teacher assessment outcomes. 'Since teacher assessment in the core subjects is to be reported alongside results from national tests both systems of assessment should be designed to be complementary and need to be undertaken according to the same criteria' (SCAA, 1993: 57). Dearing also predicted the inevitability of a 'two tier curriculum' because of the decision to confine national tests to the core subjects (SCAA, 1993: 60). Ten years later, in 2004, David Bell, then HMCI, in his annual report stated that 'we cannot afford and our children do not deserve a two-tier curriculum' adding 'there is still some way to go in ensuring that all pupils in our primary schools enjoy a rich and fulfilling curriculum as well as being taught the basics of English and maths effectively' (BBC News Education, 2004). Dearing's two predictions were confirmed in 1997 with the newly elected Labour administration ushering in a standards agenda based on two subjects (or more factually, the testable aspects of two subjects), English and mathematics, and on testing rather than on teacher assessment. National performance targets were set in 1997 (although originally mooted by the Conservative government in 1995) based around end of key stage tests, not teacher assessment judgements. (Targets were initially set at 75% of 11 year olds to reach level 4 in mathematics and 80% to reach the same level in English; in 2007 85% of the annual cohort is

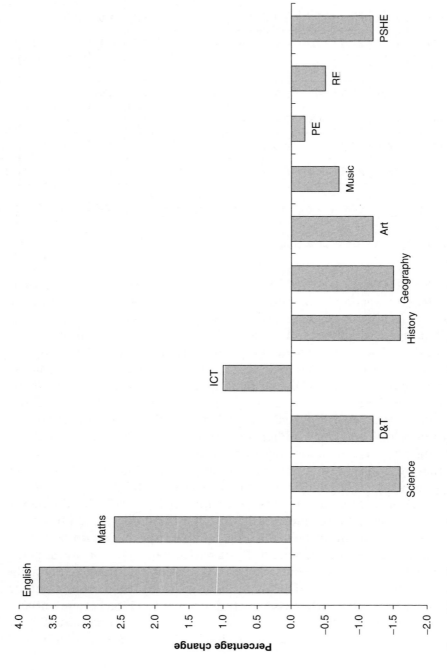

Figure 12.4 Key stage 2: percentage change 1997–2004 (Berj, 2006)

expected to achieve level 4 in both English and mathematics in the end of key stage 2 national tests.) To ensure that these percentages were achieved New Labour introduced the literacy and numeracy 'pedagogical prescriptions' (Alexander, 2004) strategies which further narrowed teaching and learning (Alexander, 2004; Brehony, 2005).

This obsession with 'standards' has resulted in a situation in the middle years of the first decade of the twenty-first century in which we have a majority of primary schools in which 'assessment is synonymous with testing' and 'SATs success is the main driver for the models of pupil-dom available' (Hall et al., 2004: 804). 'Assessment as learning' (Torrance, 2007: 281) signified that assessment, or testing which is what assessment had become, had displaced learning by procedural compliance, a state which Torrance describes as 'achievement without understanding' (Torrance, 2007: 291). The period from 1991 to date of publication can be summarised in assessment terms as a 'problematic mix of mere compliance and of going ever so systematically through all the steps instrumental in subverting the goal of assessment, distorting both the learning itself and teachers' and students' understanding of what learning entails' (Sadler, 2007: 389) Gone are the opportunities for pupils to offer alternative evidence of their expertise, as Linn states (1992: 179): 'multiple indicators are essential so that those who are disadvantaged on one assessment' are not excluded from demonstrating achievement.

In the *Guide to Teacher Assessment* packs for primary teachers (SEAC, 1989, Pack C: 6), we had stressed that 'assessment is designed to be an integral part of the teaching process and to provide continuous feedback to both the teacher and the pupil regarding progress'. However, the discussion about the purpose of assessment was firmly fixed in the summative purposes lobby during the 1990s through the millennium as excellence in schools was conceptualised in policy terms through a singular expression: percentage of pupil cohorts at target levels as outcomes from national end of key stage tests and public examinations (Blair, 2004; Brehony, 2005).

There have been attempts to strategically insinuate formative assessment into the standards agenda, e.g. by Black and Wiliam, through percentagising 'the evidence of learning gains … [which] restates and reinforces the claim for priority of formative work' (Black and Wiliam, 2003: 12). Clearly Black[10] et al. felt that the best hope of returning to the TGAT principles was to embrace the prevailing national outcomes accountancy and accountability mentality rather than try to win the day by emphasising the more 'reform' virtues of formative assessment, such as promoting the child at the centre of the learning process through a more active involvement of the pupil in his/her own learning, transferring some of the

---

[10]Professor Paul Black had been the Chair of the TGAT.

control for learning from teacher to pupil, encouraging pupils to take responsibility for their own learning, etc. This is understandably so as these are less palatable, harder to digest and to sell concepts, unlikely to find favour within an education policy agenda which now stands well to the right even of the Thatcherite conceptualisation of the 1988 version of the National Curriculum and its assessment (TGAT, 1988a).

Philosophical context

In 1989 Sadler defined formative assessment as being concerned with 'how judgements about the quality of student responses can be used to shape and improve the student's competence by short-circuiting the randomness and inefficiency of trial-and-error learning' (Sadler, 1989: 120). This definition, for me, raises several separate but 'related' issues at the core of a conceptualisation of formative assessment: the role of the pupil in the learning process, the quality of the information being exchanged between the pupil and the teacher and the teacher's appreciation of the quality of the work expected from the pupil in response to a task.

The role of the pupil

In *A Guide to Teacher Assessment*, we refer to 'sharing responsibility (for learning) with the child' (SEAC, 1989, Pack C: 12); Perrenoud (1991: 93) similarly alludes to the change from passive to active learning role required from the pupil: 'Every teacher who wants to practice formative assessment must reconstruct the teaching contracts so as to counteract the habits acquired by his pupils'. One example of this classroom regulation would be to outlaw 'the forest of hands-up' enculturation which is still the prevailing model of response in the teacher – class/group question strategy, the learned competitive behaviour of fastest hand answers the question. From years of experience of working in classrooms, it seems that teachers, because of several issues – e.g. concerns about classroom control, keeping the lesson moving, 'covering' what they set out as the 'learning objectives' for the lesson etc. – find it hard to circumvent this culture and to improve the quality of classroom dialogue whether it be teacher–pupil or pupil–pupil. The ideal of 'waiting time' causing pupils (individually or collaboratively) to think through their responses at present remains in the main just that, an ideal. The norm sadly in our classrooms is the traditional didactic model (reinforced by the teaching methodologies promoted by the various national strategies) of the teacher presenting, managing, controlling and dominating the information exchange rather than supporting dialogue.

An example of active learning is the acceptance of self- and peer-assessment as a desirable classroom practice. Sadler (1989) stated that self-assessment is essential to learning because pupils can only achieve a learning goal if they understand that goal and can assess what they need to do to achieve it. 'Anita', a recently qualified Y5 teacher in one of the Manchester primary schools with which we work, explained what her pupils felt about doing self- and peer-assessment: 'they enjoy doing it, they like the immediacy of the feedback and have a clear understanding of where they need to go next in their learning'. She also said that the pupils are far blunter with each other in their comments on the quality of each other's work outputs than she would be. Unfortunately, much of what we see portrayed as 'peer-assessment' is the exchanging of books for the marking of answers while sometimes as a variant these are read out by the teacher – another example of the dangers of the shallow, spread thinly but quickly philosophy behind the centre-periphery process which has become known as national 'roll-out' (see Smith and Gorard, 2005).

If the goal of teaching is that the pupil improves in performance then the pupil's role needs to change or be changed from passive recipient to active participant. There are two elements here. These are: raising of the level of *self-interest* of the pupil in being involved in the *self-improvement* process and increasing the pupil's understanding of 'how' to improve. 'The research tells us that successful learning occurs when learners have ownership of their learning, when they understand the goals they are aiming for; when crucially they are motivated' (ARG, 1999: 2). The pupil has to have an active involvement, i.e. be self-motivated to be involved in their own learning and to see the learning process as a collaboration with their peers rather than as a competition; then they need to be supported to understand how to improve. 'A child may seem to have missed the point or not recognised the learning involved in the activity' (SEAC, 1989, Pack C: 12). In 'big picture' national 'assessment for learning' strategy terms, one of the current commonly suggested techniques or micro-strategies is to refer to this process as the pupil 'sharing the learning objectives with the teacher' (Ofsted, 2003; QCA, 2003). At its concrete operational level this has resulted in classrooms with lists titled as 'learning objectives' or 'lesson objectives' pinned on walls or written on whiteboards. It's a start, but are these 'learning objectives' or are they 'lesson outcomes' which soon become 'tasks to be got through', and is this strategy actually addressing the issue of teacher and pupils 'sharing' and defining the learning objectives (Boyle, 2007a)? So with the benefit of the lessons learned through hard experience of the problems inherent in 'rolling out' anything nationally within the context of 19 years of misunderstandings of 'assessment', caution has to be advised (Smith and Gorard, 2005). Our preferred model is that from working daily in a classroom environment where they are actively involved in their own learning, pupils will gradually and naturally 'possess a concept of the standard being aimed for, compare their current level of performance with the standard and engage in appropriate action which leads to some closure of the gap' (Sadler, 1989: 121). This leads us into the issue of the quality of the information which is 'fed back' to the pupil to enable them to address 'the gap'.

Quality of the information being exchanged with the pupil

Ramprasad (1983: 4) defines the process of information exchange with the pupil as the transmission of 'information about the gap between the actual level and the reference level of a system parameter which is used to alter the gap in some way'. The definition seems to have been generally accepted, the problem appears to have been the practicalities of addressing Ramprasad's call to 'alter the gap'.

In 1990 Christie and Boyle (SEAC, 1989) suggested the mnemonic INFORM (hardly original but designed as a 'hook' for an audience which at that time had not been exposed to any national formalised professional development in 'assessment') to capture the relationship between teacher assessment information and future planning for the teaching of pupils. The letter 'F' of INFORM advised the teacher to 'focus on the performance, looking for evidence of achievement', while the letter 'O' suggested that the teacher 'offer the pupil a chance to discuss what was achieved' (SEAC, 1989, Pack C: 20). Focusing on the pupil's work finally seems to be now generally accepted as the obvious starting point for feedback (see Black and Wiliam, 1998; Boyle, 2007a) as it is this focus by teacher and pupil on the learning steps in the pupil's work which enables support for pupil improvement in those specific areas of misconception to be developed. 'Talking with the pupil will allow an opportunity for positive reinforcement and enable the teacher to guide future learning' (SEAC, 1990, Pack C: 12). The specificity, quality and depth of the dialogue is crucial. It should provide pupils with sufficient focused support to understand how to make the necessary improvements. In Vygotskyian terms it means the pupil is being 'pushed' onwards using external support (the teacher, their peers) to reach their potential level (Vygotsky, 1987). 'Properly understood it means providing appropriate supports during learning so that learners are better able to bridge the gap between what they bring to the learning task and where they need to be to achieve a deep level of learning' (Sadler, 2007: 390). This support can best be described as a series of feedback loops. 'These usually include a teacher who can recognise and describe a fine performance, demonstrate a fine performance and indicate how a poor performance can be improved' (Sadler, 1989: 120).

Through this supported process the pupil comes to know what constitutes quality of performance and is enabled, if so motivated, to self-monitor the quality of their work. Therefore there is a need for pupils to be actively involved in self-assessment as an integral and acknowledged part of their learning process. Sadler posits two approaches to specifying standards, i.e. through descriptive statements and exemplars. 'While neither of these is sufficient in itself, a combination of verbal descriptions and associated exemplars provides a practical and efficient means of externalising a reference level' (Sadler,1989: 127). There is the concern that the use of exemplars as indicators of standards would encourage pupils to copy the exemplars and produce stereotyped responses at the expense of creativity and originality. The response to this concern would be the expectation that pupils were presented with a range of exemplars as illustration that there are diverse expressions for outputs of quality for a task. As Sadler strictures, 'Unless [pupils] come to this understanding and learn how to abstract the qualities that run across cases with different surface features but which are judged equivalent they can hardly be said to appreciate the concept of quality' (Sadler, 1989: 128). Surely if all stakeholders in the learning process understand the meaning and purpose of the 'analysis and feedback' process, its richness in developing dialogue and co-construction of knowledge and focus that process on supportive dialogue related to the individual pupil's work, then marks and grades will be seen as redundant – a scenario beyond Utopian in the current norm-referenced climate. However, as Stiggins et al. (2004: 236) says: 'Descriptive feedback points out to [pupils] their work's strengths and weaknesses ... and models the kind of thinking we want them to do for themselves about their work'. Reinforcing that this feedback dialogue is a two-way process, a two-way communication line is an essential first step for many teachers, as in too many classrooms the traditional 'teacher instructs from a rigid plan – pupil responds' model is still in operation. Sadler does, however, pose a cautionary note: 'I refer to the concept of "scaffolding" the learning. But "scaffolding" is supposed to be a temporary arrangement that supports the building process. After the scaffolding has done its job, it is dismantled. The building then stands on its merits' (Sadler, 2007: 390). In the current rush towards assessment *for* learning rather than assessment *of* learning, Sadler is concerned that the meaning of assessment is not lost. 'Learners can be said to have learned something when three conditions are satisfied. They must be able to do, on demand, something they could not do before. They have to be able to do it independently of particular others, e.g. the teacher and members of a learning group, and they must be able to do it well' (Sadler, 2007: 391). In his view, one shared by myself, assessment should be focused towards gathering evidence for drawing inferences about capability under these conditions, not the scaffolded conditions.

Teacher's appreciation of the quality of the pupil's work

To quote from Sadler again, the teacher must 'possess a concept of quality appropriate to the task and be able to judge the student's work in relation to that concept' (Sadler, 1989: 121). However, this will only lead to improvement if the pupil 'comes to hold a concept of quality roughly similar to that held by the teacher, is able to monitor continuously the quality of what is being produced during the act of production itself and has a repertoire of alternative moves or strategies from which to draw at any given point' (Sadler, 1989: 121). ·

Some researchers, e.g. Bell and Cowie (2001) and Torrance (1993), attribute the low level of use of formative assessment information not only to the problems teachers find inherent in flexible planning after the whole school/whole department/whole key stage planning sessions – which became common practice in the 1990s as a means of coming to terms with 'covering' the National Curriculum programmes of study and which initiated a form of 'rigidity through compliance' – but also to limitations in teachers' pedagogical knowledge. For teachers to make short-term future teaching and learning decisions based on assessment (information), the teacher needs to be able to interpret the pupil's work appropriately and to understand the 'next steps' in pupils' learning across the range of subjects taught in the primary school.

'Planning for progression' cannot afford to be 'hit and miss' (see Sadler, 1989), and the role of formative assessment in this planning is well served by Black's (1998: 26) description that 'formative assessment has to provide some guidance about the ways in which a pupil might progress in learning, linked to a clear conception of the curriculum and its learning goals'.

Ramprasad's (1983: 21) concern was that 'if the [assessment] information is simply recorded, passed to a third party who lacks either the knowledge or the power to lead to appropriate action, the control loop cannot be closed'.

Developing formative assessment within the curriculum

As the Director of a Centre for Formative Assessment during this period we are fully aware that formative assessment is no 'quick fix' to improving pupil achievement and that 'this can only happen relatively slowly and through sustained programmes of professional development' (Black and Wiliam, 1998: 15). We have also become aware of the self-evident truth that since the reforms of 1988 and in particular since the arrival of the standards agenda in 1997, 'the grading function is over-emphasised and the learning function under-emphasised' (Black, 1998: 111) in the evaluation of children's progress. This must be one of the concerns related to the national strategy espousal of 'assessment for learning' with its focus on the dissemination of the processes, i.e. sharing objectives, open questions, comment-only marking and peer- and self-assessment, becoming a mantra for professional development days – rather than the professional development focusing on the key teaching, learning and assessment change agenda issues such as the radical rethinking in the roles of the teacher and pupil in the learning situation, a more active involvement of the pupils in their own learning, emphasising the collaborative rather than the competitive nature of learning and strengthening two-way communication between pupil and teacher on learning needs/information. In the classroom example below children were consciously or sub-consciously connecting prior learning to a present theme and they were redrafting openly and orally their developing conceptualisation of counting in tens in a non-rigidly controlled classroom context. This is an example, sadly rare in current observations of teaching and learning, of co-construction between the teacher and the child enabling the children's dialogue to expand by non-intervention from the teacher at the point of the first child's question thereby enabling the children themselves to drive the learning.

Mathematics lesson Year 1 children

Learning focus: Counting in tens (10 more/10 less)

Context: The previous week the children had explored the concept of odd and even numbers. In this lesson the whole class was on the carpet with the teacher exploring counting. The teacher recorded the following dialogue which took place as the children worked on 'grouping numbers' as part of the process of understanding the concept.

Teacher (T):	Let's count to 100 in tens.
Burhan:	Three sets of 10 make 30 but it is an odd number.
Mohammed:	Is it an odd number?
Burhan:	Yes, it is odd.
T:	Well is it an odd number?
Burhan:	If you had three people one would get 10, one would get 10 and one would get 10.
T:	What about two people?
Reem:	One person would get five, five and five.
T:	How many is that?
Reem:	Fifteen.
T:	What is that doubled?
Reem:	Thirty.
T:	Burhan, you can share 30 as 15 and 15.

However, the norm that we witness is that far from formative principles of involving children in their own learning, teachers are controlling the learning agenda even more firmly. 'Many schools are giving the impression of having implemented AfL when in reality the change in pedagogy that it requires has not taken place. This may happen when teachers feel constrained by external tests over which they have no control. As a result they are unlikely to give pupils a greater role in directing their [own] learning' (ARG, 2007: 9)

How far formative assessment principles are removed from the actual position in classrooms was illustrated in the summer of 2008 when the stranglehold that summative testing holds over pedagogy was made clear. The end of key stage test results were delayed and teachers' complaints were widely reported. Typical of the comments was 'I am teaching Year 6 next year and am appalled that all their hard work (and mine) could end up in another fiasco like this' (TES, 4/7/08). This reveals a lot about that teacher and the many other teachers who seemed paralysed by the lack of marks from the tests. Whichever way one analyses the comment the conclusion is not positive: either the teacher sees his role and philosophy of teaching and learning in a paradigm of whatever the children will achieve in that Year 6 class next year is expressed in a very summative, test-outcomes model, or it reveals that teacher's sanguine 'real politic' view of teaching in which he is resigned to the fact that whatever teaching and learning goes on throughout the year, the only measurement of learning that is externally esteemed is the national test score. So that teacher could be telling us that his exciting, creative, formative teaching which involves, motivates, engages and supports learning progress for the children in Year 6 and is seminal to those children becoming lifelong learners (one of the government's ambitions for the whole population unless we are mistaken?) is all in vain – because in this era of accountability, the percentage of the tested cohort (note the official language of conformity, not that of a child as an individual learner) which achieves level 4 is all that matters.

Our question is: why are the schools waiting on the results of a summative set of tests to tell them how well their children have learned? Surely despite national government pressure, relayed through Ofsted and local authority intermediaries, to achieve and report percentage success at specified levels (and sub-levels), teachers as professionally trained educators must know better? Has the teaching profession with its many thousands of professionally trained and qualified teachers become so weak under this standards agenda that individually and corporately it cannot raise enough muscle to demonstrate to central government that there are other ways of illustrating and measuring children's progress?

Or have teachers been deluded by the continued bombardment from the national strategies that there is only one way to prove that learning is taking place? There is another route, that of formative teaching and learning. That route is exemplified through commentaries which provide exemplifications of children's learning progress over time and chronicle the micro-steps of development of that learning – richness of information a test cannot supply or replicate. There are models of this practice 'out there' in schools needing support and nurture. In our research we have identified and praised them because they are not getting the necessary support from their respective local authorities, support which would enable them to be identified as models of good practice and to flourish.

In an important paper Baroudi (2007) follows this line of thought. He comments on the 'tension [which] exists between formative and summative assessments specifically because they both compete for the limited time available in the classroom' and suggests that 'a model for combining both functions advocates collecting information about student learning using formative assessment instruments and later reinterpreting the same information when a summative assessment is required' (Baroudi, 2007: 46). That tension of course becomes multiplied even more when a national government defines whole cohort testing as the sole form of summative assessment for reported performance measurement immediately turning it into a 'high stakes' process. Somewhere in the mix formative assessment is squeezed of any purpose in the eyes of the teaching profession – in the eyes of the politicians it had no purpose anyway because it looks too messy and untidy and is difficult to aggregate into 'league table' ranking-style data.

Similarly Popham (2008) relates the plight of 'instructionally oriented classroom assessment' (his descriptor for formative assessment) in the context of the testing policy underpinning America's No Child Left Behind federal legislation. 'The current indicator of a school's success – the indicator regarded by the world as the definitive reflection of instructional effectiveness – is the performance of a school's students on its state's NCLB tests' (Popham, 2008: 269). The 'high stakes' element is supplied through the threat that 'schools that fail to make their adequate yearly progress targets are generally viewed as failing, that is as ineffective schools' (Popham, 2008: 269). So there you have it, just as in England the threat of identification as ineffective and failing leading subsequently to closure is the warning. Echoing similar criticism to that of the tests administered in England for quality, validity and reliability (Tymms, 2004; Tymms and Merrell, 2007), Popham describes the NCLB tests as 'instructionally insensitive, incapable of detecting improved instruction even if such improved instruction were present'

(Popham, 2008: 269). Repeating the criticism of academics in England (Whitty, 2001; Lupton, 2004; Thrupp, 2005), Popham also asserts that the 'NCLB tests are so directly tied to students' socio-economic status (SES) that the resultant NCLB customized tests tend to measure the SES composition of a school's students rather than the effectiveness of the school's instructional efforts' (Popham, 2008: 273). He adds worry-ingly, 'if a school's teachers enthusiastically adopt instructionally oriented classroom assessment and thus do a superb job of enhancing student learning, the odds are that the student NCLB scores won't reflect it', leading to the inevitability in Popham's view that 'a few years of big-time effort coupled with no NCLB pay-off will soon lead to the abandonment of instructionally oriented classroom assessment – a measurement approach that benefits children' (Popham, 2008: 269). The pervasive influence and pressure of international governments' one-dimensional standards agenda (i.e. the one dimension of paper and pencil testing of narrowly domained aspects of subjects) inevitably means that just as Popham is sure that children will be advantaged by formative assessment strategies he is just as sure that 'teachers will scurry from such an assessment approach if the state's NCLB tests indi-cate year after year that instructionally oriented classroom assessment does little good on the test that *really* counts' (Popham, 2008: 270). This sadly is what has happened in England and accounts for the situ-ation that Baroudi presents, i.e. that put under accountability pressure teachers will select to prepare children for test performance rather than teach formatively to improve learning (Perrenoud, 1991; Allal and Lopez, 2005) as they will not risk that there will be a mismatch between that improvement and the requirements of a national test which is not constructed in such a way as to show the improvement. The answer is to use formative teaching and learning to supply its own method of demonstrating children's progress.

Improving learning outcomes

Formative assessment will improve learning outcomes but this will not happen without there being a specific action by teacher/pupil resulting from the assessment information generated. The current climate is one of 'delivering' teaching programmes and 'covering' subject material rather than one of supporting pupils to learn with understanding. As seasoned observers (former Local Authority Advisers) we have watched many lessons and so soon see 'the plan' being revealed and although the rhetoric of sharing the 'learning objectives' and 'involving the pupils in learning with the teacher' is much in evidence, there is little deviation from the teacher's planned agenda of the lesson to enable the teacher and pupils to follow in any depth issues or concerns raised by or evidenced from the pupils to adapt planning post-reflection on learning needs. Instead we see the 'formalism of highly structured lessons, whole class plenaries' (Alexander, 2005). Phrases such as 'differentiation' are used but examples are harder to see, e.g. an 'extended activity' for 'those pupils who complete the task' is the depressing result of a strategies-dominated teaching culture. If we see assessment as integral to improving pupil learning, then formative assessment strategies are the road maps to follow on that route as they inform both teacher and pupil about learning needs and they enable the teacher to intervene to support the pupils' learning during the learning activity. It is the possibility for that intervention to address a need at point of use which makes the assessment formative.

Assessment to support rather than just to measure learning has now been accepted as part of the government's teaching and learning strategies (QCA, 2006) and a range of teacher support materials is now being produced (Boyle and Charles, 2013). This would be progress if it actually meant that teachers and schools were being enabled to leave behind a decade memorable only for accountability driven, externally set performance targets. However, pronouncements emanating from the government, such as this from the (then) Education Secretary, Alan Johnson, stating that 'league tables are absolutely the right thing for raising standards' and that he backed 'the whole kit and caboodle of school accountability' (BBC News, 2006a) are hardly promising signals. DCSF's recent decision (QCA seminar, 16 November 2007) to introduce single level testing throughout key stages 2 and 3, testing to be carried out during two 'testing windows' per annum, is not even being true to the anticipated 'assessment when ready' paradigm which would have moved towards empowering both child and teacher. But for the present we still have to ask, have we learned nothing? 'Under pressure from bureaucrats to achieve, schools which desperately need to cater to their pupils' diverse requirements are having to tailor teaching to the tests' (de Waal, 2006). This has resulted in a huge distortion in primary school teaching and learning activity with the teaching timetable skewed towards the tested subjects (Boyle and Bragg, 2006).

From auditing and accounting to learning

To enable a change from an auditing to a teaching and learning culture in our schools to take place in the short term we need to accept that some thorough professional development in understanding how to plan for using assessment to support learning will have to take place – basically because after more than a decade in which summative 'assessment' (testing) has held sway, teachers have either forgotten how to or lost whatever confidence that they had originally to incorporate formative assessment into their teaching and learning planning. So what does assessment in support of learning really mean and how can teachers use or make use of it in their classrooms? How can they change the culture of their classrooms from one in which pupils are being passively prepared against testable curriculum sub-domains and then tested, into one in which pupils become active learners and their learning deepened and enriched by the assessment information which is gathered from dialogue between teacher and pupil, and from pupil working collaboratively with pupil?

Firstly, the teacher needs to understand that there is no entity called 'assessment' which has an existence on its own and stands alone as a process. There is something called 'testing' which is not the same thing as assessment – although the last decade might make one think otherwise (Hall et al., 2004). The whole and only purpose of assessment is to produce information which is then used to support pupil and teacher in the learning process. This is assessment as one of an integrated set of processes labelled teaching, learning and assessment, which are mutually linked and supportive of learning. Assessment in support of teaching and learning puts the pupil and their learning needs at the centre of teaching and learning so that the pupils become actively involved in their own learning.

That sounds fine, and is nice rhetoric but what is it that *enables* assessment to support learning? The short response would be that teachers through formative assessment principles access specific information on pupils' learning processes which then support their interventions in the pupils' learning processes, actions and activities. The strategies through which teachers access, process and focus, and use that information to intervene appropriately in pupil learning, is what renders the assessment 'in support of learning' or 'formative'.

We think there are four key areas in which focused professional development would enable teachers to use assessment in support of teaching and learning.

Development area 1

We currently are hearing a lot about pupils being 'active' in their own learning. One of the 'official' suggestions to achieve this is through sharing learning objectives and success criteria with the pupil. It has become almost a mantra. All the official publications about assessment for learning (see QCA's AfL website: www.qca.org.uk/3.html) list 'sharing learning objectives with the pupil' but they don't clearly explicate that learning objectives are not lists of tasks to be covered during the lesson; that learning objectives need to be differentiated to take account of learning styles and learning pace of the teaching group; that the teacher needs to make a decision as to when pupils understand the learning objectives and their relevance to their learning when they are ready to start a task; that the teacher needs to be constantly observant of and alert to pupil progress against the learning objectives and that in some cases this may mean redefining or consolidating against the learning objectives. Quite a professional development agenda in its own right! Also the verb 'sharing' implies not just 'telling' pupils what the objectives are or regularly checking out their understanding of the learning objectives – e.g. 'What are you learning? What do you think you are learning?' – but also both teacher and pupils being involved in originating and generating the learning objectives and success criteria for the lesson or piece of work. This is quite a step from our recent (and ongoing) observations in primary classrooms of teaching and learning following national strategy prescriptions such as Assessment for Learning and Assessing Pupil Progress.

Development area 2

The second key aspect in our list of professional developments of assessment for learning strategies is that of 'involving pupils in their own learning'. So, what does that mean? You may well ask. How do you involve pupils in their own learning? An indication of whether assessment in support of learning is taking place is if pupils are active in their own learning. You can achieve this involvement by making sure that the pupils are included in discussing and sharing planning of all aspects of the learning process, i.e. 'What am I doing and why am I doing it?'. Over time pupils will become more confident as independent learners and will be secure in taking responsibility for their own learning.

Development area 3

The third key aspect is that of making learning more collaborative. We are sure not all would subscribe to this. Certainly those who believe in didactic methods would not subscribe to the notion that learning is a collaborative social process in which pupils have to be active and work together sharing knowledge with their peers. Within that description of learning, teachers need to understand that the learning process is a dialogue. Through that dialogue, teacher and pupil access richer information to support their teaching and learning. Through support, pupils will develop their own confidence and competence in learning. The use of learning partners encourages the sharing and talking through of learning issues.

Development area 4

The fourth aspect is our belief in the centrality of peer- and self-assessment in the learning process. These two forms of pupil involvement assessment are at the core of pupil learning.

An observer who understands learner-centred teaching can see instantly if peer- and self-assessment are working in a classroom if pupil learning is being taken forward specifically within individual learning trajectories. By enabling peer- and self-assessment to take place in the class, this does not mean that the teacher is losing control of the learning. The teacher has the opportunity to plan their interventions to focus and support pupil learning.

It is not a new statement but if education standards are to be measured and publicly reported, shouldn't they be measured across a wider front than tested or testable curriculum sub-domains of two or three subjects which are judged suitable for production in 'national test' format on 'national test day'? These tests are then presented to primary school pupils who have gone through an intensive coaching process of test preparation (as distinct from a focus on teaching and learning) by teachers who know that it is in their (and their school's) accountability interest to produce 'test wise' pupils who will, in turn, produce acceptable performances against the test, so that the tested cohort's results will be around or above the DFCS's required percentage target. These teachers will ensure that this will be the case by teaching the two 'performance measured' subjects for a disproportionate amount of time (Boyle and Bragg, 2006). This is a very neat strategy and solution and has been and still is used by successive education ministers to claim that 'no government has done more to improve attainment in these basic skills' (BBC News, 2006b). However, the claim has proved to be very shallow in the succeeding nine years since it was made. Accountability has reached new heights of pressure on schools; pace and coverage are the key words to service the coaching for factory-style, production-line examinations success; the curriculum only serves a purpose to supply testable domains for score and grade production within the norm-referenced centrally controlled ranking systems which apply to schools. The education system at the micro-levels of the school and the pupil is based on compliance and pressure and bears minimal resemblance to anything connected to a school's role in developing teaching and learning or 'humanistic individuals' (Boyle and Charles, 2011). Until political priorities shift to viewing education as supplying an 'entitlement development curriculum' through offering the learner the time and pace, in terms of opportunities to reflect and self-regulate the range of learning experiences, and a reduction in the 'assessment' (testing) weighting which defines success, then a broad and balanced curriculum will remain the myth that it has been since 1989.

Appendix

Allocating subject time within the curriculum

B Allocating time for your school's curriculum

There are no statutory time allocations for National Curriculum subjects. It is up to each school to determine the amount of time needed for its children to cover the programmes of study successfully in all subjects.

B1 In your school, what is the teaching time for the following subjects over one year? Please give the *approximate percentage of the time* spent on each subject.

Please note: Where subjects are taught together in a topic, please estimate the percentage of time spent on individual subjects.

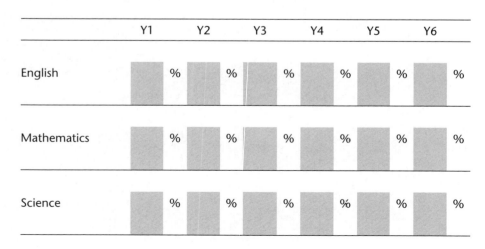

	Y1	Y2	Y3	Y4	Y5	Y6
English	%	%	%	%	%	%
Mathematics	%	%	%	%	%	%
Science	%	%	%	%	%	%

	Y1	Y2	Y3	Y4	Y5	Y6
Design and technology	%	%	%	%	%	%
ICT	%	%	%	%	%	%
History	%	%	%	%	%	%
Geography	%	%	%	%	%	%
Art and design	%	%	%	%	%	%
Music	%	%	%	%	%	%
PE (including swimming)	%	%	%	%	%	%
RE	%	%	%	%	%	%
Sex and relationship education *(if taught)*	%	%	%	%	%	%
PSHE *(if taught)*	%	%	%	%	%	%

(Continued)

(Continued)

	Y1	Y2	Y3	Y4	Y5	Y6
MFL *(if taught)*	%	%	%	%	%	%

Other timetabled subjects *(Please specify)*

	Y1	Y2	Y3	Y4	Y5	Y6
	%	%	%	%	%	%
	%	%	%	%	%	%
	%	%	%	%	%	%
	%	%	%	%	%	%
	%	%	%	%	%	%
Total	**100** %	**100** %	**100** %	**100** %	**100** %	**100** %

Glossary

Key technical terminology (with specific literature references)

Adjustment: *retroactive adjustment*: takes place after a shorter or longer learning sequence, on the basis of micro-evaluation; *interactive adjustment*: takes place through the learning process; *proactive adjustment*: takes place when the pupil is set an activity or enters a teaching situation.

Allal, L. (1988) 'Vers un elargissement de la pedagogie de Maitrise: processus de regulation interactive, retroactive et proactive', in M. Huberman (ed.), *Assurer la reussite des apprentissages scolaires? Les propostions de la pedagogie de maitrise*. Neuchatel: Delachaux et Niestle.

Heritage, M. (2011) 'Knowing what to do next: the hard part of formative assessment?' Special issue of *CADMO: An International Journal of Education Research*, 19 (1): 67–84.

Popham, W.J. (2008) *Transformative Assessment*. Alexandria, VA: Association of Supervision and Curriculum Development.

Affective domain: the area of the social development of the learner (self-esteem, self-motivation, self-worth) which secures progress in learner cognition.

Bandura, A. (1977) 'Self-efficacy: towards a unifying theory of behavioural change', *Psychology Review*, 84: 191–215.

Huitt, W.G. and Cain, S.C. (2005) 'An overview of the conative domain', *Educational Psychology Interactive*. Available at: www.edpsycinteractive. org/brilstar/chapters/conative.pdf (accessed 11 June 2015).

Schunk, D.H. and Zimmerman, B.J. (2007) 'Influencing children's self-efficacy and self-regulation of reading and writing through modelling', *Reading & Writing Quarterly*, 23: 7–25.

Analysis and feedback: analysing pupil outcomes against task criteria and supplying specific feedback to the pupil related to those criteria, indicating positive achievement as well as what and how to improve.

Coffey, J., Hammer, D., Levin, D.M. and Grant, T. (2011) 'The missing disciplinary substance of formative assessment', *Journal of Research in Science Teaching*, 48(10): 1109–36.

Perrenoud, P. (1998) 'From a formative evaluation to a controlled regulation of learning processes towards a wider conceptual field', *Assessment in Education: Principles, Policy and Practice*, 5(1): 85–102.

Strike, K.A. and Posner, G.J. (1992) 'A revisionist theory of conceptual change', in R. Duschl and R. Hamilton (eds), *Philosophy of Science, Cognitive Psychology, and Educational Theory and Practice*. Albany, NY: SUNY Press.

Assessment: a continuous iterative process taking place day by day and enabling the teacher and pupil to adjust their respective actions to the teaching/learning situations. The word 'assessment' derives from the Latin word *assidere* meaning to 'sit beside' – this can be taken to mean a close proximity between the assessor and the learner in the assessment process (Good, 2011).

Audibert, S. (1980) 'En d'autres mots ... l'evaluation des apprentissages!', *Mesure et evaluation en education*, 3: 59–64.

Good, R. (2011) 'Formative use of assessment: it's a process, so let's say what we mean', *Practical Assessment, Research & Evaluation*, 16(3): 1–6.

Morrissette, J. (2011) 'Formative assessment: revisiting the territory from the point of view of teachers', *McGill Journal of Education*, 46(2): 247–64.

Autonomy of learner: pupils develop the process of self-regulation through instrumental support from teachers and peers through the forms of modelling and 'scaffolding' (supporting the development of) attitudes and actions.

Meyer, D.K. and Turner, J.C. (2002) 'Discovering emotion in classroom motivation research', *Educational Psychologist*, 37(2): 107–14.

Paris, S.G. and Paris, A.H. (2001) 'Classroom applications of research on self-regulated learning', *Educational Psychologist*, 36(2): 89–101.

Perry, N.E, Hutchinson, L. and Thauberger, C. (2007) 'Mentoring student teachers to design and implement literacy tasks that support self-regulated reading and writing', *Reading & Writing Quarterly*, 23: 27–50.

Child-centred teaching and learning: the child's learning needs are at the centre of planning for teaching and learning; rather than a 'one size fits all' syllabus being 'covered' and worked through and children 'moved through' it at the same pace.

Hayes, N. (2008) 'Teaching matters in early educational practice: the case for a nurturing pedagogy', *Early Education and Development*, 19(3): 430–40.

Makin, L. and Whiteman, P. (2006) 'Young children as active participants in the investigation of teaching and learning', *European Early Childhood Education Research Journal*, 14(1): 33–41.

Matthews, J. (1999) *The Art of Childhood and Adolescence: The Construction of Meaning*. London: The Falmer Press.

Closed questions: usually require only short responses, demand only recall of facts, decision between a number of choices or no choice at all; they restrict pupils' time, opportunities to reflect and internalise a new concept.

Myhill, D. (2006) 'Talk, talk, talk: teaching and learning in whole class discourse', *Research Papers in Education*, 21(1): 19–41.

Scardemalia, M. and Bereiter, C. (1992) 'Text-based and knowledge based questioning by children', *Cognition and Instruction*, 9(3): 177–99.

Siraj-Blatchford, I. and Manni, L. (2008) 'Would you like to tidy up now? An analysis of adult questioning in the English Foundation Stage', *Early Years Journal*, 28(1): 5–22.

Co-construction: the active involvement of pupils in sharing the development of learning alongside the teacher; the individualisation of the learning trajectory.

Alexander, R.J. (2008) *Essays on Pedagogy*. London: Routledge.

Allal, L. and Lopez, M. (2005) *Formative Assessment of Learning: A Review of Publications in French*. Paris: OECD.

Yarrow, F. and Topping, K.J (2001) 'Collaborative writing: the effect of meta-cognitive prompting and structured peer interaction', *British Journal of Educational Psychology*, 71(2): 261–82.

Code: (elaborated/restricted codes: Bernstein, 1973) in the range of limiting or widening expectations of pupil learning capability; teacher in traditional role of 'power' in learning situation.

Alexander, R.J. (2004) 'Still no pedagogy? Principle, pragmatism and compliance in primary education', *Cambridge Journal of Education*, 34(1): 7–33.

Bernstein, B. (1973) *Class, Codes and Control*. London: Routledge and Kegan Paul.

Haberman, M. (1991) 'The pedagogy of poverty versus good teaching', *Phi Delta Kappan*, 73 (4): 290–4.

Collaborative learning: collaborative tasks are deliberately presented to groups of pupils so that the contributions of more than one pupil are necessary for an achieved outcome; social mediation of learning (Vygotsky, 1978).

Blatchford, P., Kutnick, P. and Baines, E. (2007) 'Pupil grouping for learning in classrooms: results from the UK SPRinG study', paper presented at

Symposium 'International Perspectives on Effective Groupwork: Theory, Evidence and Implications', AERA Annual Meeting, Chicago.

Vygotsky, L. (1978). *Mind in Society*. Cambridge, MA: Harvard University Press.

Vygotsky, L. (1986) *Thought and Language*. Cambridge, MA: MIT Press.

Williams. P. (2008) *Independent Review of Mathematics Teaching in Early Years Settings and Primary Schools. Final Report*. London: Department for Children, Schools and Families.

Correlation: a measure of the strength and direction of the relationship between the scores of the same people on two tests.

Owen, D. and Doerr, M. (1999) *None of the Above: The Truth Behind the SATs*. Lanham, MD: Rowman and Littlefield Publishers.

Rummel, R.J. (1976) *Understanding Correlation*. Department of Political Science, University of Hawaii.

Criterion referenced: a pupil is assessed in relation to a criterion for a task and not in relation to how other pupils perform a task.

Dunn, L., Parry, S. and Morgan, C. (2002) 'Seeking quality in criterion referenced assessment', paper presented at the Learning Communities and Assessment Cultures Conference by EARLI Special Interest Group on Assessment and Evaluation, University of Northumbria, 28–30 August.

Swaminathan, H., Hambleton, R.K and Algina, J. (1974) 'Reliability of criterion-referenced tests: a decision-theoretic formulation', *Journal of Educational Measurement*, 11: 263–7.

Demythologising: the search for theoretical frameworks for assessment could lead to an increasingly abstract vision of formative assessment cut off from the realities of classroom practice. That is why it is essential to articulate theoretical work with the study of how assessment is actually practised in the classroom.

Allal, L. and Lopez, M. (2005) *Formative Assessment of Learning: A Review of Publications in French*. Paris: OECD.

Boyle, B. and Charles, M. (2010) 'Leading learning through assessment for learning?', *School Leadership and Management*, 30(3): 285–300.

Boyle, B. and Charles, M. (2013) *Formative Assessment for Teaching and Learning*. London: Sage.

Depth of learning: this equates with the immersion of the teacher *and* the pupil within the teaching and learning process. Teachers bring skills in devising and constructing tasks to involve pupils in the learning process and to elicit revealing and pertinent researched responses from those pupils.

Alexander, R.J. (2008) 'Education for all: the quality imperative and the problem of pedagogy', Consortium of Research on Educational Access, Transitions and Equity. April.

Dadds, M. (2001) 'The politics of pedagogy', *Teachers and Teaching: Theory and Practice*, 71(1): 43–58.

Graziano, K.G. (2008) 'Walk the talk: connecting critical pedagogy and practice in teacher education', *Teaching Education*, 19(2): 153–63.

Deregulation: changes in classroom practice are central to the effectiveness of formative assessment. One of the focal points of pre-service teacher training must be an awareness of this changing of roles for teacher and pupil in the learning context with teaching situations being interactive and with spontaneous feedback to support and enrich learning.

David, M. (2007) 'Deregulation in the classroom: parents have more "choice" over schools: how have they reacted?', *New Economy*, 1(2): 79–82.

Perrenoud, P. (1991) 'Towards a pragmatic approach to formative evaluation', in P. Weston (ed.), *Assessment of Pupils' Achievement: Motivation and School Success*. Amsterdam: Swets and Zeitlinger.

Pryor, J. and Crossouard, B. (2008) 'A socio-cultural theorisation of FA', *Oxford Review of Education*, 34(10): 1–20.

Dialogic: the avoidance of the initiation-response (IR) rote model of two-part classroom exchange between teacher and pupils; replacing it by encouraging pupils' active verbal contributions and reducing teacher intervention.

Eke, R. and Lee, J. (2004) 'Pace and differentiation in the literacy hour: some outcomes of an analysis of transcripts', *The Curriculum Journal*, 15(3): 219–31.

Myhill, D. (2006) 'Talk, talk, talk: teaching and learning in whole class discourse', *Research Papers in Education*, 21(1): 19–41.

Well, G. (1999) *Dialogic Enquiry: Towards a Socio-cultural Practice and Theory of Education*. Cambridge: Cambridge University Press.

Dialogue: explicitly seeking to make attention and engagement mandatory and to chain exchanges of talk into meaningful sequences.

Radford, J., Blatchford, P. and Webster, R. (2011) 'Opening up and closing down: how teachers and TAs manage turn-taking, topic and repair in mathematics lessons', *Learning and Instruction*, 21(5): 625–35.

Tharp, R.G. and Gallimore, R. (1991) *Rousing Minds to Life: Teaching, Learning and Schooling in a Social Context*. Cambridge: Cambridge University Press.

Wells, G. (1995) 'Language and the inquiry-oriented curriculum', *Curriculum and Inquiry*, 25(3): 233–69.

Differentiation: if formative assessment is carried out in classrooms on a regular basis, the result is pressure to differentiate. 'Diversity in people + appropriate teaching treatment for each = diversity in teaching treatments' (Perrenoud, 1998: 86).

Boaler, J. (2005) 'The "psychological prison" from which they never escaped: the role of ability grouping in reproducing social class inequalities', *Forum*, 47(2/3): 135–44.

Bourdieu, P. (1966) 'Condition de classe et position de classe', *Archives europeennes de sociologie*, 7(2): 201–23.

Perrenoud, P. (1998) 'From formative evaluation to a controlled regulation of learning processes: towards a wider conceptual field', *Assessment in Education*, 5(1): 85–101

Tomlinson, C.A. (2001) *How to Differentiate Instruction in Mixed-ability Classrooms*, 2nd edn. Alexandria, VA: ASCD.

Focused chain: assessing narrative development of pupils' writing skills, teachers need to be aware of the writer developing a sequential series of events through 'focused and unfocused chains' (Applebee, 1978). Narratives expand on the focused chain by including additional features – the centre of the story is developed while a new idea or situation evolves from a previous idea.

Applebee, A. (1978) *The Child's Concept of Story: Ages Two to Seventeen*. Chicago, IL: University of Chicago Press.

Hudson, J.A. and Shapiro, L.R. (1991) 'From knowing to telling', in A. McCabe and C. Peterson (eds), *Developing Narrative Structure*. Hillsdale, NJ: Laurence Erlbaum Associates.

Simmons, V. and Gebhardt, A. (2010) *Concept of Story* (summer 2010). http://red6747.pbworks.com/w/page/8522525/Concept–of–Story (accessed 11 June 2015).

Formative assessment: through its structural philosophy of evidence elicitation, analysis and action supplies the strategy to make teaching effective and learning deep and sustained. Formative assessment requires teachers to pay attention to pupils' thinking and to adjust their planning accordingly.

Boyle, B. and Charles, M. (2012) 'David, Mr Bear and Bernstein: searching for an equitable pedagogy through guided group work', *The Curriculum Journal*, 23(1): 117–33.

Coffey, J., Hammer, D., Levin, D.M. and Grant, T. (2011) 'The missing disciplinary substance of formative assessment', *Journal of Research in Science Teaching*, 48(10): 1109–36.

Perrenoud, P. (1996) 'The teaching profession between proletarianism and professionalization: two models of change', *Outlook*, 26: 543–62.

Group composition and **group work**: group work is part of the composition of many classrooms and pupils are often assessed through teacher observation while working in those groups. This can raise classroom management issues such as the organisation of pupils not in the target group and how best to observe and therefore assess what each pupil in the target group is doing.

Boyle, B. and Charles, M. (2012) 'David, Mr Bear and Bernstein: searching for an equitable pedagogy through guided group work', *The Curriculum Journal*, 23(1): 117–33.

Hallam, J.V., Ireson, J. and Davis, J. (2004) 'Primary pupils' experiences of different types of grouping in school', *British Journal of Educational Research*, 30: 515–33.

Harris, E.L. (1995) 'Toward a grid and group interpretation of school culture', *Journal of School Leadership*, 56(6): 617–46.

Guided group work: a form of guided, co-operative learning. It requires expert 'scaffolding' by the teacher and direct instruction, modelling and practice in the use of the four simple strategies (questioning, clarifying, summarising, predicting) that underpin all teaching. It offers four things: (1) a strategic organisational device; (2) an optimal opportunity for specific and focused teaching; (3) the small group situation enables learning to be planned tightly to learning needs and offers accessibility for the pupil to the teacher; (4) optimal opportunity for the teacher to focus their observations of learning behaviours within a small group situation.

Allal, L. and Ducrey, G.P. (2000) 'Assessment of – or in – the zone of proximal development', *Learning and Instruction*, 10(2): 137–52.

Mercer, N. and Dawes, L. (2008) 'The value of exploratory talk', in N. Mercer and S. Hodgkinson (eds), *Exploring Talk in School*. London: Sage.

Ruthven, K., Hofmann, R. and Mercer, N. (2011) 'A dialogic approach to plenary problem synthesis', *Proceedings of the 35th Conference of the International Group for the Psychology of Mathematics Education*, 4: 81–8.

Initiation, Response, Feedback (IRF): research by Sinclair and Coulthard (1975) originated the notion of the three-part exchange of teacher recitation demonstrated as 'directive forms of teaching' and which consisted of a series of teacher questions which require convergent answers and pupil display of known information. The opposite to a teacher's pedagogy being learner-centred.

Atkins, A. (2001) 'Sinclair and Coulthard's IRF model in a one-to-one classroom: an analysis'. Available at: www.birmingham.ac.uk/documents/college-artslaw/cels/essays/csdp/atkins4.pdf (accessed 11 June 2015).

Sinclair, J. and Coulthard, M. (1975) *Toward an Analysis of Discourse: The English Used by Teachers and Pupils*. Oxford University Press.

Wells, G. (1993) 'Re-evaluating the IRF sequence: a proposal for the articulation of theories of activity and discourse for the analysis of teaching and learning in the classroom', *Linguistics and Education*, 5(1): 1–37.

Interrogatives: probing questioning techniques to elicit evidence of understanding 'how' and 'why'.

Ball, D.L. and Forzani, F.M. (2011) 'Teaching skilful teaching', *The Effective Educator*, 68(4): 40–6.

Galton, M., Hargreaves, L., Comber, C., Wall, D. and Pell, T. (1999) 'Changes in patterns of teacher interaction in primary classrooms: 1976–1996', *British Educational Research Journal*, 25(1): 23–37.

Kirkby, P. (1996) 'Teacher questions during story-book reading: who's building whose building?', *Literacy*, 30(1): 8–15.

Intrinsic motivation: the self-directed need to be involved in the learning process through the pupil's understanding of the meaningfulness and relevance of what and why they are doing classroom tasks.

Makin, L. and Whiteman, P. (2006) 'Young children as active participants in the investigation of teaching and learning', *European Early Childhood Education Research Journal*, 14(1): 33–41.

McCombs, B.L. and Marzano, R.J. (1990) 'Putting the self in self-regulated learning: the self as agent in integrating skill and will', *Educational Psychologist*, 25(6): 51–69.

Paris, S.G. and Cunningham, A. (1996) 'Children become students', in D. Berliner and R. Calfee (eds), *Handbook of Educational Psychology*. New York: Macmillan.

Involvement in own learning (co-construction): the pupil's learning needs should dictate the planning for teaching and learning, not the reverse, where the teacher writes a plan based on the curriculum but without involving the children in developing that planning, and therefore having 'ownership' of the learning.

Monteil, J.M. and Huguet, P. (2001) 'The social regulation of classroom performances: a theoretical outline', *Social Psychology of Education*, 4: 359–72.

Rogoff, B. (1990) *Apprenticeship in Thinking*. New York: Oxford University Press.

Rogoff, B., Baker-Sennett, J., Lacasa, P. and Goldsmith, D. (1995) 'Development through participation in socio-cultural activity', in J.J. Goddnow, P.J. Miller and F. Kessel (eds), *Cultural Practices as Contexts for Development*. San Francisco: Jossey-Bass.

Learner behavioural analysis: the teacher formatively assesses the pupil's thinking by paying close attention to the demonstrations through behaviours and outcomes of that thinking. The teacher wants to understand what the pupil is thinking and why they are thinking that way – the evidence that the teacher gains in this way, forms their next teaching steps.

Coffey, J., Hammer, D. and Grant, D.M. (2011) 'The missing disciplinary substance of formative assessment', *Journal of Research in Science Teaching*, 48(10): 1109–36.

Organisation for Economic Co-operation and Development (OECD) (2004) *Lifelong Learning*. Policy Brief, February, Paris: OECD.

Pollard, A. with Anderson, J., Maddock, M., Swaffield, S., Warin, J. and Warwick, P. (2008) *Reflective Teaching: Evidence-informed Professional Practice*, 3rd edn. London: Continuum.

Learner-centredness: teaching interventions that are suited to the taught group of pupils' potential levels of learning. This 'learner-centred' pedagogy is serviced by adult–pupil verbal interactions, differentiation and formative assessment.

Shepard, L.A. (2000) 'The role of assessment in a learning culture', *Educational Researcher*, 29(7): 4–14.

Shepard, L.A. (2005) 'Linking formative assessment to scaffolding', *Educational Leadership*, 63(3): 66–70.

Shor, I. and Freire, P. (1987) *A Pedagogy for Liberation: Dialogues on Transforming Education*. South Hadley, MA: Bergin and Garvey Publishers.

Learning objectives (sharing): in most classrooms, there is a single objective for a lesson, the objective is selected and 'planned' by the teacher. However, the teacher always has to be responsive to the learner's goals as these emerge in the course of a classroom activity and by collaborating with the pupils as they work towards and achieve their individual goals (learning objectives) to enable them to extend their mastery and their potential for further development. From the teacher's perspective 'learning objectives' are always a 'moving target'.

Bower, J. and Thomas, P.L. (2013) De-Testing and *De-grading Schools*: *Authentic Alternatives to Accountability and Standardization*. New York: Peter Lang Publishing Inc.

Dweck, C.S. (1999) *Self-theories: Their Role in Motivation, Personality, and Development*. Philadelphia, PA: The Psychology Press.

Lesson planning: the teacher is trying to identify and support learning strengths and misconceptions and to do that they have to facilitate opportunities for all the pupils in the group to demonstrate their learning. The teacher needs to understand that they need to be flexible enough to deviate from the planned lesson (during the course of the lesson) if they notice that learning is not taking place with some pupils.

Moss, G. (2007) 'Lessons from the National Literacy Strategy', paper presented at the Annual Conference of the British Educational Research Association, September.

Mottier Lopez, L. and Allal, L. (2007) 'Socio-mathematical norms and the regulation of problem solving in the classroom', *International Journal of Educational Research*, 46: 252–65.

Raveaud, M. (2005) 'Hares, tortoises and the social construction of the pupil: differentiated learning in French and English primary schools', *British Educational Research Journal*, 31(4): 459–79.

Mean score: the average score, computed by summing the scores of all test-takers and dividing by the number of test-takers.

Page, M., Davis, U.C. and Jackson, E. (2013) 'Smaller classes yield higher test scores among young children', *Policy Brief Center for Poverty Research*, 1(9).

Wenglisky, H. (2001) 'Teacher classroom practices and student performance: how schools can make a difference', Research Report, RR-01-19, Educational Testing Service. Statistics and Research Division.

Misconceptions (analysis of): there is a view that misconceptions are inaccurate or incorrect conceptions which pupils hold that are contrary to the learning objectives. Research challenges the idea that it is sufficient to 'explain the correct concepts' and supports the rationality of the pupils' initial conceptions. Strike and Posner (1992) argued that if conceptual change theory suggests anything about instruction it is that the handles to effective instruction are to be found in persistent attention to the argument and less in the attention to right answers. Research (Taber, 2000; Nobes et al., 2003) has raised empirical and theoretical reasons to doubt the view of prior conceptions as obstacles to learning.

Newman, D., Griffin, P. and Cole, M. (1989) *The Construction Zone: Working for Cognitive Change in School*. New York: Cambridge University Press.

Nobes, G., Moore, D., Martin, A., Clifford, B., Butterworth, G., Panayiotaki, G. and Siegal, M. (2003) 'Children's understanding of the earth in a multicultural community: mental modes of fragments of knowledge?', *Developmental Science*, 6(1): 72–85.

Strike, K.A. and Posner, G.J. (1992) 'A revisionist theory of conceptual change', in R. Duschl and R. Hamilton (eds), *Philosophy of Science, Cognitive Psychology, and Educational Theory and Practice*. Albany, NY: SUNY Press.

Taber, K.S. (2000) 'Exploring conceptual integration in student thinking: Evidence from a case study', *International Journal of Science Education*, 30(14): 1915–43.

Modelling of desirable (learning) behaviours: developing social-educative norms. It is important that teachers model, for example, active listening by focusing on non-verbal communication, such as good eye contact, interest by facial expression, gesture, posture, nodding, emotions and feelings and other aspects of paralanguage elements, all known as kinesics (Birdwhistell, 1970). Teachers should be aware of and understand the power and effects of paralanguage within their teaching, learning and assessment contexts. All of these desirable social-educative norms being modelled by the teacher are for the purpose of demonstrating and handing over desirable behaviours for good teaching and learning models.

Ambady, N. and Rosenthal, R. (1993) 'Half a minute: predicting evaluation from thin slices of non-verbal behaviour and physical attractiveness', *Journal of Personality and Social Psychology*, 64: 431–44.

Birdwhistell, R.L. (1970) *Kinesics and Context: Essays on Body Motion Communication*. Philadelphia: University of Pennsylvania.

Tizard, B., Hughes, M., Carmichael, H. and Pinkerton, G. (1983) 'Language and social class: is verbal deprivation a myth?', *Journal of Child Psychology*, 24(4): 533–42.

Nurturing pedagogy: pedagogy has to capture the multi-layered and dynamic practice necessary to support a pupil's holistic development. The importance of nurturing pedagogy is that if we take quality of teaching and learning seriously then the teacher has to get closer to our learners, their needs, their motivations and their learning styles. It is crucial that the teacher realises that they are working with 30–35 discrete individuals all with learning and learning needs, not just delivering an atomised centrally devolved 'one-size-fits-all' curriculum.

Dadds, M. (2001) 'The politics of pedagogy', *Teachers and Teaching: Theory and Practice*, 7(1): 43–58.

Hayes, N. (2008) 'Teaching matters in early educational practice: the case for a nurturing pedagogy', *Early Education and Development*, 19(3): 430–40.

Noddings, N. (1992) *The Challenge of Care in Schools: An Alternative Approach to Education Advances in Contemporary Educational Thought*, New York: Teachers College Press.

Observation and evidence elicitation: teachers who use formative assessment strategies are constantly observing and responding through flexible adjustment in the planning of their teaching strategies to match the learning and support needs of pupils. Observation must be planned for the information gained to usefully support the learning process. The link between interpretation of the evidence from these observations and the formative assessment process is integral. If the teacher does not form an appropriate picture of what is going on in the pupil's thinking then there is minimal likelihood of that teacher's actions having a decisive effect in adjusting positively the pupil's learning process.

Cardinet, J. (1986) *Evaluation scolaire et pratique*. Brussels: De Boeck.

Perrenoud, P. (1991) 'Towards a pragmatic approach to formative evaluation', in P. Weston (ed.), *Assessment of Pupils' Achievement: Motivation and School Success*. Amsterdam: Swets and Zeitlinger.

Rijlaarsdam, G. and Van Den Bergh, H. (2008) 'Observation of peers in learning to write: practise and research', *Journal of Writing Research*, 1(1): 53–63.

'One size fits all': a pedagogy which usually focuses on teaching in a very prescriptive and formulaic way only the elements of the curriculum which are going to be tested; the pupil is usually a passive respondent to the process rather than being an involved learner.

Boyle, B. and Charles, M. (2011) 'Re-defining assessment: the struggle to ensure a balance between accountability and comparability based on a "testocracy" and the development of humanistic individuals through assessment', Special issue of *CADMO: An International Journal of Educational Research*, 19(1): 55–65.

Freire, P. (1970) *Pedagogy of the Oppressed*. New York: Continuum.

Guinier, L. and Torres, G. (2003) *The Miner's Canary: Enlisting Race, Resisting Power, Transforming Democracy*. Cambridge, MA: Harvard University Press.

Pace of teaching: often a teacher's pedagogical style will dominate a teaching and assessment session. The teacher should not set a 'fast pace' which the pupils must all keep to, rather they should model taking time for reflection, for collaborating, for investigating, for discussion. This maintains the pupils' level of interest and motivation and demonstrates that the teacher understands the importance of linking the pupil's affective domain to the development of cognition.

Brown, M., Askew, M., Baker, D., Denvir, H. and Millet, A. (1998) 'Is the National Numeracy Strategy research-based?', *British Journal of Educational Studies*, 46(4): 362–85.

Dadds, M. (2001) 'The politics of pedagogy', *Teachers and Teaching: Theory and Practice*, 7(1): 43–58.

Smith, F., Hardman, F., Wall, K. and Mroz, M. (2004) 'Interactive whole class teaching in the national literacy and numeracy strategies', *British Educational Research Journal*, 30(3): 295–411.

Pedagogy: has to be informed by learning theory and to be focused on the learning needs of the individual pupil. Teachers should have high pedagogical content knowledge and strong levels of pedagogical skills. Each teacher should have a strong, informed theoretical construct underpinning their teaching, learning and assessment practice.

Alexander, R.J (2001) *Culture and Pedagogy: International Comparisons in Primary Education*. Oxford: Blackwell.

Simon, B. (1985) 'Why no pedagogy in England?', in B. Simon and W. Taylor (eds), *Education in the Eighties: The Central Issues*. London: Batsford.

Sylva, K., Melhuish, E., Sammons, P. and Siraj-Blatchford, I. (2004) 'The effective provision of the pre-school education (EPPE) project: findings from the Pre-school to the end of Key Stage 1'. Available at: www.ioe.ac.uk/RB_Final_Report_3-7.pdf (accessed 11 June 2015).

Percentile of a distribution: the score having a given percentile rank. The 80th percentile of a score distribution is the score having a percentile rank of 80. (The 50th percentile is also called the median; the 25th and 75th percentiles are also called the 1st and 3rd quartiles.)

Boyle, B. and Bragg, J. (2006) 'A curriculum without foundation', *British Educational Research Journal*, 32(4): 569–82.

Reeves, D., Boyle, B. and Christie, T. (2001) 'The relationship between teacher assessments and pupil attainments in standard tests/tasks at key stage 2, 1996–98', *British Educational Research Journal*, 27(2): 141–60.

Standards for Educational and Psychological Testing (1999) Washington, DC: American Educational Research Association.

Percentile rank of a score: the percentage of test-takers with lower scores, plus half the percentage with exactly that score. (Sometimes it is defined simply as the percentage with lower scores.)

Ehrenberg, R.C., Brewer, D.J., Gamoran, A. and Willms, J.D. (2001) 'Class size and student achievement', *American Psychological Society*, 2(1): 1–30.

Programme for International Student Assessment (PISA) (2012) *2012: National Report for England* (revised April 2014). London: Department for Education.

Rees, D.L., Argus, L.M. and Brewer, D.J. (1996) 'Tracking in the United States: descriptive statistics from NELS', *Economics of Education Review*, 15: 83–9.

Positive (and negative) feedback: Research has found that both positive and negative feedback can have beneficial effects on pupil learning (Kluger and DeNisi, 1996). However, Hattie and Timperley (2007) found that negative feedback is more positive at the 'self' level while both negative and positive feedback can be effective at the 'task' level. While there are differential effects relating to commitment, mastery or performance orientation and self-efficacy at the self-regulatory level. Feedback on a task will be ignored by pupils if it is poorly presented or if their knowledge (of the concept being taught or assessed) is insufficient to accommodate additional feedback information.

Hattie, J. and Timperley, H. (2007) 'The power of feedback', *Review of Educational Research*, 77(1): 81–112.

Kluger, A.N. and DeNisi, A. (1996) 'The effects of feedback interventions on performance: a historical review, a meta-analysis and a preliminary feedback intervention theory', *Psychological Bulletin*, 119(2): 254–84.

Kulvaney, R.W., White, M.T., Topp, B.W., Chan, A.L. and Adams, J. (1985) 'Feedback complexity and corrective efficiency', *Contemporary Educational Psychology*, 10: 285–91.

Proactive adjustment: takes place in the classroom context when a pupil is set an activity or takes part in a teaching situation.

Allal, L. (1988) 'Vers un elargissement de la pedagogie de maitrise: processus de regulation interactive, retroactive et proactive', in M. Huberman (ed.), *Assurer la reussite des apprentissages scolaires? Les propositions de la pedagogie de maitrise*. Neuchatel: Delachaux et Niestle.

Heritage, M. (2007) 'Formative assessment: what teachers need to know and do?', *Phi Delta Kappan*, 89: 140–5.

Popham, J. (2008) 'Formative assessment: seven stepping stones to success', *Principal Leadership*, 9: 16–20.

Process (observation of): such observation (for assessment purposes) has to be analytical, moving beyond a general impression to seeing what the pupil is actually doing – even thinking. Popham (2008) stated that 'formative assessment is not a test but a process' which produces a qualitative insight into pupil understanding.

Burenbaum, M., Kimron, H., Shilton, H. and Shahaf-Barzilay, R. (2010) 'Cycles of inquiry: formative assessment in service of learning in classrooms and in school-based professional communities', *Studies in Educational Evaluation*, 35: 135–49.

Gallimore, R., Ermeling, B.A., Saunders, W.M. and Goldenberg, C. (2009) 'Moving the learning of teaching closer to practice: teacher education implications of school-based inquiry teams', *The Elementary School Journal*, 109: 537–53.

Gattulo, F. (2000) 'Formative assessment in ELT primary (elementary) classrooms: an Italian case study', *Language Testing*, 17: 278–88.

Popham, W.J. (2008) *Transformative Assessment*. Alexandria, VA: Association of Supervision and Curriculum Development.

Questioning: poor quality 'closed' questions do not contribute to learning. Some teachers, despite being aware that learning is not taking place, continue to ask or paraphrase their questions, cueing or even 'mouthing' the required answers until these emerge. This is not learning. The pupils' responses become monosyllabic and never develop into 'chained responses' linking dialogue with their peers or the teacher. Communication, in this style of questioning, is not viewed by the teacher as a valuable tool both in cognition and its social mediating effects. 'Language not only manifests thinking but also structures it and speech shapes the higher mental processes necessary for so much learning' (Alexander, 2005).

Alexander, R.J. (2005) 'Culture, dialogue and learning: notes on an emerging pedagogy', paper presented at International Association for Cognitive Education and Psychology Conference, Durham, UK, July.

Hunter, J. (2009) 'Developing a productive discourse community in the mathematics classroom', in R. Hunter, B. Bicknell and T. Burgess (eds), *Crossing Divides: Proceedings of the 32nd Annual Conference of the Mathematics Education Research Group of Australasia* (Vol. 1). Palmerston, North NZ: MEDGA.

Minstrell, J. and Van Zee, E.H. (2003) 'Using questioning to assess and foster student thinking', in J.M. Atkin and J.E. Coffey (eds), *Everyday Assessment in the Science Classroom*. Arlington, VA: National Science Teachers Association.

Siraj-Blatchford, I. and Manni, L. (2008) 'Would you like to tidy up now? An analysis of adult questioning in the English Foundation Stage', *Early Years Journal*, 28(1): 5–22.

Reflection: reflective teaching is applied in a cyclical or spiralling process, in which teachers monitor, evaluate and then revise their own practice continuously (Pollard et al., 2008). The most distinctive feature of very good teachers is that their practice (pedagogy) is the result of careful reflection. They themselves learn lessons each time they teach, evaluating what they do and, using these self-critical evaluations, adjust what they do next time (Ofsted, 2004).

Ofsted (Office for Standards in Education) (2004) *Annual Report of Her Majesty's Chief Inspector of Schools*. Ofsted: London.

Pollard, A. with Anderson, J., Maddock, M., Swaffield, S., Warin, J. and Warwick, P. (2008) *Reflective Teaching: Evidence-informed Professional Practice*, 3rd edn. London: Continuum.

Schon, D.A. (1983) *The Reflective Practitioner*. Farnham, UK: Ashgate Publishing.

Regulation of learning: individual pupil learning achievement targets are not imposed but negotiated with the learner; feedback comments are clear and specific to the learning objective of the task being undertaken by the pupil. This is the 'regulation of learning' (Cardinet, 1986). Allal (1988) clarifies this as 'interactive regulation contributes to the progression of pupil learning by providing feedback and guidance that stimulate pupil involvement at each step of instruction'.

Allal, L. (1988) 'Vers un elargissement de la pedagogie de Maitrise: processus de regulation interactive, retroactive et proactive', in M. Huberman (ed,.), *Assurer la reussite des apprentissages scolaires? Les propostions de la pedagogie de maitrise*. Neuchatel: Delachaux et Niestle.

Cardinet, J. (1986) *Evaluation scolaire et pratique*. Bruxelles: De Boeck.

Schunk, D.H. and Zimmerman, B.J. (1997) 'Social origins of self-regulatory competence', *Educationalist Psychologist*, 32(4): 195–208.

Yackel, E. and Cobb, P. (1996) 'Socio-mathematical norms, argumentation and autonomy in mathematics', *Journal for Research in Mathematics Educational*, 27(4): 458–77.

Zimmerman, B.J. (2000) 'Attaining self-regulation: A social-cognitive perspective', in M. Boekarts, P.R. Pintrich and M. Zeidner (eds), *Handbook of Self-regulation*. San Diego: Academic Press.

Restricted code: exemplified through the teacher controlling language transactions with pupils at the monologic level – denying the pupils access to real, meaningful dialogue and then the autonomy (necessary for learner development) of dialogic interactions. Restricted code is produced when the teacher assumes the traditional role of 'power' (Bernstein, 1973) in which they ask (the majority of) the questions and therefore structure the pupils' thinking. The teacher takes the position of control and models for the pupils that the teacher's role is as architect (of learning) and problem-solver and the pupils' role is recipient of instructions which they then carry out to produce quite firmly controlled outcomes.

Bernstein, B. (1973) *Class, Codes and Control*. London: Routledge and Kegan Paul.

Blote, A.W. (1995) 'Students' self-concept in relation to perceived differential teacher treatment', *Learning and Instruction*, 5(3): 221–36.

Bourdieu, P. and Passeron, J.C. (1970) *Reproduction in Education, Society and Culture*. London: Sage.

Retroactive regulation: in traditional classes, teaching is giving a class or taking a lesson; assessment is a specific event, a written test or assignment or oral questions. Traditional teaching inevitably reduces regulation to its simplest expression and confines assessment to tests, which are quite distinct from lessons, even if those tests are sequenced post-lesson. 'The ensuing retroactive regulation is often restricted to re-working notions which have not been understood by a significant proportion of pupils' (Perrenoud, 1998).

Bennett, R.E. (20011) 'Formative assessment: a critical review', *Assessment in Education*, 18(1): 5–25.

Katzman, J., Lutz, A. and Olson, E. (2004) 'Would Shakespeare get into Swarthmore?', The Atlantic.com.

Perrenoud, P. (1998) 'From a formative evaluation to a controlled regulation of learning processes towards a wider conceptual field', *Assessment in Education: Principles, Policy and Practice*, 5(1): 85–102.

'Scaffolding': teachers need to understand the learning capability and pace of working of the pupils in the group being taught. With this information, the teacher can 'scaffold' (structure) the learning experience accordingly through differentiating the questions or prompts being used to support pupil learning to achieve the concept being taught.

Ash, D. and Levitt, K. (2003) 'Working within the zone of proximal development: Formative assessment as a professional development', *Journal of Science Teacher Education*, 14(1): 23–48.

Englert, C.S., Berry, R. and Dunsmore, K.L. (2001) 'A case study of the apprenticeship process: another perspective on the apprentice and the scaffolding metaphor', *Journal of Learning Disabilities*, 34(2): 152–71.

Shepard, L.A. (2005) 'Linking formative assessment to scaffolding', *Educational Leadership*, 63(3): 66–70.

Score distribution: the number (or the percentage) of test-takers at each score level.

Brookhart, S.M. (2003) 'Developing measurement theory for classroom assessment purposes and uses', *Educational Measurement: Issues and Practice*, 22: 5–12.

Moss, P.A. (2003) 'Re-conceptualizing validity for classroom assessment', *Educational Measurement: Issues and Practice*, 22: 13–25.

Willms, J.D. and Raudenbush, S.W. (1992) 'A longitudinal hierarchical linear model for estimating school effects and their stability', *Journal of Educational Measurement*, 26: 209–32.

Self-regulated learning (learner autonomy): involves the interplay between pupil commitment, control and confidence. It addresses the ways in which pupils monitor, direct and regulate actions towards the learning goal. It implies the development by the pupil (supported by the teacher and the active learning strategies used by the teacher) of autonomy, self-control, self-direction and self-discipline.

Schunk, D.H. and Zimmerman, B.J. (1997) 'Social origins of self-regulatory competence', *Educationalist Psychologist*, 32(4): 195–208.

Yackel, E. and Cobb, P. (1996) 'Socio-mathematical norms, argumentation and autonomy in mathematics', *Journal for Research in Mathematics Educational*, 27(4): 458–77.

Zimmerman, B.J. (2000) 'Attaining self-regulation: a social-cognitive perspective', in M. Boekarts, P.R. Pintrich and M. Zeidner (eds), *Handbook of Self-regulation*. San Diego: Academic Press.

Setting: has to be understood as the opposite to 'differentiation'. Setting is the locking of pupils into ability groups which (rarely) change. Differentiated teaching is a diversified approach – one that is required because of the diverse and complex nature of all pupils. Avoiding all pupils doing the same learning at the same time is not an end in itself; it is only a consequence of differentiated teaching which attempts to locate each pupil in a learning situation which is optimal for them. 'To the extent that all pupils do not have the same abilities nor the same needs nor the same way of working, an optimal situation for one pupil will not be optimal for another' (Perrenoud, 1998).

Boaler, J. (2005) 'The "psychological prison" from which they never escaped: the role of ability grouping in reproducing social class inequalities', *Forum*, 47(2/3): 135–44.

McAdamis, S. (2001) 'Teachers tailor their instruction to meet a variety of student needs', *Journal of Staff Development*, 22(2): 1–5.

Perrenoud, P. (1998) 'From a formative evaluation to a controlled regulation of learning processes towards a wider conceptual field', *Assessment in Education: Principles, Policy and Practice*, 5(1): 85–102.

Rosenthal, R. and Jacobson, L. (1968) *Pygmalion in the Classroom: Teacher Expectations and Student Intellectual Development*. New York: Holt.

Social mediation of learning: knowledge is socially constructed and not perceived as a fixed entity but rather in terms of an incremental view of learning, experiences and information gathering. For example, the social genesis of language and its development: 'any utterance is a link in a very complexly organised chain of other utterances', in learning to speak we do not take words from a dictionary but from the utterances of other speakers (Bakhtin, 1986: 69–70).

Bakhtin, M.N. (1986) *Speech Genres and Other Late Essays*. Austin: University of Texas Press.

Brockner, J. (1979) 'The effects of self-esteem, success-failure, and self-consciousness on task performance', *Journal of Personality and Social Psychology*, 37(10): 1732–41.

Vygotsky, L. (1978) *Mind in Society*. Cambridge, MA: Harvard University Press.

Socio-cognitive apprenticeships: establishment of communities of practice in which 'pupils participate in inquiry-based conversations about text, learning to treat written words as thinking devices' (Englert et al., 2006: 211). When pupils interact on a frequent basis they have a greater opportunity to internalise and understand – talk is an important component of learning whether that learning is in the domain of creativity or numeracy.

Alexander, R.J. (2010) 'Speaking but not listening? Accountable talk in an unaccountable context', *Literacy*, 44(3): 103–11,

Boyle, B. and Charles, M. (2012) 'David, Mr Bear and Bernstein: searching for an equitable pedagogy through guided group work', *The Curriculum Journal*, 23(1): 117–33.

Cowie, J. and Ruddock, H. (1988) *Co-operative Group Work: An Overview* (Vol. 1). UK: BP Educational Service.

Englert, C.S., Mariage, T.B. and Dunsmore, K. (2006) 'Tenets of sociological theory in writing instruction research', in C.A. MacArthur, S. Graham and J. Fitzgerald (eds), *Handbook of Writing Research*. New York: The Guilford Press.

Socio-constructivist learning theory: individuals assimilate knowledge and concepts after restructuring and reorganising it through negotiation with their surroundings, including with their fellow learners. Each pupil has their own unique socially constructed context – ideas, concepts and meanings are not fixed nor standardised across a class or group of pupils. Therefore the individual outcomes of learning situations will be diverse.

Bandura, A. (1989) 'Social cognitive theory', in R. Vasta (ed.), *Annals of Child Development*, 6. Greenwich, CT: JAI.

Cobb, P., Yackel, E. and Wood, T. (1992) 'A constructivist alternative to the representational view of mind in mathematics education', *Journal for Research in Mathematics Education*, 23: 2–33.

Hickey, D. (1997) 'Motivation and contemporary socio-constructivist instructional perspectives', *Educational Psychologist*, 32(3): 175–93.

Standard deviation: a measure of the dispersion (spread, amount of variation) in a score distribution. It can be interpreted as the average distance of scores from the mean, where the average is a special kind of average called a 'root mean square', computed by squaring the distance of each score from the mean, then averaging the squared distances, and then taking the square root.

Bangert-Drowns, R.L., Kulik, J.A and Kulik, C.L.C. (1991) 'Effects of frequent classroom testing', *Journal of Educational Research*, 85(2): 89–99.

Livingston, S. (2004) *Equating Test Scores (without IRT)*. Portland, OR: Educational Testing Service.

Moss, P.A. (2003) 'Re-conceptualizing validity for classroom assessment', *Educational Measurement: Issues and Practice*, 22: 13–25.

Summative assessment: 'a way to identify students' skills at key transition points such as entry into the world of work or for further education' (OECD, 2005).

Bennett, R. (2007) 'Assessment of, for and as learning: can we have all three?', paper presented at the National Assessment Agency and the Institute of Educational Assessors' National Assessment Conference, London, UK.

OECD (Organisation for Economic Co-operation and Development) (2005) *Formative Assessment: Improving Learning in Secondary Classrooms*. Policy Brief, November, Paris: OECD.

Stiggins, R. (2006) *Balanced Assessment Systems: Redefining Excellence in Assessment*. Portland, OR: Educational Testing Service.

Transmission model: the teacher is the controller and originator of discourse (communication) patterns in the classroom with monologic uses of language as a high priority. Too often the transmission model of communication is chosen which inevitably leads to the pupil being cast in the role of 'passive recipient of knowledge' (Freire, 1970 – 'banking' analogy).

Freire, P. (1970) *Pedagogy of the Oppressed*. New York: Continuum.

Gerson, H. and Bateman, E. (2010) 'Authority in an agency-centred, inquiry-based university calculus classroom', *Journal of Mathematical Behaviour*, 29(4): 195–206.

Nystand, M. (1997) 'Dialogic instruction: when recitation becomes conversation', in A. Nystand, R. Gamoran, R. Kachur and C. Prendergast (eds), *Opening Dialogue: Understanding the Dynamics of Language and Learning in the English Classroom*. New York: Teachers College Press.

Zone of proximal development: for Vygotsky, pupils learn by working on and solving problems with peers (and adults) more capable than themselves, who take them through their zone of proximal (or potential) development (Vygotsky, 1986). Vygotsky saw social interaction as the essential factor in pupil learning development.

Allal, L. and Ducrey, G.P. (2000) 'Assessment of – or in – the zone of proximal development', *Learning and Instruction*, 10(2): 137–52.

Ash, D. and Levitt, K. (2003) 'Working within the zone of proximal development: formative assessment as a professional development', *Journal of Science Teacher Education*, 14(1): 23–48.

Vygotsky, L. (1986) *Thought and Language*. Cambridge, MA: MIT Press.

References

Aldrich, R. (1988) 'The national curriculum: an historical perspective', in D. Lawton and C. Chitty (eds), *The National Curriculum, Bedford Way, Paper 3*. London: Institute of Education, University of London.

Alexander R.J. (1997) *Policy and Practice in Primary Education: Local Initiative, National Agenda*. London: Routledge.

Alexander, R.J. (2004) 'Still no pedagogy? Principle, pragmatism and compliance in primary education', *Cambridge Journal of Education*, 34 (1): 7–33.

Alexander, R.J. (2005) 'Culture, dialogue and learning: notes on an emerging pedagogy', paper presented at International Association for Cognitive Education and Psychology Conference, Durham, UK, July.

Alexander, R.J. (2008) 'Education for all: the quality imperative and the problem of pedagogy', Consortium for Research on Educational Access, Transactions and Equity, April.

Allal, L. and Ducrey, G.P. (2000) 'Assessment of – or in – the zone of proximal development', *Learning and Instruction*, 10: 137–52.

Allal, L. and Lopez, M. (2005) *Formative Assessment of Learning: A Review of Publications in French*. Paris: OECD.

Anning, A. (1995) *A National Curriculum for the Early Years*. Buckingham: Open University Press.

Anning, A. (1997) 'Developing the school curriculum', School Curriculum and Assessment Authority Conference, *The Primary Curriculum: The Next Steps*. London: SCAA.

Appk, M.W. (1975) 'The hidden curriculum and the nature of conflict', in W. Pinar (ed.), *Curriculum Theorizing: The Reconceptualists*. Berkeley: McCutchan, pp. 95–119.

Apple, M.W. (1996) *Cultural Politics & Education*. New York: Teachers College Press.

ARG (Assessment Reform Group) (1999) *Beyond the 'Black Box'*. Cambridge: Assessment Reform Group.

ARG (Assessment Reform Group) (2002) *Assessment for Learning: 10 Principles*. Cambridge: Assessment Reform Group.

ARG (Assessment Reform Group) (2007) *The Role of Teachers in the Assessment of Learning*. Cambridge: Assessment Reform Group.

Bain, B. (1975) 'Toward an integration of Piaget and Vygotsky: Bilingual considerations', *Linguistics*, 16: 5–20.

Balkan, L. (1970) *Les Effets du bilingualism Francais-Anglais sur les aptitudes intellectuelles*. Brussels: AIMAV.

Ball, S.J. (1994) *Education Reform: A Critical and Post-structural Approach*. Buckingham: Open University Press.

Barger, R.N. (2000) *A Summary of Lawrence Kohlberg's Stages of Moral Development*. Robert, N. Barger, Ph.D. University of Notre Dame 2000.

Baroudi, Z.M. (2007) Formative assessment: Definition, elements and role in instructional practice', *Postgraduate Journal of Education Research*, 8(1): 37–8.

BBC News Education (2004) 'Ofsted "two-speed lessons" alarm', 4 February [online]. Available at: http://news.bbc.co.uk/2/hi/uk_news/education/3458037.stm (accessed 11 June 2015).

BBC News Education (2006a) 'Testing should be intensified', 19 July [online]. Available at: http://news.bbc.co.uk/2/hi/uk_news/education/5196188.stm (accessed 11 June 2015).

BBC News Education (2006b) 'Primary school test target missed', 24 August [online]. Available at: http://news.bbc.co.uk/2/hi/uk_news/education/5281132.stm (accessed 11 June 2015).

BBC News Education (2007) 'Testing "deprives primary pupils"' [online]. Available at: http://news,bbc.co.uk/1/hi/education/7080794.stm (accessed 6 November 2007).

Bell, B. and Cowie, B. (2001) *Formative Assessment and Science Education*. Dordrecht: Kluwer Academic.

Bennett, R. (2011) 'Formative assessment: a critical review', *Assessment in Education: Principles Policy and Practice*, 18(1): 5–25.

Berninger, V., Abbott, R. and Jones, J. (2006) 'Early development of language by hand: composing, reading, listening and speaking connections; three letter writing modes and fast mapping in spelling', *Developmental Neuropsychology*, 29(1): 61–2.

Black, P. (1998) *Testing: Friend or Foe? Theory and Practice of Assessment and Testing*. Falmer Press: London.

Black, P. and Wiliam, D. (1998) *Inside the Black Box: Raising Standards Through Classroom Assessment*. London: King's College London School of Education.

Black, P. and Wiliam, D. (2003) 'In praise of educational research: formative assessment', *British Educational Research Journal*, 29(5): 623–37.

Blair, A. (2004) 'Universal education and care for under fives' [speech]. The National Association of Headteachers Conference, Cardiff.

Blair, A. (2005) 'Education speech', 25 October, BBC News. Available at: http://news.bbc.co.uk/1/hi/uk_politics/4372216.stm (accessed 11 June 2015).

Bloom, B.S., Engelhart, M.D., Furst, E.J., Hill, W.H. and Krathwohl, D.R. (1956) *Taxonomy of Educational Objectives: The Classification of Educational Goals. Handbook I: Cognitive Domain*. New York: David McKay Company.

Boaler, J. (2005) 'The "psychological prison" from which they never escaped: the role of ability grouping in reproducing social class inequities', FORUM, 47(2–3): 135–44.

Bogdan, R.C. and Biklen, S.K. (1982) *Qualitative Research for Education: An Introduction to Theory and Methods*. Boston: Allyn & Bacon.

Bourdieu, P. (1990) *The Logic of Practice*, translated by Richard Nice. California: Stanford University Press.

Boyle, B. (2000) *The Aims and Priorities of the School Curriculum in (1999): A Self-report by Schools*. Report to QCA based on the author's national consultation prior to Curriculum 2000 revisions.

Boyle, B. (2005–6) *Integrated Curriculum Manual*. Gulf Arab States Educational Research Council.

Boyle, B. (2006) *Assessment for Learning (Primary): A Teacher's Guide to Formative Assessment* [DVD]. Manchester: 186 Media/University of Manchester.

Boyle, B. (2007a) 'Learning through assessment', *School Leadership Today*, 2(2): 50–5.

Boyle, B. (2007b) 'A curriculum without breadth and balance: teaching to the targets', *School Leadership Today*, 2(7): 22–5.

Boyle, B. (2008) 'Testing to the limits – a very "accountable" 20-year period in primary education in England', *Managing Schools Today*, 17(4): 20–3.

Boyle, B. and Bragg, J. (2002) *Curriculum Trends 1997–2002*. Manchester: CFAS/QCA.

Boyle, B. and Bragg, J. (2003) *Curriculum Trends 1997–2003*. Manchester: CFAS/QCA.

Boyle, B. and Bragg, J. (2004) *Survey of Foundation Stage Education in England*. Manchester: CFAS/QCA.

Boyle, B. and Bragg, J. (2005) 'No science today: the demise of primary science teaching', *The Curriculum Journal*, 16(4): 423–37.

Boyle, B. and Bragg, J. (2006) 'A curriculum without foundation', *British Educational Research Journal*, 32(4): 569–82.

Boyle, B. and Bragg, J. (2008a) 'Making primary connections: the cross-curriculum story', *The Curriculum Journal*, 19(1): 5–21.

Boyle, B. and Bragg, J. (2008b) 'What is the relationship between disadvantage and primary school performance standards?', *School Leadership Today*, 2(9): 25–8.

Boyle, B. and Bragg, J. (2009) 'What a waste of money', *The Education Journal*, 114: 44–7.

Boyle, B., Bragg, J. and Pearson, D. (2007) *Testing and Assessment: Report to the Children, Schools and Families Committee*. London: Houses of Parliament, 17 December.

Boyle, B. and Charles, M. (2008) 'Excellence and enjoyment 2003–8: a five year review of its Assessment for Learning Strategy: has it encouraged formative teaching and learning in primary schools?', CFAS, School of Education, University of Manchester.

Boyle, B. and Charles, M. (2010a) 'Assessment for future generations: the struggle to ensure a balance between accountability and comparability based on a "testocracy" and the development of humanistic individuals through assessment', keynote lecture presented at the Annual Conference of the International Association of Educational Assessment (IAEA), Bangkok, Thailand, August.

Boyle, B. and Charles, M. (2010b) 'Leading learning through assessment for learning', *School Leadership & Management*, 30(3): 285–300.

Boyle, B. and Charles, M. (2011) 'Re-defining assessment: the struggle to ensure a balance between accountability and comparability based on a "testocracy" and the development of humanistic individuals through assessment', Special issue of *CADMO: An International Journal of Educational Research*, 19(1): 55–65.

Boyle, B. and Charles, M. (2013) *Formative Assessment for Teaching and Learning*. London: Sage.

Boyle, B. and Christie, T. (eds) (1996) *Issues in Setting Standards: Establishing comparabilities*. London: Falmer Press.

Boyle, B., Lamprianou, I. and Boyle, T. (2005) 'A longitudinal study of teacher change: what makes professional development effective? Report of the second year of the study', *International Journal of School Effectiveness and School Improvement*, 16(1): 1–27.

Boyle, P. J., Norman, P. and Popham, F. (2009) 'Social mobility: evidence that it can widen health inequalities', *Social Science and Medicine*, 68(10): 1835–1842.

Bradbury, A. (2013) 'Education Policy and the "ideal learner": producing recognisable learner-subjects through early years assessment', *British Journal of Sociology of Education*, 34(1): 1–19.

Brehony, K.J. (2005) 'Primary schooling under New Labour: the irresolvable contradiction of excellence and enjoyment', *Oxford Review of Education*, 31(1): 29–46.

Broadfoot, P. (1996) *Education, Assessment and Society*. Open University Press.

Broadfoot, P., Osborn, M., Planel, P. and Pollard, A. (1996) 'Assessment in French Primary Schools', *The Curriculum Journal*, 7(2): 227–246.

Brown, M., Askew, M., Baker, D.H.D. and Millett, A. (1998) 'Is the national numeracy strategy research based?', *British Journal of Educational Studies*, 46(4): 362–385.

Bruce, T. (1997) 'Adults and children developing play together', *European Early Childhood Education Research Journal*, 5(1): 89–99.

Bruce, T. (2001) *Learning Through Play: Babies, toddlers and the foundation years*. London: Hodder and Stoughton.

Buck, M. and Inman, S. (1993) *Curriculum Guidance no. 2, Reaffirming Values*. Centre for Cross-Curricular Initiatives. London: Goldsmiths.

Burgess, S. and Greaves, E. (2009) 'Test scores, subjective assessment and stereotyping of ethnic minorities', Working Paper No. 09/221, Centre for Market and Public Organisation Bristol Institute of Public Affairs University of Bristol.

Campbell, J. (1997) 'Towards curricular subsidiarity?' Paper presented at the School Curriculum and Assessment Authority Conference, Developing the Primary Curriculum, the next steps. June.

Campbell, T. (2013) 'Stereotyped at 7? Biases in teacher judgements of pupils' ability and attainment', Institute of Education, London, Centre for Longitudinal Studies.

Carr, W. (1997) 'Philosophy and method in educational research', *Cambridge Journal of Education*, Special issue: Philosophy and Educational Research.

Carr, W. (1997) 'Professing education in a postmodern age', *Journal of Philosophy of Education*, 31(2): 309–327.

Casti, J.L. (1989). *Alternate Realities. Mathematical Models of Nature and Man*. New York: Wiley-Interscience.

CFAS (Centre for Formative Assessment Studies) (2003) *School Sampling Project Curriculum Survey: Summary of Primary School Findings 2001–2*. Available at: www.education.man.ac.uk/cfas/mca/summaries.htm.

Chitty, C. (1988) 'Central control of the school curriculum, 1944–87', *History of Education*, 17(4): 321–334.

Clark, P. and Christie, T. (1995) 'Assessment led curriculum development in action: a study of seven primary schools responses to statutory requirements', *International Journal of Education Management*, 9(4): 19–27.

Clarke, A. (1999) *Evaluation Research*. London: Sage.

Clycq, N., Ward Nouwen, M.A. and Vandenbroucke, A. (2014) 'Meritocracy, deficit thinking and the invisibility of the system: discourses on educational success and failure', *British Educational Research Journal*, 40(5): 796–819.

Cohen, L. and Manion, L. (1994) *Research Methods in Education*. London: Routledge.

Covey, S.R. (1990). *The 7 Habits of Highly Effective People*. New York: Simon & Schuster.

Crawford, K. (2000) 'The political construction of the whole curriculum', *British Educational Research Journal*, 26 (5): 615–30.

Cummins, J. and Gulutsan, M. (1974) 'Bilingual education and cognition', *The Alberta Journal of Educational Research*, 20: 259–69.

DCSF (Department for Children, Schools and Families) (2007) *Improving Writing with a Focus on Guided Writing*. DCSF: London.

Depree, H. and Iversen, S. (1994) *Early Literacy in the Classroom*. Desoto, TX: Wright Group Publishing.

DES (Department of Education and Science) (1967) *Children and their Primary Schools* (The Plowden Report). London: HMSO.

DES (Department of Education and Science) (1985) *Better Schools*. London: DES.

DES (Department of Education and Science) (1987) *The National Curriculum 5–16: A Consultation Document*. London: HMSO.

DES (Department of Education and Science) (1988) *The Education Reform Act*. London: HMSO.

DeVries, R. and Kohlberg, L. (1990) *Constructivist Early Education: Comparison with other programs*. Washington D.C. National Association for the Education of Young Children.

Di Angelo, R. (2011) 'White fragility', *International Journal of Critical Pedagogy*, 3(3): 54–70.

de Waal, A. (2006) 'Do targets work?', *Times Educational Supplement*, 20 August: 19.

DfEE (Department for Education and Employment) (1999a) *All Our Futures: Creativity, Culture and Education*. London, DfEE.

DfEE (Department for Education and Employment) (1999b) *The National Curriculum Handbook for Primary Teachers in England*. London: DfEE.

DfES (Department for Education and Skills) (2003) *Excellence and Enjoyment: A Strategy for Primary Schools*. London: DfES.

DfES (Department for Education and Skills) (2004) *Five Year Strategy for Children and Learners*. London: DfES.

Donovan, M.S., Bransford, J.D. and Pellegrino, J.W. (eds) (1999) *How People Learn. Bridging Research & Practice*. Washington, DC: National Academy Press.

Dunphy, L. (2008) 'Developing pedagogy in infant classes in primary schools in Ireland', *Learning from Research*, 27 (1): 55–70.

Dyson, L. (2004) 'The effect of neighbourhood poverty and low-income on the school context: teachers' expectations for achievement and rating of achievement motivation of elementary school children', paper presented to the Canadian Society for the Study of Education, Winnipeg, Canada.

Early Years Foundation Stage (2008) Statutory Framework for the Early Years Foundation Stage: Setting the Standards for Learning, Development and Care for children from birth to five. Department for Children, Schools and Families.

Education Institute (2004) *Curriculum Standards for the State of Qatar. Science: Grades K–12*. Doha, Qatar: The Education Institute of the Supreme Education Council. Available at: www.ibe.unesco.org/curricula/qatar/qa_al_sc_2004_eng.pdf (accessed 10 June 2015).

Education Institute (2005) *Science Scheme of Work for the State of Qatar. Science: Grades K–12*. Doha, Qatar: The Education Institute of the Supreme Education Council. Available at: https://csomathscience.wordpress.com (accessed 10 June 2015).

Edwards, A. (2001) 'Researching pedagogy: a sociocultural agenda', *Pedagogy, Culture and Society*, 9: 161–86.

Elliott, J. (1994) 'Clarifying values in schools', *Cambridge Journal of Education*, 24(3): 413–22.

Ericsson, K.S. and Charness, N. (1994) 'Expert performance: Its structure and acquisition', *American Psychologist*, 49, 725–74.

Fletcher, C.L. and Barufaldi, J.P. (2002) 'Evaluating professional development with student data: challenges and successes for project ESTT', paper presented at the Annual Meeting of the National Association of Research in Science Teaching, New Orleans, LA.

Flower, L., Hayes, J.R., Carey, L., Schriver, K. and Stratman, J. (1986) 'Detection, diagnosis and the strategies of revision', *College Composition and Communication*, 37(1): 16–53.

Fogelman, K. (1991) *Citizenship in Schools*. London: David Fulton.

Frankenberg, R. (2001) 'The mirage of an unmarked whiteness', in Brander, R.K., Klinenberg, M., Nexica, I.J and Wray, M. (Eds.), *The Making and Unmaking of Whiteness*. Durham: NC, pp. 72–96.

Freire, P. (1970) *Pedagogy of the Oppressed*. New York: Continuum.

Fullan, M. (2003) *Change Forces with a Vengeance*. London: Routledge Falmer.

Galton, M. and McBeath, J. (2002) *A Life in Teaching? The Impact of Change on Teachers' Working Lives*. London: National Union of Teachers.

GAO (Government Accountability Office) (2003) 'Characteristics of tests with influence expenses: information sharing may help states realize efficiencies'. Available online at: www.gao.gov/new.items/d03389.pdf

Gentner, D. and Stevens, A. (1983) *Mental Models*. Hillsdale, NJ: Erlbaum.

Giere, R.N. (1992) *Cognitive Models of Science.* Minnesota Studies in the Philosophy of Science, Vol. XV. Minneapolis: University of Minnesota Press.

Giere, R.N. (1994). 'The cognitive structure of scientific theories', *Philosophy of Science*, 61: 276–96.

Glas, E. (2002) 'Klein's Model of Mathematical Creativity', *Science and Education*, 11(1): 95–104.

Glaser B.C. and Strauss A.L. (1976) *The Discovery of Grounded Theory: Strategies for Qualitative Research*. Chicago: Aldine.

Glaser, B.G. (1978) *Theoretical Sensitivity: Advances in the Methodology of Grounded Theory*. Mill Valley, CA: Sociology Press.

Goodson, I. (1989) 'Curriculum reform and curriculum theory: a case of historical amnesia', *Cambridge Journal of Education*, 19(2): 131–41.

Goouch, K. (2008) 'Understanding playful pedagogies, play narratives and play spaces', *Journal of Early Years Education*, 28(1): 93–102.

Gorard, S. (2010) 'Serious doubts about school effectiveness', *British Educational Research Journal*, 36(5): 745–66.

Gorard, S. and Smith, E. (2004) 'What is "underachievement" at school?', *School Leadership & Management*, 24(2): 205–25.

Gordon H. Bower and Daniel G. Morrow (1990) 'Mental Models in Narrative Comprehension', *American Association for the Advancement of Science*, 24(4938): 44–48.

Gray, J. (2001) *Success Against the Odds: Five Years On*. London: Routledge

Gray, J. (2004) 'Frames of reference and traditions of interpretation: some issues in the identification of "under-achieving" schools', *British Journal of Educational Studies*, 52(3): 293–309.

Graziano, K.G. (2008) 'Walk the talk: connecting critical pedagogy and practice in teacher education', *Teaching Education*, 19(2): 153–63.

Guinier, L. (2003) 'The Supreme Court, 2002 Term: Comment: admissions rituals as political acts: guardians at the gates of our democratic ideals', *Harvard Law Review*, November.

Guinier, L. and Torres, G. (2003) *The Miner's Canary: Enlisting Race, Resisting Power, Transforming Democracy*. Cambridge, MA: Harvard University Press.

Hall, K., Collins, J., Benjamin, S., Nind, M. and Sheehy, K. (2004) 'Assessment and inclusion/exclusion: SATurated models of pupildom', *British Educational Research Journal*, 30(6): 801–17.

Halloun, I. (2001) *Apprentissage par modélisation: la physique intelligible*. Beyrouth: Librairie du Liban Publishers.

Halloun, I. (2004/2006) *Modelling Theory in Science Education*. Dordrecht: Kluwer Academic Publishers/Boston: Springer.

Halloun, I. (2007) 'Mediated modelling in science education', *Science and Education*. 16(7): 653–97.

Halloun, I. (2011a) 'Profile shaping education: a paradigm shift in education to empower students for success in modern life', *Proceedings of the 11th International History, Philosophy and Science Teaching Group Biennial Conference*. Aristotle University, Thessaloniki, Greece.

Halloun, I. (2011b) 'From modelling schemata to the profiling schema: modelling across the curricula for profile shaping education', in M.S. Khine and I.M. Saleh (eds), *Models and Modelling in Science Education*. Boston: Springer.

Hansard (1987) 1 December, Vol. 123, Col. 771.

Hansen, K. and Jones, E.M. (2011) 'Ethnicity and gender gaps in early childhood', *British Educational Research Journal*, 37 (6): 973–91.

Harlen, W. (2004) 'Re-thinking the teacher's role in assessment', Paper presented at the British Educational Research Assessment Annual Conference, University of Manchester, 16–18 September.

Harlen, W. (2007) *The Quality of Learning: Assessment Alternatives for Primary Education*, Primary Review Research Survey 3/4. Cambridge: University of Cambridge.

Harlen, W. and Deakin-Crick, R. (2003) 'Testing and motivation for learning', *Assessment in Education*, 10(2): 169–208.

Hayes, N. (2008) 'Teaching matters in early education practice: the case for a nurturing pedagogy', *Early Education and Development*, 19(3): 430–40.

Helm, H. and Novak, J.D. (1983) Proceedings of the International Seminar on Misconceptions in Science and Mathematics. Ithaca, NY: Cornell University.

Holt, D. (ed.) (1997) *Primary arts education: Contemporary Issues*. London: The Falmer Press.

House of Commons (2009) *National Curriculum: Fourth Report of Session 2008–09* (Children, Schools and Families Committee). London: Stationery Office.

Huitt, W. (1999) 'Conation as an important factor of mind', *Educational Psychology Interactive*. Valdosta, GA: Valdosta State University. Available at: www.edpsycin teractive.org/topics/conation/conation.html (accessed 11 June 2015).

Humphreys, A., Post, T. and Ellis, A. (1981) *Interdisciplinary Methods: A Thematic Approach*. Santa Monica, CA: Goodyear Publishing Company.

Hutt, C. (1979) 'Play in the under 5s: form, development and function', in J.G. Howells (Ed.) *Modern Perspectives in the Psychiatry of Infancy*. New York: Brunner/Marcel.

IEA (International Association for the Evaluation of Educational Achievement) (2008) *TIMSS 2007 Technical Report*. Amsterdam, The Netherlands: IEA.

Isaacs, S. (1971) *The Nursery Years: The Mind of the Child from Birth to Six Years*. Routledge: London.

Jackson, P.W. (1968) *Life in Classrooms*. New York: Holt, Rinehart and Winston.

Jeff, S. and Julie, N. (1991) *Accuracy of Self-reported Course Work and Grade Information of High School Sophomores*. American College Testing Research Report Series, REPORT_NO: ACT-RR-91-6.

Johnson-Laird, P.N. (1983) *Mental Models*. Cambridge: Cambridge University Press.

Karsten, S., Visscher, A. and De Jong, T. (2001) 'Another side to the coin: the unintended effects of the publication of school performance data in England and France', *Comparative Education*, 37(2): 231–42.

Kirschner, P.A., Sweller, J. and Clark, R.E. (2006) 'Why minimal guidance during instruction does not work: an analysis of the failure of constructivist, discovery, problem-based, experiential, and inquiry-based teaching', *Educational Psychologist*, 41(2): 75–86.

Lakoff, G. (1987) *Women, Fire, and Dangerous Things. What Categories Reveal About the Mind*. Chicago: University of Chicago Press.

Lambert, R.G. (2003) 'Considering purpose and intended use when making evaluations of assessments: a response to Dickinson', *Educational Researcher*, 32(4): 23–6.

Lawton, D. (1987) 'Fundamentally flawed', *Times Educational Supplement*, 18 September.

Lee, P. (1996) 'Cognitive development in bilingual children: a case for bilingual instruction in early childhood education', *Journal of Bilingual Research*, 20(3): 499–522.

LeCompte, M.D. and Goetz, J.P. (1982) 'Problems of reliability and validity in ethnographic research', *Review of Educational Research*, 52(1): 31.

Le Métais, J. and Tabberer, R. (1997) *International Review of Curriculum Assessments and Frameworks: Comparative Tables*. Slough: NFER.

Lerner, M.J. (1980) *The Belief in a Just World: A Fundamental Delusion*. New York: Plenum Press.

Liebeck, P. (1984) *How Children Learn Mathematics*. London: Penguin.

Linn, M.C. (1992) *Gender Differences in Educational Achievement: Sex Equity in Educational Opportunity, Achievement and Testing*. Princeton, NJ: Educational Testing Services.

Lupton, R. (2004) *Schools in Disadvantaged Areas: Recognising Context and Raising Quality*, CASE paper 76, January, Centre for Analysis of Social Exclusion, London School of Economics and Political Science.

Maden, M. (1997) 'Curriculum planning: some OECD lessons', in P. Mortimore and V. Little (eds), *Living Education*. London: Paul Chapman.

Makin, L. and Whiteman, P. (2006) 'Young children as active participants in the investigation of teaching and learning', *European Early Childhood Education Research Journal*, 14(1): 33–41.

Marenbon, J. (1996) *A Moral Maze: government values in education*. London: Politeia.

Margolis, E. (2001) *The Hidden Curriculum in Higher Education*. New York: Routledge.

Martin, E.L., Segraves, R., Thacher, S. and Young, L. (2003) 'The writing process: three first grade teachers and their students reflect on what was learned', *Reading Psychology*, 26(3): 200.

Maxey, E.J. and Ormsby, V.J. (1971) *The Accuracy of Self-report Information Collected on the ACT Test Battery: High School Grades and Items of Non-academic Achievement*. Research and Development Division, The American College Testing Programme, REPORT _NO: ACT-RR-45.

Maykut, P. and Morehouse, R. (1994) *Beginning Qualitative Research*. London: Falmer Press.

McLaughlin, T.H. (1992) 'Citizenship, diversity and education, a philosophical perspective', *Journal of Moral Education*, 21(3): 235–250.

Meyer, D.K. and Turner, J.C. (2002) 'Discovering emotion in classroom motivation research', *Educational Psychologist*, 37(2): 107–14.

Miles, M.B. and Huberman, A.M. (1984) *Quantative Data Analysis: A Sourcebook of New Methods*. Berkeley, CA: Sage

Morris, J.A. and Gardner, M.J. (1988) 'Calculating confidence intervals for relative risks (odds ratios) and standardised ratios and rates', *British Medical Journal*, 296: 1313–16.

Mourshed, M., Chijioke, C. and Barber, M. (2010) *How the World's Most Improved School Systems Keep Getting Better*. London: McKinsey & Company. Available at: www.mckinsey.com/client_service/social_sector/latest_thinking/worlds_most_improved_schools (accessed 11 June 2015).

Mullis, I.V.S., Kennedy, A.M., Martin, M.O. and Sainsbury, M. (2006) *PIRLS 2006 Assessment Framework and Specifications*, 2nd Edition. Chestnut Hill, MA: Boston College.

Mullis, I.V.S., Martin, M.O., Smith, T.A., Garden, R.A., Gregory, K.D., Gonzalez, E.J., Chrostowski, S.J. and O'Connor, K.M. (2003) *TIMSS Assessment Frameworks and Specific Actions*, 2nd Edition. Chestnut Hill, MA: Boston College.

Myhill, D. (2006) 'Talk, talk, talk: teaching and learning in whole class discourse', *Research Papers in Education*, 21(1): 19–41.

NAGB (National Assessment Governing Board) (2011a) *Mathematics Framework for the 2011 National Assessment of Educational Progress*. Washington, DC: US Government Printing Office.

NAGB (National Assessment Governing Board) (2011b) *Science Framework for the 2011 National Assessment of Educational Progress*. Washington, DC: US Government Printing Office.

NCC (National Curriculum Council) (1990) *Curriculum Guidance 3: The Whole Curriculum*. York: NCC.

NCC (National Curriculum Council) (1993) *Planning the National Curriculum at Key Stage 2*. York: NCC.

NCTM (National Council of Teachers of Mathematics) (1989) *Curriculum and Evaluation Standards for School Mathematics*. Reston, VA: NCTM.

NCTM (National Council of Teachers of Mathematics) (1991) *Professional Teaching Standards for School Mathematics*. Reston, VA: NCTM.

NCTM (National Council of Teachers of Mathematics) (1995) *Assessment Standards for School Mathematics*. Reston, VA: NCTM.

NCTM (National Council of Teachers of Mathematics) (2000) *Principles and Standards for School Mathematics*. Reston, VA: NCTM.

Nezhnov, P. and Kardanova, E. (2011) *SAM Framework*. Moscow, Russia: Center for International Cooperation in Education Development.

Nichols, S.L. and Berliner, D.C. (2007) *Collateral Damage: How High-stakes Testing Corrupts America's Schools*. Cambridge, MA: Harvard Education Press.

Nilsson, M. (2010) 'Developing voice in digital storytelling through creativity narrative and multimodality', *International Journal of Media, Technology and Lifelong Learning*, 6(2): 1–11.

Norwegian Ministry of Education and Research (1990) *Curriculum Guidelines for Compulsory Education in Norway*. Oslo: Aschehoug.

Novak, J. (ed.) (1993) *Proceedings of the Third International Seminar on Misconceptions and Educational Strategies in Science and Mathematics*. Cornell University, Ithaca.

Novak, J.D. (1987) Proceedings of the Second International Seminar on Misconceptions and Educational Strategies in Science and Mathematics. Ithaca, NY: Cornell University.

NRC (National Research Council) (1996) *National Science Education Standards*. Washington, DC: National Academy Press.

NRC (National Research Council) (2011) *A Framework for K–12 Science Education: Practices, Crosscutting Concepts, and Core Ideas*. Washington, DC: National Academies Press.

NUT (National Union of Teachers) (2006) *NUT Briefing: The Impact of National Curriculum Testing on Pupils*, September.

OECD (Organisation for Economic Co-operation and Development) (2005) *Formative Assessment: Improving Learning in Secondary Classrooms*. Policy Brief November. Paris: OECD.

OECD (Organisation for Economic Co-operation and Development) (2009) *PISA 2009 Assessment Framework: Key Competencies in Reading, Mathematics and Science*. Paris: OECD.

OECD (Organisation for Economic Co-operation and Development) (2011) *PISA in Focus*, 9 (October). Paris: OECD.

Ofsted (2001) *Standards and Quality in Education: The Annual Report of Her Majesty's Chief Inspector of Schools*. London: Office for Standards in Education.

Ofsted (2002a) *Standards and Quality in Education: The Annual Report of Her Majesty's Chief Inspector of Schools*. London: Office for Standards in Education.

Ofsted (2002b) *The Curriculum in Successful Primary Schools*. London: Office for Standards in Education.

Ofsted (2003) *Good Assessment Practice in Mathematics*. London: Office for Standards in Education.

Ofsted (2005) *The Annual Report of Her Majesty's Chief Inspector of Schools 2003/04*. London: Office for Standards in Education.

Ofsted (2006) *The Annual Report of Her Majesty's Chief Inspector of Schools 2005/06*. London: Office for Standards in Education.

Ofsted (2007) *Standards and Quality in Education: The Annual Report of Her Majesty's Chief Inspector of Schools*. London: Office for Standards in Education.

O'Hear, P. and White, J. (1991) *A National Curriculum for All: Laying the foundation for success*. London: Institute for Public Policy Research.

O'Hear, P. and White, J. (ed.) (1993) *Assessing the National Curriculum*. London: Paul Chapman Publishing.

Osborn, M., with Croll, P., Broadfoot, P., Pollard, A., McNecs, E. and Triggs, P. (1997) 'Policy into practice – creative meditation in the primary classroom', in Helsby, G. and McCulloch, G. (eds.) *Teachers and the National Curriculum*. London: Falmer Press, p. 15.

Osborne, J. and Dillon, J. (2008) *Science Education in Europe: Critical Reflections*. London: The Nuffield Foundation.

Palmer, J. (1991) 'Planning wheels turn curriculum around', *Educational Leadership*, 49 (2): 57–60.

Paris, S.G. and Paris, A.H. (2001) 'Classroom applications of research on self-regulated learning', *Educational Psychologist*, 36(2): 89–101.

Patrick, F., Forde, C. and McPhee, A. (2003) 'Challenging the "new professionalism": from managerialism to pedagogy?', *Journal of In- Service Education*, 28(2): 237–53.

Patton, M.Q. (1990) *Qualitative evaluation and research methods*, 2nd edition. Thousand Oaks, CA: Sage.

Perrenoud, P. (1991) 'Towards a pragmatic approach to formative evaluation', in P. Weston (ed.), *Assessment of Pupils' Achievement: Motivation and School Success*. Amsterdam: Swets and Zeitlinger.

Perrenoud, P. (1996) 'The teaching profession between proletarianism and professionalization: two models of change', *Outlook*, 26: 543–62.

Perrenoud, P. (1998) 'From formative evaluation to a controlled regulation of learning processes: towards a wider conceptual field', *Assessment in Education*, 5(1): 85–101.

Perrenond, P. (2001) 'The key to social fields: Competencies of an autonomous actor', in D.S. Rychen and L.H. Salganik (Eds.) *Defining and selecting key competencies*. Göttingen: Hogrefe and Huber.

Perry, N.E, Hutchinson, L. and Thauberger, C. (2007) 'Mentoring student teachers to design and implement literacy tasks that support self-regulated reading and writing', *Reading and Writing Quarterly*, 23: 27–50.

Piazza, C.L. (2003) *Journeys: The Teaching of Writing in Elementary Classrooms*. Upper Saddle River, NJ: Pearson Education Inc.

Popham, J. (2008) 'Classroom assessment: staying instructionally afloat in an ocean of accountability', in C.A. Dwyer (ed.), *The Future of Assessment: Shaping Teaching and Learning*. Lawrence Eribaum Associates.

Popham, W.J. (2001) *The Truth About Testing: An educator's call to action*. Alexandria, VA: ASCD.

Porter, A.C. (2001) *The Condition of Education*. National Centre for Education Statistics [online]. Available at: nces.ed.gov/pubs2001/2001072.pdf (accessed 11 June 2015).

Pryor, J. and Crossouard, B. (2008) 'A socio-cultural theorisation of FA', *Oxford Review of Education*, 34(10): 1–20.

QCA (Qualifications and Curriculum Authority) *Assessment for Learning*. London: QCA.

QCA (Qualifications and Curriculum Authority) *Aims for the School Curriculum: What Does Your School Think?* London: QCA.

QCA (Qualifications and Curriculum Authority) (1999) *Key Stage 2 Assessment and Reporting Arrangements*. London: QCA.

QCA (Qualifications and Curriculum Authority) (2002) *Designing and Timetabling the Primary Curriculum: A Practical Guide for Key Stages 1 and 2*. London: QCA.

QCA (Qualifications and Curriculum Authority) (2006) Primary Framework for Literacy and Mathematics. Available at: http://www.educationengland.org.uk/documents/pdfs/2006-primary-national-strategy.pdf

QCA Seminar (2007) Assessment for Learning Seminar. Downing College, University of Cambridge, Friday 16th November, 2007.

Radnor, H. and Shaw, K. (1994) 'Developing a collaborative approach to moderation: the moderation and assessment project – southwest', in H. Torrance (ed.), *Evaluating Authentic Assessment*. Buckingham: Open University Press.

Ramprasad, A. (1983) 'On the definition of feedback', *Behavioural Science*, 28(1): 4–13.

Reeves, D., Boyle, B. and Christie, T. (2001) 'The relationship between teacher assessments and pupil attainments in standard tests/tasks at key stage 2, 1996–98', *British Educational Research Journal*, 27(2): 141–60.

Resnicow, K., Davis, M., Smith, M., Lazarus-Yaroch, A., Baranowski, T., Baranowski, J., Doyle, C. and Wang, D.T. (1998) 'How best to measure implementation of school health curricula: a comparison of three measures', *Health Education Research: Theory and Practice*, 13(2): 239–50.

Ribbins, P. and Sherratt, B. (1997) *Radical Educational Policies and Conservative Secretaries of State*. London: Cassell.

Riggs, E.G. (2004) 'Conation: cultivating the will to succeed among middle and high school students', Forum on Public Policy. Available at: forumonpublicpolicy.com/archivesum07/riggs.pdf (accessed 11 June 2015).

Roe, E. (1994) *Narrative Policy Analysis*. Durham, NC: Duke University Press.

Rothman, R. (2001) 'One hundred and fifty years of testing', in *The Jossey Bass Reader on School Reform*. San Francisco: Jossey Bass.

Rowsell, J., Kosnik, C. and Beck, C. (2008) Fostering multiliteracies pedagogy through pre-service teacher education', *Teaching Education*, 19(2): 109–22.

RSA (2005) *Opening Minds: Giving Young People a Better Chance*. London: RSA.

Ruttle, K. (2004) 'What goes on inside my head when I'm writing? A case study of 8–9 year-old boys', *Literacy*, July: 71–7.

Sadler, D.R. (1989) 'Formative assessment and the design of instructional systems', *International Science*, 18: 119–44.

Sadler, D.R. (2007) 'Perils in the meticulous specification of goals and assessment criteria', *Assessment in Education*, 14(3): 387–92.

SCAA (School Curriculum and Assessment Authority) (1993) *The National Curriculum and its Assessment* (The Dearing Review). London: SCAA.

SCAA (School Curriculum and Assessment Authority) (1996) 'Nursery education: Desirable outcomes for children's learning on entering compulsory education', one-day conference. London: SCAA and Department for Education and Employment.

SCAA (School Curriculum and Assessment Authority) (1997) 'Developing the primary school curriculum: the next steps', proceedings from invited conference, June. SCAA: London.

Schunk, D.H. and Zimmerman, B.J. (1997) 'Social origins of self-regulatory competence', *Educational Psychologist*, 32(4): 195–208.

Schunk D.H. and Zimmerman, B.J. (2007) 'Influencing children's self-efficacy and self-regulation of reading and writing through modelling', *Reading & Writing Quarterly*, 23: 7–25.

SEAC (Schools Examinations and Assessment Council) (1989) *A Guide to Teacher Assessment, Packs A, B, C*. London: Heinemann.

SEAC (Schools Examinations and Assessment Council) (1990) *A Guide to Teacher Assessment, Pack C*. London: Heinemann.

SEC (Supreme Education Council) (2010) *The Early Years Foundation Curriculum for Qatar 2010*. Doha, Qatar: Supreme Education Council/Early Years Specialist Team.

Shepard, L.A. (2000) 'The role of assessment in a learning culture', *Educational Researcher*, 29(7): 4–14.

Shepard, L.A. (2005) 'Linking formative assessment to scaffolding, *Educational Leadership*, 63(3): 66–70.

Shoemaker, B. (1989) 'Integrative education: a curriculum for the twenty-first century', *Oregon School Study Council*, 33: 2.

Shor, I. (1992) *Empowering Education: Critical Teaching for Social Change*. Chicago: University of Chicago Press.

Siraj-Blatchford, I. (2009) 'Quality teaching in the Early Years', in Anning, A., Cullen, J. and Fleer, M. *Early Childhood Education and Culture*, p. 147.

Smith, E. (2003) 'Understanding underachievement: an investigation into the differential attainment of secondary school pupils', *British Journal of Sociology of Education*, 24 (5): 576–86.

Smith, E. and Gorard, S. (2005) 'They don't give us our marks: the impact of formative assessment techniques in the classroom', *Assessment in Education*, 12(1): 21–38.

Smith, F., Hardman, F., Wall, K. and Mroz, M. (2004) 'Interactive whole class teaching in the National Literacy and Numeracy Strategies', *British Educational Research Journal*, 30(3): 395–441.

Smith, K. and McCann, C.W. (1998) 'The validity of students' self-reported family incomes', paper presented at the 38th Annual Forum of the Association for Institutional Research, Minneapolis, MN.

STAIR Consortium (1990) *Evaluation Report of the Standard Assessment Task Pilot Study*. CFAS/SEAC, University of Manchester.

Stiggins, R.J., Arter, J.A., Chappuis, S. and Chappuis, J. (2004) *Classroom Assessment for Student Learning*. Portland, OR: Assessment Training Institute.

Taylor, P.J., Lamers, A., Vincent, M.P. and O'Driscoll, M.P. (1998) 'The validity of immediate and delayed self-reports in training evaluation: an exploratory field study', *Applied Psychology: An International Review*, 47(4): 459–79.

TDA (2008) *Professional Standards for Qualified Teacher Status and Requirements for Initial Teacher Training*. London: Training and Development Agency for Schools.

TES (1987) '1904 and all that', *Times Educational Supplement*, 31 July.

TES (2008) 'What the markers told us'. Available at: https://www.tes.com/article.aspx?storycode=2644175 (accessed 4 July 2008).

Te Whāriki (1996) He Whāriki Màtauranga mò ngà Mokopuna o Aotearoa Early Childhood Curriculum, Ministry of Education, Learning Media Limited, Wellington, New Zealand.

TGAT (Task Group on Assessment and Testing) (1988a) *National Curriculum Task Group on Assessment and Testing: A Report*. London: Department for Education and Science.

TGAT (Task Group on Assessment and Testing) (1988b) *National Curriculum Task Group on Assessment and Testing: Three Supplementary Reports*. London: Department for Education and Science.

Tharp, R.G. and Gallimore, R. (1991) *Rousing Minds to Life: Teaching, Learning and Schooling in a Social Context*. Cambridge: Cambridge University Press.

Tharp, R.G. and Gallimore, R. (1988) 'A theory of teaching as assisted performance', in *Rousing Minds to life: teaching, learning and schooling in social context*. New York: Cambridge University.

Thatcher, M. (1993) *The Downing Street Years*. London: Harper Collins.

Thrupp, M. and Tomlinson, S. (2005) 'Introduction: education policy, social justice and "complex hope"', *British Educational Research Journal*, 31: 549–556.

Tobias, M. and Howden-Chapman, P. (2000) *Social Inequalities in Health, New Zealand, 1999: A Summary*. Wellington: Ministry of Health.

Tooley, J. (1997) 'Choice and diversity in education: A defence', *Oxford Review of Education*, 23(1): 103–16.

Torrance, H. (1993) 'Formative assessment: some theoretical problems and empirical questions', *Cambridge Journal of Education*, 23(3): 333–43.

Torrance, H. (2007) 'Assessment as learning?' *Assessment in Education*, 14(3): 281–294.

Traub, R.E. and Weiss, J. (1982) 'The accuracy of teachers' self-reports: evidence from an observational study of open education', paper presented at the Annual Meeting of the American Educational Research Association, New York.

Twing, J., Boyle, B. and Charles, M. (2010) 'Integrated assessment systems for improved learning', paper presented at the 36th Annual Conference of the International Association of Educational Assessment, Bangkok, Thailand, August.

Tyler, K. (1992) 'Differentiation and integration of the primary curriculum', *Journal of Curriculum Studies*, 24(6): 563–7.

Tymms, P. (1996) *The Value Added National Project: Second Primary Technical Report: An Analysis of the (1991) Key Stage 1 Assessment Data Linked to the 1995 KS2 Data Provided by Avon LEA*. London: School Curriculum and Assessment Authority.

Tymms, P. (2004) 'Are standards rising in English primary schools?', *British Educational Research Journal*, 30(4): 477–94.

Tymms, P. and Merrell, C. (2007) *Standards and Quality in English Primary Schools Over Time: National Evidence*. Primary Review Research Survey 4/1. Cambridge: University of Cambridge.

Tytler, R. (2011) 'Socio-scientific issues, sustainability and science education', *Research in Science Education*, 41.

UNESCO (1990) *World Declaration on Education for All*. Paris: UNESCO. Available at: unesdoc.unesco.org/images/0009/000975/097552e.pdf (accessed 11 June 2015).

UNESCO (2000) *The Dakar Framework for Action*. Available at: www.unesco.at/bildung/basisdokumente/dakar_aktionsplan.pdf (accessed 11 June 2015).

Viau, E.A. (1994) 'The mind as a channel: a paradigm for the information age', *Educational Technology Review*, Autumn/Winter: 5–10.

Vulliamy, G. and Nikki, M.L. (1997) 'The comparative context for educational reform in England and Finland', paper presented at the British Educational Research Association symposium on 'A Comparative Analysis of Curriculum Change in English and Finnish Primary Schools: The York-Finnish Project'.

Vygotsky, L. (1978). *Mind in Society*. Cambridge, MA: Harvard University Press.

Vygotsky, L. (1986) *Thought and Language*. Cambridge, MA: MIT Press.

Vygotsky, L. (1987) *The Collected Works of L.S. Vygotsky*. New York: Plenum Press.

West, C. (2008) *Hope on a Tightrope*. Carlsbad, CA: Smiley Press.

White, J. (1997) *Education and the End of Work*. London: Cassell.

White, J. (2004) *Rethinking the School Curriculum: Values, Aims and Purposes*. London: Routledge Falmer.

Whitty, G. (2001) 'Education, social class and social exclusion', *Journal of Education Policy*, 16(4): 287–95.

Wiggins, A. and Tymms, P. (2002) 'Dysfunctional effects of league tables: a comparison between English and Scottish primary schools', *Public Money and Management*, January–March: 43–8.

Willis, S. and Mann, L. (2000) 'Differentiating instruction finding manageable ways to meet individual needs', *Curriculum Update*, Winter. Available at: http://www.ascd.org/publications/curriculum-update/winter2000/Differentiating-Instruction.aspx (accessed 11 June 2015).

Wragg, T. (1990) 'Who put the ass in assessment?' *The Times Educational Supplement*, 16 February.

Wragg, E.C. (1997) *The Cubic Curriculum*. London: Routledge.

Wyse, D., McCreery, E. and Torrance, H. (2007) *The Trajectory and Impact of National Reform: Curriculum and Assessment in English Primary Schools*. Primary Review Interim Report. Cambridge: University of Cambridge.

Young, M. (1999) 'The curriculum of the future', *British Education Research Journal*, 25(4): 463–77.

Zimmerman, B.J. (2000) 'Attaining self-regulation: a social-cognitive perspective', in M. Boekarts, P.R. Pintich and M. Zeidner (eds), *Handbook of Self-regulation*. San Diego: Academic Press.

Index